# UNDER-GROUND MOVE-MENTS

Modern Culture on the New York City Subway

A VOLUME IN THE SERIES
*Science/Technology/Culture*

EDITED BY
Carolyn de la Peña
Siva Vaidhyanathan

# UNDER-GROUND MOVE-MENTS

Modern Culture on the New York City Subway

Sunny Stalter-Pace

UNIVERSITY OF MASSACHUSETTS PRESS
Amherst and Boston

Printed in the United States of America

ISBN 978-1-62534-055-9 (paper); 054-2 (hardcover)

Designed by Sally Nichols
Set in Quadraat OT
Printed and bound by IBT/Hamilton, Inc.

Library of Congress Cataloging-in-Publication Data
A catalog record for this book is on file at the Library of Congress.

British Library Cataloguing-in-Publication Data
A catalogue record for this book is available from the British Library.

For L.B.

# Contents

Acknowledgments
ix

Introduction
Subway Stories
1

1. Forming the Subway Habit
24

2. How the Subway Became Sublime
52

3. Minding the Gaps in Modernist Poetry
78

4. Underground Assimilation in Ethnic Drama
110

5. Uncanny Migration Narratives
140

Conclusion
The Private Subway in the Postmodern City
166

Notes
191

Works Cited
205

Index
225

# Acknowledgments

My book explores the impersonal community created in the underground space of the New York City subway. I want to take a moment to acknowledge the network of friends, colleagues, and family members that helped me bring these shadowy ideas to light.

First, I express my warmest gratitude to my mother, Jill. She has been a cheerleader, a sounding board, and a friend. This book would not have been possible without her. Thanks to all of my family: Michael, Casey and Jeff, Chad and Lorraine, Bradley, Brooke, Addison, Andrew, and Gram. Though my immediate family has lived with this project longer, my in-laws have heard more about the ins and outs of the publication process. I'm especially grateful to Paula and Simeon Pace, Jennie R. Davis, and Hannah Atkins, who had better return the favor and thank me in a book of her own.

I've explored Chicago and New York City with a wonderful group of people. Steph Sola, Rachel Benoit, Amy Kalbster, Ri Pierce-Grove, and Gabby Warshawer, thank you all for your help and love along the way. If I've written a book that interests you all, I have done my job.

The Rutgers English Department is my intellectual family, and I am so grateful to all of the faculty, staff, and students there—past and present. My committee deserves particular thanks: director Elin Diamond, Meredith McGill, Matthew Buckley, Harriet Davidson, and Jackson Lears. My dissertation writing group provided welcome intellectual community in what can otherwise be an isolating time. Thanks to Kristie Allen, Alison Shonkwiler, and Alex Socarides. Carrie Preston, Danielle Bobker, Kathy Lubey, and Liz Reich have all provided feedback, encouragement, or a combination of the two. Ben Johnson is still the best writer I know. I consider myself lucky that he's also a wonderful reader and friend.

Much of the work in this book was possible only because of the archival riches available in New York City. My thanks to the Museum of the City of

New York; the Billy Rose Theatre Division at the New York Public Library for the Performing Arts; and the Manuscripts and Archives Division and the Milstein Division of U.S. History, Local History, and Genealogy at the New York Public Library's Stephen A. Schwarzman Building. Not all of the work got done at those archives, so I'm also grateful for the many coffee shops where I wrote first drafts of these chapters, especially Gorilla Coffee. In spite of what Alfred Kazin says, I also thank the Bergen Street stop on the 2/3, where I still feel like I'm coming home.

Since I have arrived at Auburn University, my colleagues in the English Department have all done so much to help this project toward its fruition. Hilary Wyss offered helpful advice, a sympathetic ear, and an introduction to my editor. Jim Ryan read my manuscript and talked transportation early on. Michael Frazer provided research assistance. I received funding for summer research leave through the College of Liberal Arts and the Research Culture Committee. For general support, both scholarly and psychological, I thank Chase Bringardner, Rebecca Brunson, Emily Friedman, Susana Morris, Erich Nunn, Kathryn Olsen, Anya Riehl, and Matt Zarnowiecki. In the past few years Twitter has become a useful venue for me to share ideas and links with other scholars of New York City. Liana Silva and Bryan Waterman have been the most generous and enthusiastic of my online collaborators. Beatrice Smedley provided a translation used in chapter 4.

Carolyn de la Peña and Siva Vaidhyanathan gave me my first platform for talking about transportation and American culture in *American Quarterly.* I thank them for their work as coeditors of the Science/Technology/Culture series as well. Carolyn in particular has seen this project go through a number of revisions; she has always pushed me to make my work more accessible and more interdisciplinary, and for that I am grateful. Two anonymous readers and Cotten Seiler offered attentive notes and challenging questions. I appreciate their time and generosity. Thanks to the *Journal of Modern Literature* for permission to reprint a revised and expanded version of my article "Subway Ride and Subway System in Hart Crane's 'The Tunnel,'" which first appeared in volume 33, number 2 (Winter 2010). I am grateful to the University of Massachusetts Press and especially Clark Dougan, the best advocate and demystifier an author could want. Thanks are also due to Carol Betsch (a Broadway Local rider), Mary Bellino, and Amanda Heller.

Finally to Paul. You are my husband and my best friend. This book is dedicated to you and to the many journeys we will take together.

# UNDER-GROUND MOVE-MENTS

Modern Culture on the New York City Subway

# INTRODUCTION

# SUBWAY STORIES

Stories about technology proliferate in contemporary culture. In online forums, in mass media, and in everyday conversation, Americans narrate their relation to the world through their machines: my smartphone makes me feel connected, perhaps too connected; my car offers freedom of movement and shields me from fellow commuters. Technologies do not inherently shape these new forms of sociability, though they do make some ways of relating easier than others. Instead, stories told about technologies model the new modes of interaction they bring about. Stories bestow cultural capital on some machines, allowing them to play a symbolic role in US culture that extends beyond the sphere of their producers and consumers. And when they are prevalent and powerful enough, stories about technology can orient its users to the world in new ways.

In *Underground Movements* I focus on the stories told about the New York City subway in the first half of the twentieth century. In this period, a remarkable variety of writers took up the challenge of narrating a new technology that simultaneously reshaped the consciousness of its riders and the metropolis through which they moved. The underground transit system plays an outsized role in experimental writing of the time that has come to be called modernist.[1] These particular texts describe and evaluate the New York subway system as a representative space for exploring the difficulty of navigating the city, the commercialization of art, and the impact of immigration on local and national identity. They belong to a number of microgenres, specific forms of subway writing bound by their own aesthetic rules; these texts isolate different elements of the subway ride and use them to embody different aspects of urban life. Although the types of literature under discussion differ widely in tone, theme, and publishing venue, they all attempt to explain what difference the subway makes to particular riders.

The infrastructure of the subway system has remained relatively unchanged since the New York City subway opened to the public in October 1904,[2] and so has the infrastructure of the subway story.[3] Then as now, these stories articulate a relationship to the city and to fellow city dwellers through their depiction of the subway ride. Whether nonfiction or fiction, poetry or drama, certain elements remain. The comfort level of the passenger suggests her familiarity with the city as a whole: Is she sure of her final destination or constantly watching the map? The commuters with whom the protagonist shares the train become a representative sample of the urban public. Do they leer and press against her, read newspapers in foreign languages, shut her out with headphones? Stories of crosstown movement explore cultural mobility as well, highlighting the aspirations of modern New Yorkers. In a city where change has been the only constant, the subway serves as a stable setting for writers who want to test the cosmopolitan mettle of urban types. With the exception of a few texts that appear in newspapers and business-oriented periodicals, these subway stories share publication venues that might be characterized as middle- to highbrow. That is to say, these technological stories aspire to both contemporary relevance and a certain degree of aesthetic complexity. Whereas Cotten Seiler examines the ways in which stories about American automobility construct a neoliberal individualist, I argue that these subway stories construct the passenger as a knowing urban subject, but one who is still part of the crowd.

Although I pay closest attention to literature, I do not want to make an old-fashioned Myth and Symbol School–style argument that the writers I have chosen reveal some timeless truth about the American need for mobility. Their writings demonstrate that technology stories are eminently *local:* they reckon with the various ways that technology reshapes the possibilities for urban dwellers, for example, when a subway line is built beneath one avenue instead of another. Reading these stories with an eye to local history is equally important for understanding the canonical writers I discuss as well as their lesser-known compatriots. Without knowledge of the Interborough Rapid Transit train's path from Times Square to Brooklyn Heights, Hart Crane's poem "The Tunnel" loses its everydayness; its setting becomes a merely mythic vehicle. Similarly, the American Yiddish playwright Osip Dymov maps the mental journey of a Jewish immigrant dreaming about assimilation onto the man's physical journey from Manhattan to the Bronx. By doing so, Dymov reminds audience members that technology might facilitate assimilation and at the same time reinforce cultural isolation. By examining how different texts address the subway movement of particular groups of New Yorkers, I mean to work against the idea that every subway ride is the same. Mark Simpson's discussion of nineteenth-century American mobility narratives opens up that concept by listing the different forms of movement in the era, including "travel, transport, placement, displacement, fugitivity, migration, immigration, removal, traffic, [and] circulation" (xxii). There are important distinctions between a conventional travel narrative, which assumes a stable home to which the narrator will return, and one of removal or what Simpson calls fugitivity (71). Similarly, I discuss how subway riding functions differently for tourists, commuters, poets, laborers, immigrants, and migrants. Situating technological stories within specific geographic and cultural frameworks helps us understand how machines take on their meaning through an overlapping and sometimes conflicting set of affiliations.

These texts deal with different experiences of subway riding, but they all identify the same underlying feeling shared by modern subway passengers—the sensation of being pulled in opposing directions, of simultaneously paying attention to the particulars of your ride and imagining yourself as part of an immense system. The *New York Times*'s "Tunnel Vision" columnist Randy Kennedy points to the difficulty of capturing the lived reality of technology use in language when he says: "Trying to describe a day in the subway is a little like trying to take a snapshot of the wind. It's everywhere and nowhere in particular. You can feel it and hear it yet chase in vain to capture the essence of the life lived along some 700 miles of track, inside 468 stations, where New Yorkers have done everything they've done on the streets above and more." Concrete details such as track length fail to account for the lived reality of the passengers and workers. The texts that I discuss represent the infrastructural facts and the embodied feelings as inextricably linked.

The subway becomes emblematic of a particular version of New York–based literary modernism that theorizes new formal relationships between the part and the whole. This concern helps us better understand the navigation of subway space and the accommodations made by passengers in this period. The lines of influence between texts and technologies move in both directions. Rather than suggesting that modernist writers wrote works influenced by the subway or that they influenced the reception of it, I want to "help us see how experiences of mobility become textualized and how textual forms have been affected by mobility" (Seiler 11).[4] The literature of this period is engaged with modernization both as a subject and as a model for formal innovation. Eric Schocket makes the parallel between the two explicit. Modernist texts, he says, have "a substructure that connects them to the social and economic processes of industrial modernization." That is, "first, [they] express a commitment to atomization and fragmentation, a desire to separate the object, scene, or theme into a set of disparate, elemental parts. Second, they reconnect these parts through an external system, logic, or in more familiar terms, aesthetic technique" (148–49).[5] The literature that I discuss shares this "commitment" to breaking down its literary subjects into their minimum component parts, isolating and defamiliarizing the heteroglossic slogans of advertisements as well as the emotions of passengers. These components are reconstructed into aesthetic systems bound by their own logic. In this way, the texts self-reflexively explore both the coherence of their own forms and the logic of the subway system that holds together such a diverse set of impressions.

Carolyn de la Peña has commented on the difficulty of interdisciplinary technology studies, noting that "technology is slippery; to understand it one must simultaneously consider the 'body' and the 'system' " ("Slow and Low Progress" 916). In this book I suggest that literature from this period is chiefly concerned with this "slippery" form of navigation. Mobility studies scholars have paid attention to the affective power of transportation technology; Mimi Sheller in particular points out that the American attachment to the automobile should be understood in terms of the "embodied sensibilities" of the driver and not just the access that the car provides (222). As I show throughout *Underground Subjects,* descriptions of subway rides abandon the bird's-eye perspective used by riders of the elevated train, giving accounts of the "subway crush" that echo and amplify complaints about crowds on buses and streetcars. Yet this intense physical experience is balanced with the contemplation of the subway route. When moving through underground space, passengers can orient themselves only by looking at the map, observing the names of passing stations, and listening to the conductor's often inaudible announcements. I suggest that modern passengers habituate to the subway by modulating between these two ways of seeing the city. Indeed, John Urry suggests that nineteenth-century hikers felt a similar sense of mobility, one that draws on the landscape painting as well as the map (87). Subway movement necessitates a visual relation that synthesizes two distinct and opposing perspectives. The subway rider brings immediate visual (and auditory) cues together with a preexisting knowledge of mapped representations of the landscape. As I discuss in the first chapter, modern writers were fascinated by the habits of the subway rider which facilitated movement through the crowded space of transit. A regular passenger engrossed in a book, for instance, seems to navigate the subway system more easily than a tourist nervously studying the map. How do riders feel themselves moving through underground space? How do they keep track of stops while ignoring them? And how does this form of mobility differ for women, minorities, and other passengers whose embodiment makes them stand out within the crowd?

Earlier studies have approached the New York subway from perspectives that range from the Marxist to the mythic, yet none has explored how it manages to operate simultaneously as a technology of embodiment and abstraction. Through interwoven historical, technological, spatial, and literary analysis, I show how this tension undergirds representations of the modern New York City subway. These local interrogations overlap in their concerns with the body and the system as the twin poles of urban modernity. Avant-garde engagements with subway space interrogate a peculiar form of what Mark Seltzer calls "the American body-machine complex" (1). In this particular combination of man and machine, passengers are physically restricted, but their attention (to their discomfort, to their reading material, to the people around them) is heightened. Modernist texts are deeply engaged with the partial perceptions of individual passengers;

overheard bits of conversation, slogans from advertisements, and isolated thoughts all play equally central roles in modernist subway poetics. At the same time, authors from this period show these bits of sensory data subsumed into the flow of the subway crowd within the stations and the planned movement of the trains throughout the city. Their aesthetic strategies, then, depict subway movement as following modern tenets of efficiency similar to those of Frederick Taylor.[6] Each passenger in the subway moves in a particular direction, but those particularities must conform to the collective movement of the subway crowd.[7] The physical strain of the subway ride and the abstract reach of the subway system analogically show their readers what it feels like to move through modernity. Like automobile driving manuals, subway stories teach city dwellers how to get where they want to go without interrupting the flow of the crowd.

## A Critical History of the Subway

In its first fifty years, the New York City subway was a multivalent symbol. It could be depicted as both a hellish underworld and a thoroughly modern miracle, even in the same text. But cultural analysis of the subway has been restricted by its dependence on a framework for understanding the subway that focuses on ascent and descent at the expense of other forms of movement. As a central technology in the American urban imaginary, the subway has been the subject of two cultural histories, Michael Brooks's *Subway City: Riding the Trains, Reading New York* (1997) and Tracy Fitzpatrick's *Art and the Subway: New York Underground* (2009). Brooks examines the political debates surrounding the elevated trains and subways, from their conception to their construction and expansion. He also traces the changing attitudes toward race, class, and gender depicted in subway art. As her title suggests, Fitzpatrick addresses the subway from the perspective of an art historian; yet she "begins with the subway itself as a work of art" (3) and juxtaposes analyses of the built environment with visual and textual representations of subway space throughout her book. Their books are essentially surveys of the genre, and as such they aspire toward inclusiveness rather than the presentation of a central argument about the subway as an imaginative structure.

While the subway may serve as a reflection of New York's modernization or a manifestation of underground space more broadly, it is equally important to unpack its meaning on its own terms.[8] When it comes to the analysis of technology, Lisa Gitelman reminds us, "specificity is key" (8). Technology is not monolithic in its influence; in order to understand its cultural impact, we must explore its embeddedness in regional, spatial, and historical particularities. As John Stilgoe makes clear through *Metropolitan Corridor,* there is no singular American railroad, nor is there a singular American railroad landscape. In early twentieth-century America, riding on a cross-country luxury liner is far different from taking a commuter train into and out of the city; similarly, riding a train in contemporary America has a far different resonance than does either of these examples (ix). I examine the modern subway because it serves a number of rhetorical purposes in this period, each with its own complex discursive history. When tropes and images overlap, I take care to highlight their differences. Both Jewish and African American writers discuss migration and the railroad, for example, but the former might cite Sholem Aleichem while the latter uses the language of a spiritual. The New York subway of the early twentieth century is resolutely multiple in its associations.

The subway's construction and opening were widely celebrated. The cachet of the space grew as it became a common setting for both highbrow and popular interpretations of the city. The majority of positive literary and artistic depictions of the subway appeared from the mid-1920s to the mid-1950s (Fitzpatrick 4; Brooks 5). This attitude would change, however, in the wake of postwar suburbanization. By the late 1950s, New Yorkers had begun to perceive the subway as a dangerous place (Brooks 190), and by the early 1960s, crime in the subway system had increased dramatically. The model of the subway as a system that enables underground connection began to compete with an emergent model of the subway as marginal, criminal, completely cut off from the city above. The subway was both increasingly policed and increasingly beautified: the MTA Arts for Transit program was founded in 1985 in order to return the system to the "ideals of the original subway builders" (qtd. in Fotsch 121). As I note in the conclusion, however, the early twentieth-century model recurs in postmodern writing, suggesting that when crime and graffiti decline, the sense of the subway as a unifying force resurges.

For too long the New York subway has been restrictively understood through the lens of 1960s and 1970s urban history. My chronological frame, 1904–1955, roughly follows the first rise and fall of the subway as a cultural icon. Though my conclusion discusses late twentieth- and twenty-first-century responses to the subway, I suggest that these postmodernist texts are better understood in dialogue with both their immediate predecessors and their modernist counterparts. Telling a story beginning at a specific point in a technology's past can serve a number of strategic purposes. Carolyn Marvin attends to the period "when old technologies were new" in order to frustrate our sense of inevitability about technological development; Lisa Gitelman does so in order to argue that the materiality of media shapes the stories that get told about it. Cultural agencies tell stories about technology's history just as often as academics do: when it was founded in 1985, the Metropolitan Transit Authority's Arts for Transit program allied itself with the aesthetic standards of the subway's founders in order to break away from the then current image of the subway system as a graffiti-covered dystopic space ("MTA—Arts for Transit"). My conclusion demonstrates that critics and city dwellers alike retain an investment in the "subway hell" of the 1970s and 1980s as a badge of authenticity and a sign of identification with the counterculture. Michael Brooks concludes, "The mundane reality of the New York City subway system is increasingly obscured by the mythology it generates" (206). I find that returning to the subway's first fifty years helps both to remind us of the mundane realities of the present day and to illuminate some of the mythologies of the past that have been obscured by later ones.

With a focus on the modern subway I contest the image of an ominous underworld, one that owes more to the crime-ridden cars of twenty or thirty years ago than it does to the everyday realities of riding today (Allen, "Elmgreen").[9] Following the lead of prior technological historians, I do so not to give a more correct history of the subway but to highlight the complex relationship that critics have to this cultural artifact. The poetics of the subway have often been described in archetypal terms, but they should nevertheless be understood within the framework of the historical present. Different academic and popular accounts of transit technologies are inescapably shaped by the periods in which they are written; the historical present structures the way we interpret and even choose the data to describe the past. Lewis Mumford, never a fan of the subway, could still see the aesthetic appeal of the system when he wrote *Technics and Civilization* in 1934 (333). By the time he publishes *The City in History* in 1961, however, the subway appears to have prefigured the "underground city" of the Atomic Age, where man is entirely cut off from nature in an artificially controlled environment. Mumford warns that this space may become the "burial crypt of our incinerated civilization" (478–81). Similarly, Michael Brooks begins his cultural history with a personal account of his desire to ride the subway, which is interrupted by a tabloid headline screaming "SUBWAY HELL" (1). This scaremongering takes place in a very specific period of New York's history, when the city was rebuilding infrastructure that had been ignored during the budget crisis of the 1970s. Even that seemingly infernal title can tell a number of different stories, depending on the state of the city and the subway being described. The newspaper that Brooks spotted describes a stalled car and passengers groping through a dark tunnel; a 2011 *New York Post* article with the same title warns passengers of impending difficulty in their weekend plans due to subway service changes (Namako). Depending on the decade, hell can mean ominous underground passageways or impeded crosstown journeys.

Subway discourse, like subway space, can be inflected differently in different times. That is why I try simultaneously to historicize my subway history with the thickest possible description and to keep in mind why the histories that I choose resonate in the present day. Bruno Latour suggests that critics should foreground their own experience and think about how it might inform the stories they tell; he asks us to "keep track of all our moves, even those that deal with the very production of the account" (133). This account of the subway is shaped by my background as a literary scholar. I have chosen the most formally interesting texts, as well as those that tell the most interesting stories about the subway. The history I trace, then, is necessarily partial. It is also shaped by my life in New York City in the post-9/11 era. My subway has never been the subway of Bernie Goetz or Keith Haring; my subway has instead been a panoptic form of transit, one where an abandoned backpack poses a threat and suspicious behavior should always be reported. In part, this self-surveillance informs my critical model of the subway as a place where passengers constantly monitor their positions and chart their progress through a system. The request made of the subway passenger in the twenty-first century—"If you see something, say something"—differs from the modernist injunction to "watch your step." These demands articulate different responsibilities for the single passenger within the crowd, yet both suggest that attention plays a central role in subway movement.

Modernist writers are fascinated by the ways that attention is transformed in subterranean space. The attention of the subway passenger is focused over a wide range of objects: reading material, fellow passengers, the map, conductors' announcements, and the passing stations themselves. The city above is bracketed off; a zone will return to its concrete status once the passenger emerges from a tunnel or ascends at her stop. But this abstraction does not arise from a void. To understand the unique elements of the subway's orientation, we must place the subway system in dialogue with other forms of mechanized mobility. I turn now to a brief survey of other modes of transportation in order to clarify the ways in which the subway reshapes the understanding of space, sociability, and attention.

## Mechanized Mobility

As recent cultural critics have made clear, technologies situate viewers in literal and symbolic relation to their surroundings.[10] Imagine driving past a neighborhood at seventy miles an hour on the elevated Brooklyn-Queens Expressway; though you might have a vague sense of the landscape, you couldn't familiarize yourself with the faces of the residents or the names of the businesses. As a passenger on a local bus, you would be privy to more of that local knowledge, but you'd also be subject to the set schedule and route followed by the bus driver. As Lisa Gitelman reminds us, even the most novel technologies should be understood as a response to older ones and not as a break from them (6). The processes of subway riding develop out of and in response to the cultural norms associated with earlier transportation technologies, including those associated with the railroad, the trolley, the elevated train, and the city sidewalk.

Since Manhattan is a long, thin island with business and government initially focused at its southern tip, urban development moved northward (Brooks 8). As settlement expanded, so did commutes between work and home. While the truly poor continued to walk to work, the working and middle classes soon had another option: local common carrier transportation.[11] Abraham Brower was the first entrepreneur to bring urban mass transit to New York City, and indeed to America. His modified stagecoaches ran along Broadway in the late 1820s; an omnibus designed by John Stephenson joined his fleet in early 1831. Stephenson also designed cars for the horse-drawn streetcar line that opened in New York City in 1832, the first in America. It was funded and constructed by the New York and

Harlem Railroad, the brainchild of a wealthy banker, John Mason. Originally intended to be the first section of a conventional steam-powered railroad, this line ran along the Bowery between Prince and Fourteenth streets in Manhattan. The horsecar improved on the design of its chief competitor in the realm of urban transit, the omnibus. An omnibus ride was far from comfortable for passengers, who bounced and jostled over cobblestone streets. Since streetcars ran on rails, they provided a far smoother ride.[12]

Rapid transit developed concurrently with American migration from country to city, and it made that process increasingly more feasible.[13] The omnibus and the streetcar were important predecessors to the subway because they enabled city dwellers to live considerably farther from their workplaces than they had in the past. They also made possible a more modern sense of time and space; though on a smaller scale than the train, streetcars and buses compress the distance between a journey's beginning and end, replacing a sense of miles traveled with one of time spent.[14] In addition to its reshaping of the urban landscape by extending the distance between work and home, rapid transit came to embody the conception of "urban haste" (Stilgoe 25). Public transportation, then, defined the era when Americans moved from the country to the city and their pace once they moved there.

In the early nineteenth century, omnibuses, streetcars, and private carriages all jockeyed for space on the congested north-south avenues, funneling people downtown for work and back uptown to their homes. Elevated trains, a mid-century innovation, were meant to lift passengers above the avenues, leaving the streets for business and freight traffic. Charles T. Harvey opened the world's first elevated line in lower Manhattan in 1868 (Hood, *722 Miles* 49). Rufus Gilbert wished to follow suit with a line on Sixth Avenue. Both men lost funding as a result of the financial panics of the 1870s, but they eventually succeeded; by 1879, elevated lines ran down Second, Third, Sixth, and Ninth avenues.[15] Although the trains were noisy and dirty, these problems fell on the poor New Yorkers who lived near the tracks. For its riders, however, the elevated train combined efficient movement and an ever-changing panorama of neighborhoods.[16]

It's important to understand the subway as an extension of these earlier forms of mass transportation, ones in which the schedules and routes are predetermined. Standardized mobility carries over from the railroad to the subway. The period when the subway rises to prominence in New

York City is also one when railroad lines consolidate, track mileage peaks, and equipment and timetables are standardized (Stover 133). The American railroad in the Progressive Era creates a relatively uniform ride across a varied terrain. Indeed, it's far more successful at standardization than the New York subway: the system is not consolidated under city control until 1940; the track gauges for former IRT and BMT trains differ to this day. Yet the earliest writing about the subway establishes it as a standardized system as well, one in which passengers efficiently move through a system they cannot experience as a whole.

Standardization has a positive effect by subjecting a large swath of the urban population to the same routines. The imagined extensibility of the subway system both enacts and represents interconnection on a citywide level. American studies scholars have made the case that other forms of transportation similarly forge imagined communities. In the nineteenth century, the Transcontinental Railroad operates as a vehicle of symbolic cohesion. Proponents imagine the railroad would unify the nation, a claim that "reveals a continual anxiety that the divisive forces of regionalism might undermine the union" (Nye, *American Technological Sublime* 48). In the subway's first fifty years, we see a number of similar anxieties about urban sociability at work, including concerns related to migration and immigration, the impersonality of the crowd, and the loss of religious faith. The subway's loose association of individuals into a cohesive whole serves to assuage those anxieties. One of the most important lessons of the modern subway, I argue, is that infrastructure shapes the relation of urban communities to one another.[17]

Of course, the flip side to standardized movement is the loss of individual agency. The walker and the driver feel a sense of independence and control that the public transit passenger lacks. In his meditation on modern speed, Jeffrey Schnapp observes that a "fundamental bifurcation occurs by the beginning of the nineteenth century between *passenger*-centered and *driver*-centered modes of transportation or, to state the matter otherwise, between modes of mass transit and individual transportation" (3). At the turn of the twentieth century, when cultural commentators bemoan the loss of individualism and initiative,[18] the subway appears as a resolutely collective form of mobility, standing in sharp contrast to the freedom and individualism promised by the automobile. Passengers can enter the subway at any stop they choose, but not in between. When they enter the car, they become subject to its rules, its crowds, and its annoyances. The subway is not a space of independence so much as it is one of interdependence.

The body figures prominently in all modern descriptions of urban transit. Indeed, Carolyn Marvin suggests that the body serves as a yardstick for measuring new technologies (109). The attention to the bodies of passengers differs widely from one form of mobility to another. Omnibus and streetcar riders become accustomed to a degree of physical proximity to one another that they otherwise would shun.[19] The elevated train was often equally crowded, but first-person accounts focus on the sights outside the train's windows.[20] The elevated car windows could be opened, and on summer days the back door of the last car was often opened as well to take in the breeze. Gliding through the city, passengers felt a sensual connection to their surroundings. A 1938 editorial in the *New York Herald Tribune* describes the aesthetic pleasure and spatial mastery of riders navigating the city: "Powerful nationalistic smells of cooking, as well as odors from the leather, spice, chemical, coffee and other industries reach the traveler who is seeing New York for a nickel, and if he is a regular, he can tell with his eyes shut about where he is on his journey" ("It Won't Be Very Soon"). This sense of connection to the urban environment was impossible on the subway, a space of physical and psychological dissociation.

Wolfgang Schivelbusch in *The Railway Journey* initiated many terms in the critical discussion of transportation technology's impact on human perception. Schivelbusch finds panoramic vision to be a central feature of nineteenth-century culture. He locates this distanced, aestheticizing gaze in the sweeping views of the countryside glimpsed from a railroad's touring-car window (52–69).[21] The American railroad operates in an equally aestheticizing way. Raised above the landscape and passing rapidly through it, passengers could not take in the details of their surroundings in the way they could when riding in a carriage or coach (Nye, *Narratives and Spaces* 15). Instead of understanding the sights they saw as grounded in the place being passed through, railroad passengers understood them as "ephemeral," "theatrical," and eventually cinematic (Stilgoe 250, 252).[22] The speed of the railroad reshaped passengers' mental maps by highlighting a limited number of focal points and blurring the surroundings. Like the railroad before it, the omnibus and streetcar distance passengers from the surrounding city, which could often be seen only in glimpses through a crowd of people.

Subway movement perpetuates this technological distancing from the landscape; indeed, it renders that distance absolute by moving the ensemble underground. Now, instead of watching a rapid blur in which "only a few scenes appeared worthy of notice" (Nye, *Narratives and Spaces* 15), passengers watch the passing darkness and occasional stations flashing into view. The infrastructure itself becomes the only possible view outside the car. Acclimating to subway ridership brings about a new orientation toward the infrastructural sights. At first, passengers' gazes range wildly over the tunnels and stations. People spend their rides staring out the windows, watching the other stations and trains fly by and admiring the intricate tilework on the walls of each stop. On the playwright Elmer Rice's first subway ride, which he described in the *New Yorker* in 1928, people "gazed out of the windows brazenly and did not attempt to stifle their exclamations of wonder" ("A New York Childhood" 21). This attention to the subway system evolved rapidly: "by the end of six months," Rice wrote, "I had even stopped looking at the tiling" (23). Nineteenth-century railroad passengers read because the changing view outside their car was too exhausting (Stilgoe 251); twentieth-century subway passengers do so once the view becomes too routine. One story that I tell in *Underground Movements,* then, is the story of how a novel transportation technology becomes a normal part of city dwellers' everyday lives.

Modern literature and popular culture celebrated the subway and showed its readers how to become riders. As I discuss in chapter 1, newspaper stories imagined the subway habit long before the first station was opened to the public. Popular songs in the years that followed recast the unsteady footing of its riders as a dance.[23] Early twentieth-century poetry, drama, and fiction show the slippage between two cognitively distinct experiences—feeling technology's effects on one's body and understanding technology as a planned element of the urban infrastructure. I turn now to the implications of a technological study that focuses chiefly on literary texts as its source material.

## Riding and Writing

Earlier American studies scholars wrote about technology using literature as their primary focus, and they have been rightly criticized both for elevating one set of cultural texts over another and for extrapolating from that privileged set of texts to intuit the state of American culture as a whole.[24]

“Though poetry and fiction are not very helpful in establishing the historical record as such,” Leo Marx acknowledges in his afterword to *The Machine in the Garden,* “they are singularly useful . . . in getting at the more elusive, intangible effects of change—its impact on the moral and aesthetic, emotional and sensory, aspects of experience” (370). Even if we no longer hold literature to be *singularly* useful, we can still explore the particular usefulness of aesthetically heightened language that tries to represent new cognitive processes which arise for people living in a technologically mediated world. One reason to consider subway literature is to differentiate the experience of technologically mediated movement through the city from prior forms of mobility recorded in other ways. Lauren Berlant and John Johnston, for instance, argue that particular kinds of technology facilitate new ways of processing the present. Extrapolating from their writing about the elevator in Colson Whitehead’s novel *The Intuitionist,* we might similarly understand the subway as an “exemplary laborator[y] for sensing or intuiting contemporary life” (Berlant 845), one that serves as both “the space and trajectory of a research” (Johnston 861). Modernist writers found the subway to be such a “laboratory” for researching the affective impact of modernity and its many constituent components, including the fragmentation of consciousness, the excitement and strain of migration, and the commercialization of the public sphere. Throughout this book I consider how they translate this research into both formal innovation and content that explores the practice of subway riding.

Literary attention to the subway must be understood in dialogue with earlier forms of writing that use the stroll as the prototypical form of discursive urban mobility. By the mid-nineteenth century, descriptions of New York City in terms of its diverse population had become a common genre of newspaper and magazine writing.[25] These features were defined by their anecdotal quality and their focus on the typicality of the characters and scenes that the narrator encounters. In this way they already establish the concern for the relation between part and whole so central to subway writing: a fruit seller, for example, must display recognizable characteristics of all fruit sellers while still giving the readers a sense of his personality. Sketches like these were subsumed under the mantle of “urban picturesque” writing by the late nineteenth century. Painters and writers entered the city’s ghettoes, sketching what they saw in words and pictures. While their depictions were often facile or dismissive, they offered readers and viewers what John Urry calls "imaginative mobilities," forms not otherwise available in the academic art and moralistic writing of the Victorian era (66). Carrie Tirado Bramen theorizes that this genre "sought to make modernity less terrifying by making it familiar," and that it "promised to turn the urban realities of class disparity and ethnic heterogeneity into customary sights and even potentially pleasant aspects of the modern experience" (156). Although traces of the urban picturesque remain in subway writing, the familiar tends to be defamiliarized: rather than making the subway ride pleasant, modern writers try to make it meaningful.

Subway writing differs from its pedestrian predecessors in terms of both the speed of the journey and the agency of the guide. With what Bramen dubs the "intra-urban walking tour," readers take in a verbal or visual representation of a stroll through a particular district of the city, recording the interesting sights along the way (159). Walking defines the scope and form of this genre for a number of reasons. Although the description emphasizes visual elements of the city, they are tied together by the presumed embodiment of the figure leading the tour. The awkward tourist walks too slowly, gawking at the sights, while the purposeful native walks too quickly to see them. The ideal guide through quaint neighborhoods of New York City, by contrast, is one who "walks its streets with a degree of ease and familiarity that only a cosmopolitan *savant* can have" (Bramen 170). In this way, the narrative's authenticity is assured in part by his physical presence in and movement through the neighborhoods that he describes. In addition, the narrator's expertise and freedom manifest themselves in his choices about which path to take: it need not be "unusual" or "historically significant," but it is uniquely defined by the figure leading the tour (Zurier 89). The sketch may not present a totality of the city, but it is assumed to present a carefully crafted totality of its first-person observer's perceptions. The subway journey is at once faster and more restricted, since the sights described depend entirely on the preestablished route of the train and the chance encounter with passengers entering and exiting. Passenger populations do change over the course of the journey—bankers enter the 6 at Grand Central Station and exit downtown, for example—but it is difficult to understand sketches in picturesque terms when passengers are divorced from their native environments.

The investment in the "intra-urban walking tour" suggests that urban literature fulfilled a turn-of-the-century need for a sense of agency over one's own movements through the city. Indeed, Bramen suggests that this literary genre allows the new commuting class to experience firsthand a mode of relating to the city that would not otherwise be possible for them: "The intra-urban walking tour was a genre ideally suited for the emerging figure of the urban commuter. While sitting on the avenue 'L' or on the crosstown trolley, reading about downtown perambulations afforded a sense of contact with the 'other half,' cross-cultural encounters that the new technologies of mobility were making more difficult to express directly and meaningfully" (159–60). The peripatetic narrator of the urban picturesque sketch is set in sharp contrast to the commuting reader. Whereas the narrator takes part in direct and meaningful cross-cultural contact, the commuter can experience those things in only a secondary way. There is no single element of the commute that can be faulted; instead, the technological ensemble as a whole limits the commuter's experience. Instead of "perambulati[ng]," she sits passively; instead of wandering the streets, she fixes her path on a north-south or east-west axis; instead of experiencing the diversity of the city firsthand, she reads about it and ignores her neighbors. In this way, the intra-urban walking tour enables a brief, imagined resistance to the segmentation of the city that takes place in modernity.

The form of the urban picturesque seen in early subway writing, by contrast, decenters the agency of the narrator. He gains mobility because of the technology, not because of his own volition; the set paths of subway lines and transfer points limit the potential for wandering. Subway writing thus explores one of the underexamined experiences of the machine age. Critics from Lewis Mumford to Joel Dinerstein have identified machine aesthetics that are present in the art of the period. Streamlining, precision, and rhythm are emblematic qualities of modern plastic arts as well as modern music.[26] Yet modern subway literature does not celebrate "human mastery of machine aesthetics" (Dinerstein 12); instead it concerns itself with human passivity in relation to the machine. From enraptured poets to sleeping commuters to reluctant migrants, modernist writers explore the lack of agency engendered by subway habits.

The texts narrated by pedestrian authorities, however intimate their relation to their surroundings, create a distanced reaction on the part of the readers who experience the sights secondhand (Bramen 173). Transportation technologies began to intervene in the discourse of the urban picturesque by the late nineteenth century, creating other opportunities for distanced or mediated relations to the slums (Haenni 27–56). These forms of transportation shape the passing neighborhoods into "scenes," whether domestic pictures spotted through the windows of apartments or groupings of figures on a street. Moving through a neighborhood becomes a metonymic form of getting to know a culture. Subway writing calls into question the authority of the urban picturesque scene, even when it is mediated by technology. It does so in part through what I consider its constitutive element, underground movement. This removal from city streets lends the subway car an air of defamiliarization toward the picturesque sights that might still be glimpsed within. The modernist mode of writing the city from the confines of the subway car, then, puts forth quite a different attitude and set of associations regarding city life than does the walking tour that preceded it. As New Yorkers begin to live farther from the urban center, the subway becomes one of the few locations where extended interracial and cross-class encounters take place. This means that its distinctive quality was both subjective and collective. In an era when life in the United States is more spatially dispersed and ideologically isolated, these subway stories remind us that transportation technology can bring us into contact with people who see the world differently.

The subway pieces together New York City in a new way, one that has not been fully theorized in previous studies of the subway or the city. In a 1916 poem Ruth Comfort Mitchell describes the train as "the torrid hyphen that bridges work and home" (54). Mitchell's metaphor suggests division as well as connection: hyphens keep words stubbornly separate even as they link them. Following the lead of Mitchell and poets like her, writers in the early twentieth century defined the subway commute as an experience of suspension or in-betweenness. I argue that this spatial disconnection led to a new model of subjectivity that was discontinuous rather than developmental. Modern writers use the underground, in-between space to meditate on the liminal quality of modern life.[27]

The first stories about the New York subway were those that told New Yorkers how the train could be used. In chapter 1 I discuss narratives of underground movement, considering how they naturalized the most frightening element of the subway system. As Lisa Gitelman reminds us, new technologies must be actively acclimated to preexisting routines, often by explaining how they will supersede prior technologies. I establish the spatial framework of my project in chapter 1, where I discuss how the *New York Times* plays a central role in shaping the way that subway movement is first understood. Early twentieth-century newspaper and magazine coverage of the New York subway repeatedly invokes the mole as a metaphor for the subway rider. I examine this urban tunneling as a form of what Kevin Lynch calls "cognitive mapping." Subway movement depends less on vision than on mole-like proprioception, a movement that seems blind yet constantly orients the subject within the underground system. It thus offers an important historical corrective to Lynch's optically driven model of locating oneself. Here we see the most literal instance of the relation between an individual subject and a system of modernity. The subway rider's immediate, tactile engagement with urban space exists in tension with her imagining the body as it moves through a mapped representation of the city. I show how the experience of the subway ride is constantly in dialogue with an overall sense of the system, a distinction I develop with reference to Michel de Certeau's opposition between the *tour* and the *map*. I suggest that the subway brings into being a new relationship to city space that involves both mental distance and physical immediacy. In this way the subway marks an important break from the models of urban visuality in operation in nineteenth-century New York City. Critics such as de Certeau, John Kasson, and Douglas Tallack have contrasted overhead views of the city—which offer a godlike perspective and grant the viewer a sense of distance from the scene—with street-level views that implicate the spectator and submerge him in the crowd. Discussions of the New York subway in the first half of the twentieth century show that those perspectives have been brought together into a technologically mediated view of urban space.

In chapter 2 I unpack the first self-consciously literary mode of subway writing, the middlebrow magazine lyric. While early subway poets argued that the subway fit into preexisting models of awe-inspiring technology, they received pushback from the highbrow critics of the period. "Technologies are contested terrains," as David Nye reminds us (*Narratives and Spaces* 3), and the subway was subject to many competing narratives. In chapter 2 I reconstruct a history of magazine poetry from the New York subway's first decade, poetry that posits a link between the seemingly infinite subway system and other systems that cannot be known rationally in full, such as religion. The darkness of its tunnels and the vastness of their interlocking network suggest a kind of boundlessness that refuses perceptual mastery on the part of the individual viewer. The speed and noise of the ride also overwhelmed passengers, amplifying the initial perceptions of the railroad as the modern example of what Kant calls the "dynamic sublime." Yet subway verse was subject to harsh censure from critics of the period, who found the trend for urban poetry to be distasteful and anti-aesthetic. American studies scholars from Perry Miller to Leo Marx to David Nye have deployed the concept of the technological sublime as a means of exploring the wonder, awe, and power that American culture locates in the machine. By calling on this discourse, subway verse argues against the commodification ascribed to its choice of content and publication venue. Forgotten poets such as Margaret French Patton and Chester Firkins—as well as the better-known but currently unfashionable Joyce Kilmer—dealt with public transit as a means of grappling with the continuing relevance of their craft. They accommodate the subway through extended comparisons to other, more poetic settings that are equally vast and unknowable, such as the ocean, the firmament, and Dante's underworld.

Later subway poems abandon the pretense that the subway perpetuates sublime feelings brought about by prior technologies, instead engaging with the routine qualities of the system. In chapter 3 I discuss the poets of the interwar period who justify their elliptical style by placing it in dialogue with the subway's dissociated movement through the city. Avant-garde poetry deployed the subway not only as a sublime setting but as a sort of textual infrastructure: rather than justifying the disconnected subway ride by suggesting that it connected to a divine plan, these poets appealed to the coherence of the subway system itself as an organizing principle. Modernist poets such as William Carlos Williams, Claude McKay, and Maxwell Bodenheim paint the New York subway as a place where collage is a part of everyday life. When these modernists deal with subterranean transit, they also tend to deal with subterranean connections, exploring less obvious and less direct paths in their poetic construction. In this chapter I point out the ways in which the subway enables New York modernist writers to theorize increasingly complex poetic structures. The underground connections made possible by the subway system in effect model the underground connections made by the reader. Technology serves as a map for orienting urban subjects and the readers of urban writing. Hart Crane attends to the subway as a figure for mapping literary history: rather than a direct line of descent, he sees influences branch off and double back like a system of underground tunnels.

With its focus on dailiness and the working class, modernist writing imagines the subway as a technology for leveling differences between New Yorkers, often eliding the inequalities that are part of city life aboveground. Indeed, because of its diverse passenger population the subway is commonly characterized as a miniature "melting pot." My fourth chapter historicizes the subway's problematic role as a technology of Americanization. In 1913 construction of new subway lines increase dramatically under what were known as the Dual Contracts. Their expansion into undersettled areas of the Bronx and Brooklyn leads to an influx of immigrants in what the historian Peter Derrick calls the "subway suburbs" (7). Osip Dymov's 1919 play *Bronx Express* (originally staged in Yiddish) traces the journey of one such New Yorker, a Jewish immigrant button maker who dreams of becoming a millionaire as he rides home. The play demonstrates how Americanization takes on a spatial resonance: rather than living in Manhattan, Jews live on the fringes of the cultural mainstream in the Bronx. In an era of intense nativist sentiment, we see how the subway both assimilates and ghettoizes. A later play, William Saroyan's *Subway Circus* (1940), imagines the subway as a melting pot where no one melts. The play enacts the dreams of passengers from many different ethnic backgrounds—even some entirely in languages other than English. The dreams, and the passengers who dream them, remain separate from one another. The elaborate sequences are all self-contained manifestations of the passengers' atomized consciousness.

The 135th Street and Lenox Avenue subway stop served as the threshold for new migrants to Harlem, the locus of African American culture and politics in the twentieth century. In chapter 5 I explore how the subway functions as a trope of migration in African American prose from the 1920s through the 1950s. Given that technology studies conversations have arisen around the modern construction of African American automobility, I suggest ways that city literature complements and complicates this discourse—particularly through its dependence on class distinctions. Harlem Renaissance writers of the 1920s including Nella Larsen, Walter White, Carl Van Vechten, and Rudolph Fisher use the language of earlier migration narratives to ironize the Great Migration, discussing the subway ride from Pennsylvania Station to Harlem in terms more appropriate for nineteenth-century journeys by train and Underground Railroad. They do so, I argue, in order to gain distance from the history of the South even as they mourn the past that is left behind in that abandoned region. We see this tradition carried on in African American literature of the 1940s and 1950s, like Ralph Ellison's *Invisible Man,* where the nameless narrator tries to reconcile his own southern past and the disaffected present of the zoot-suited young men with whom he shares a subway car. The subway, like Harlem itself, brings together African Americans of radically dissimilar backgrounds as a provisional community.

Although Langston Hughes could claim in "Subway Rush Hour" (1951) that the subway "mingled / black and white / so near" that there was "no room for fear" (*Collected Poems* 423), it no longer held that utopian position in the mid-1960s. By 1965 the subway had become a representation not of the city but of its failure. Crime increased, and budget shortages kept Mayor John Lindsay from carrying out his plans for the construction of a Second Avenue subway line. Instead of offering a model of complex cohesion, the subway seemed a dangerous sign of the irrationality of city life. It continued to be understood as a reflection of the city, but by the 1970s and 1980s this association was a dangerous one. With the publication in 1993 of *The Mole People* by Jennifer Toth, "living as a mole" no longer meant riding the subway; it meant living in one of a warren of tunnels branching off the subway lines. Indeed, critics continue to conflate the subway with the underworld, whether mythological or criminal. In 1992 Governor Mario Cuomo gave a speech in which he made the thinking of outsiders all too clear: "There is a public perception out there that New York State is New York City, and New York City is Manhattan, and Manhattan is a subway that murders people every night" (Sack). Here the subway functions as a symbol not of connection but of reduction. Every step in this train of thought leaves something important behind: the rest of the state, the other boroughs of New York City, and the other modes of transportation within Manhattan. By the time Cuomo arrives at the catachresis that describes Manhattan as a murderous subway, we have lost all of the complexity associated with that form of transit in the first half of the twentieth century.

Yet in the post-9/11 era an increasing number of writers look back to the subway nostalgically, finding in it the same type of meaning that early twentieth-century writers and artists did. I conclude with a discussion of the ways in which postmodern writers such as Jonathan Lethem, Colson Whitehead, and Colum McCann reimagine the earlier model of the subway as a site of underground connection. By concluding with contemporary writers, I suggest how my literary genealogy might help us better understand the current role of the subway in New York's cultural imaginary. Even in essays that evoke the bad old days when the subway functioned as an urban hell, these writers reconceive their own pasts through the bodily knowledge of the city that they experienced as riders. Nostalgic narratives like these do not necessarily have to be retrograde in their claims. As Colin Divall points out, examining the symbolic functions of public transportation in the past helps critics, planners, and citizens understand fixed ideas about it in the present (957–58). Rather than associating a technology with an unalterable urban pathology, contemporary writers identify shared experiences in an increasingly centripetal city and mine veins of unexplored utopianism in this seemingly dystopian space.

# CHAPTER 1
# FORMING THE SUBWAY HABIT

....

Before the subway opened, New York's newspapers took sides on the issue, sensing that it would come to define the city in a new way. Some touted the possibility of traveling from City Hall to Harlem in fifteen minutes. Joseph Pulitzer's *New York Evening World* made the claim a battle cry of its own, calling it on April 5, 1893, "the definition of the term 'Real Rapid Transit' " and repeatedly invoking it in editorials and features about subway construction ("To Harlem in Fifteen Minutes").[1] Other publications, like the *New York Sun,* concerned themselves with safety issues ("How We'll Travel in the Subway"). Elmer Davis, the first writer to chronicle the history of the *New York Times,* jokingly granted that the *Sun* "was brilliantly written" but declared that its literary pretensions notwithstanding, the paper's "energies were principally devoted to the contentions that New Yorkers could never be persuaded to ride in subway trains" (197). The editors of the *New York Times,* by contrast, knew that New Yorkers *could* be persuaded to ride in subway trains. They began their campaign early, promoting a vision of underground space that was neither dangerous nor particularly modern. Instead, the paper made a concerted effort to cultivate the subway habit.

After he bought the *Times* in 1897, publisher Adolph Ochs positioned it as the sober alternative to activist journalism. Under Ochs's ownership the *Times* became the paper that we know today, the one that gives its readers "All the News That's Fit to Print." When it came to the subway, the *Times* took an uncharacteristically speculative approach: along with its coverage of the business of subway construction, the paper imagined how that transit technology would affect the thought processes of both New Yorkers and tourists.[2] Consider "The Subway Habit," an editorial published on October 4, 1903, more than a year before the subway would open to the public. The article anticipates subway travel becoming routine, asserting that "for some hundreds of thousands of people it will be a convenience so great that they will immediately acquire the habit of using it." It describes how the prototypical passenger will learn to navigate his underground commute: "He will presently become expert in distinguishing each station by its distinctive color scheme, and will probably recognize intuitively when he nears his own stopping place without looking up from his paper." It lightly mocks the middle-class mania for efficiency with a quotation from Shakespeare: "To his self-congratulation when the savings of time over present methods of transit is first experienced, and until he becomes again impatient of delay, the only appropriate reply would be that of Hamlet to the peripatetic ghost: 'Well said, old mole. Canst work i' the earth so fast?'" And it imagines that the underground movement between highly segmented spaces might provincialize New York's citizens, worrying that the passenger's "underground flight night and morning will serve to transplant him from one small and familiar neighborhood surrounding his place of business to another equally small and familiar neighborhood surrounding his home. Of the crowded square miles lying between he will learn nothing and may gradually forget what he has known." "The Subway Habit" and articles like it imagine subway passengers' daily routines as a starting point for considering how they will perceive the city from this new, technologically mediated position. Although the writers assume that the technology will play an overall positive role, they express the dissatisfactions inherent to modernity, such as the fear that any convenience gained by speeding up is immediately lost as the new speed becomes routine.

Indeed, one of the strangest things about underground movement was the pace at which it became absolutely unremarkable. For an earlier example of this acclimation we might look to the railroad, which, as Benson Bobrick argues, enabled "people to reconcile themselves to living in the Underworld" (85). This is true both because the railroad commonly ran through long tunnels, seeming effectively to be underground, and because its smoke, soot, and fire made it appear to be an infernal machine. Yet people did not reconcile themselves to *living* in this underworld; they reconciled themselves to *moving through* it. "The Subway Habit" and later stories of subway movement reveal a fascination with this subterranean space not because people dwell underground but because they can traverse the city more efficiently in a transit system that is separate from the busy and crowded city streets. The subway stories told in the *New York Times* point to an undertheorized component of subway mobility, one that emphasizes its crosstown linkages more than its ascents and descents.[3]

Throughout the subway's first decades, the *Times* characterizes it as a liminal space, not an infernal underworld. This positive spin may have been motivated by of the paper's close ties to August Belmont Jr., the man who funded the construction of the Interborough Rapid Transit line (Davis 189). Belmont was a stockholder, and he played a central role in Longacre Square's being renamed Times Square to commemorate the paper's move uptown (Tifft and Jones 55). I find, however, that the vision of the subway as a network falls in line with the paper's general pro-business attitude. The subway is not yet imagined as a five-cent pass for children of the ghetto to attend world-class museums; that would come in the 1930s and 1940s. Instead, it is seen as linking the home with the office, the office with the bar, the train station with the grand hotel. As an "organ of the investing classes" (Davis 192), the *Times* creates the vision of a subway suitable for the commuting banker and his shopping wife—a networked space of distracted movement through the city. Moreover, the business community wanted the subway to succeed; among other things, the more people rode the subway, the more likely the underground entrances to shops would prove a wise investment. While the *Sun* and the *World* fretted about the health risks associated with the "microbes" that were thought to breed on advertising placards in the subway station, the *Times* mocked their fears in multiple stories ("Subway's Dark Secret Up at Columbus Circle"; "The Subway Signs"). People who worried about the dangers of the subway, in the paper's estimation, were simply anti-progress. The depiction of subway movement in the *New York Times,* then, offers an important corrective to the visions of the underworld presented by some of the other papers of the time. Additionally, it offers a useful starting point for considering how the popular press made networked underground movement more appealing to middle- and upper-class readers.

By the turn of the twentieth century, it was no longer inconceivable that people might commute via underground transit. London's Underground had opened in 1863, the first in the world; Boston's "T," which opened in 1897, was the first in America. New York had itself been the site of a brief foray into pneumatic tube transport, with Alfred Beach's block-long demonstration tunnel built in 1870 ("Beach Pneumatic Transit"). But New Yorkers were still barraged with concerns about travel through this realm of the city. The financier and railroad tycoon Russell Sage encapsulated much of the uneasiness with this stunningly inaccurate (and possibly apocryphal) claim: "Preposterous! New York people will never go into a hole in the ground to ride to work and to their homes" (qtd. in Hymoff 264).[4] We can hear the implicit association of altitude with human refinement and depth with animal baseness in Sage's remark, a holdover from the nineteenth century that I discuss in a later section. Compare this attitude to the one that would be expressed in the 1944 musical comedy *On the Town:*

> New York, New York—
> A helluva town
> The Bronx is up and the Battery's down
> The people ride in a hole in the ground
> New York, New York—
> It's a helluva town.[5]

Although the expression is the same, it has a markedly different connotation. For the show's sailors on shore leave, calling the subway a "hole in the ground" betrays a kind of earthy enthusiasm, connecting it with the "hole in the wall" bars where they might drink. As we can see, by 1944 any associations of the underground with the underworld can be dismissed in a cavalier way: instead of proving that the city is an earthly hell, the subway merely proves that New York is "a helluva town."

## Underground, Not Underworld

By emphasizing the horizontal as well as the vertical connections made in the process of orienting oneself within subway space, this book responds specifically to the idea of the New York subway as an urban underworld, a spatial model that implies disconnection or repression. On the contrary, early twentieth-century writers repeatedly depict the subway as a world apart that nevertheless brings the city together. Bobrick's suggestion that the railroad acclimated nineteenth-century riders to "living in the Underworld" points to a larger critical tendency that casts the underground as a dwelling place. Here I should point out the distinction that has arisen in recent years between *space* and *place:* a space is roughly a location through which one moves, while a place is a location in which one stays.[6] Yi-Fu Tuan distinguished the two concepts with his observation that "place is security, space is freedom (3). Michel de Certeau situates this distinction in urban space: *place* is the domain of boundaries, fixed uses, "the street geometrically defined by urban planning," while *space* is the realm of mobility in practice (117–18). Since the subway was not a secure dwelling place (myths of "mole people" living in subway tunnels were not popularized until late in the century), and since the vast majority of subway texts deal with the system as it is used, I treat it as a space. Thus the questions that most interest me are far different from the ones Rosalind Williams has in mind when she begins *Notes on the Underground* by asking, "What are the consequences when human beings dwell in an environment that is predominantly built rather than given?" (1). Even in discussions of parts of the built environment that seem to be clearly marked as sites of flow rather than rootedness, slippage between the two concepts occurs. Martha Banta describes the material realities of New York City's "subworlds" that transport utilities and people through the city via "sewers, water mains, gas mains, steam-heating pipes, pneumatic tubes, and conduits for streetcar cables"; but when she moves to the metaphorical realm, she elides this infrastructural stratum with that of the "poor and huddled masses packed within the lower depths" (40,41). New York stories such as Ralph Ellison's *Invisible Man*, she claims, "the underground becomes the new utopia, a way out, and down, from the contested spaces of harbor views and street scenes that betray the original hope" of seventeenth-century New Amsterdam (46). As we know, utopia means "no place." The Invisible Man's imagined dwelling underground seems more permanent than the mobile and changing city as seen from ships and streets, but by the novel's conclusion, he plans to leave it. Since I discuss Ellison's novel later, I will say here in response to Banta only that the unnamed narrator's warm, bright, and solitary underground apartment stands in sharp contrast to the subway cars and platforms where he is surrounded by people who challenge his initial readings of the city. By emphasizing the subway as a place of horizontal connection and transition, I mean to highlight its importance as an urban *space*, a transitional middle ground rather than a fixed realm.

Since the 1990s a small but important critical tradition has arisen around the concept of the "underground," with both the literal and the metaphorical sense of the concept in play.[7] All of these works suggest a connection between the underground and the underworld, a critical trope that does not play a central role in my New York story. One aspect of city life that distinguishes the New York subway from its French and British counterparts is Manhattan's lack of earlier forms of symbolically resonant underground space.[8] Unlike London and Paris, New York is a city without ancient archways or the covered passages through shopping areas known as arcades. It has few significant older tunnels, since the largest tunneling projects happened around the same time as the construction of the subway. Representations of the New York subway have long borrowed from other undergrounds and underworlds, from early newspaper cartoons depicting Dante in the subway to the apocalyptic visions of 1970s and 1980s film (Brooks 71, 205).[9] Yet in the earliest evocations of the subway as underworld, the intent was not sublime but ridiculous. In a newspaper cartoon titled "Dante Tries the Subway; Finds the Air Hotter Than He Found It in Hades," Dante and Virgil are greeted not by the gadflies and wasps that sting the uncommitted souls at the gates of hell but by "microbes" that emerge from behind an advertisement for "Beaten Bananas." Says the subway Virgil, "Oh there are millions of these," adding, "They are pets of August Belmont" (qtd. in Brooks 71). Around the turn of the century, underground space was being purged of any hellish associations that it retained. The construction of the subway played an important role in redefining its status. An article in the *New-York Tribune* points to the "subway tendency" that had begun to spread even before the IRT line opened: "Heretofore underground shops in New-York have always been associated with dampness, darkness and even dirt. Now there seems to be a strong tendency toward them as the subway system approaches completion. The idea that because a place of business is beneath the street level it must of necessity be dark and given over to a cheap class of business is disappearing, and underground stores are being fitted up for the first lines of trade" ("The Growth of Underground New-York").

Because the fashionable new form of transit was being constructed in underground space, other, equally fashionable businesses followed suit. The change was made possible in part by technological innovations such as glass sidewalk bricks that let in natural light. The *Tribune* article describes an art exhibition that took place in an underground gallery, reading that event as a testament to the highbrow possibilities of lowdown storefronts. The article ends in much the same way as the many newsprint meditations on subway space, imagining a future "subsurface city" where "upper or nether side" becomes a signifying element in merchants' addresses, much as "East Side or West Side" does now ("Growth"). Underground space becomes more closely affiliated with circulation and commerce. For New Yorkers of the early twentieth century, the subway functions as an exceptional underground space that is a part of everyday life and an emblematic feature of their city. The ideas presented in articles such as these demonstrate that cultural historians of the subway must reject the too easy conflation of underground with underworld. The subway, like all urban spaces, is a production of a rich and often contradictory cultural dialogue. To consider the subway as anything other than itself, particularly when it plays such a central role as a metaphoric space for understanding other elements of city life, would be to risk "falling through the cracks into the abyss of the ahistorical" (Banta 50). Instead, I consider underground movement, defined by its horizontality as well as its verticality, as the paradigmatic mode of inhabiting the modern New York subway.[10]

The earliest subway stories help make this "hole in the ground" more homey. In some respects, they share their perspective and purpose with the genre of urban sketches, so popular at the turn of the century. By situating the diverse sights of the city within the framework of a walking tour, Carrie Tirado Bramen theorizes that this genre "sought to make modernity less terrifying by making it familiar" (156). Some *New York Times* articles take the same approach, using plain language to describe the subway's construction and assuring their readers of the expertise of its engineering ("Practical Subway Working"). A number of the subway articles in the *Times* go beyond this seemingly objective language, fancifully imagining subway riders, workers, and planners as animals. In the following section I unpack the implications of these zoomorphic tropes, suggesting that they condense a set of cultural assumptions about how underground movement would reshape the mental image of the city as a whole. Writing that imagines subway passengers as moles naturalizes the prospect of traveling underground, rendering "modernity less terrifying" in a different way than the urban sketch; it also restores a kind of agency to the riders who might feel the loss of that agency acutely. In the process, however, it highlights the blindness of underground movement and the increasingly self-contained quality of the city as a network. Many of these stories were published before a single reader could have ridden a subway train; they are prescriptive rather than descriptive. Michel de Certeau famously said that stories are a means of mass transportation (115). The stories told by the *New York Times,* and later by popular magazines such as *Life,* are meant to "organize" subway space for New Yorkers and help readers "make the journey" in their heads (de Certeau 116). In this way they suggest the role played by the press in acclimating New Yorkers to the subway and shaping conceptions of subway movement.

## Would You Live as a Mole?

Burrowing mammals appear repeatedly in the earliest coverage of the subway. Only a week after the system opened, the *Utica Saturday Globe* declared that the subway had turned New Yorkers into "human prairie dogs" that descend into one hole in the ground and reemerge from another (qtd. in Hood, *722 Miles* 98). While sometimes portrayed as a nuisance, the mole in turn-of-the-century writing is most often seen as domestic (as in Kenneth Grahame's children's classic *The Wind in the Willows*) and sometimes as an engineer (as in Royal Dixon's book *The Human Side of Animals,* which assures us that "his [the mole's] subterranean network of tunnels excels in complexity our modern city subways" [61]). Allusions to this animal render the subway more familiar, making it merely an extension of natural forms of construction. This complicates the usual reading of animalistic figurative language as a way of exploring the loss of agency and humanity in subway space. Stuart Chase imagines passengers killed in a collision as "beeves in the Chicago stockyards" (4); for him, the indignity of the subway ride is evidence of the dehumanizing doctrines of efficiency. The later use of the phrase "mole people" to describe homeless New Yorkers sleeping in the tunnels situates them in an uncomfortable space between human and animal. A focus on the burrowing of the modern subway mole, as we shall see, offers an interpretation of underground movement that ascribes agency to the individual passengers situating themselves in the subway system.

The figure of the mole condenses many elements of the subway experience as discussed in the first half of the twentieth century.[11] Perhaps the most important is its articulation of a new form of visuality. The mole's mobility within its own nest of burrows contrasts with the animal's apparent blindness to its surroundings. Subway stories repeatedly explore this paradox, marveling at men and women who seem to move easily through the subway crowd, entering and exiting trains without even looking at the station names. The sights outside the subway windows, celebrated in accounts of the system's opening, were soon relegated to tourist guidebooks; the typical subway rider buries his face in a newspaper or novel. Yet the sense of space moved through and time spent is experienced in an unconscious way. The naturalizing of underground space through the image of the mole thus offers a contrary model to that of the subway as urban underworld: networked and habitually moved-through horizontal spaces proliferate, while vertical, mythologically inflected spaces are few and far between.

Two elements distinguish the subway from prior forms of transit through New York City: its (chiefly) subterranean location, and its consequently invisible connection of widely separated locales.[12] These two facets of the system work in tandem to create the experience described by the *New York Times* of riders living "as a mole," blinded to the different neighborhoods lying between one place and another as they enter a closed system of working, shopping, dining, and transportation ("Would You Live as a Mole?"). Although this system is celebrated by the pro-business *Times,* the attitude expressed is not wholly positive. As "The Subway Habit" suggests, a New Yorker who is blind to the neighborhoods through which he passes during his commute can no longer feel connected to the city as a whole.

The subway enables mole-like living, further claims the May 8, 1904, article, by linking the various parts of the typical businessman's daily life. One could go, reads the subtitle, "From Home to Office without Going Out of Doors," with "Stopovers Too for a Sandwich and a Highball, If You Like Them." Striking a tone that is half marveling at modern efficiency and half distraught at the disconnection from nature that results, the article describes the urban development that is taking place in response to subway construction. Offices, stores, and restaurants that already had a presence on the grid system of New York City's streets were constructing underground passageways connecting their businesses directly to the nearest subway station. The article speculates on the possible impact these passageways might have on the lives of workers: "For instance, anybody who works in the new building of the *New York Times,* if he has acquired the habit of eating in a certain restaurant on Park Row need not give up the habit. From the cellar of the skyscraper in Forty-Second Street he can take a subway train, have his same old table with the same old waiter, and never once see the street, unless he takes the notion to look out of the window while he is eating" ("Would You Live as a Mole?").[13] In this reimagining of city space, the subway will not lead to the creation of new habits among New Yorkers; instead, it makes old habits easier to maintain, even under new circumstances. For the office worker of an earlier time, moving from a job downtown to one in midtown Manhattan would have meant having to find a new place to eat lunch, since the time spent traveling between the two parts of town might take up the whole hour. This in turn would have required that he leave his office building and walk the streets of the newly christened Times Square. Instead, thanks to the subway, he will be able to use modern transportation technology to keep himself separate from the surrounding neighborhood. The subway maintains connections to the past—the "same old table with the same old waiter"—while making connections to the present optional. The businessman need not see the street where he now works "unless he takes the notion to look out of the window."

This article correctly anticipates the centrality of the subway to the lives of New Yorkers in the twentieth century, as well as the disconnection from the life of the city streets that it facilitates. But it also complicates the association of the subway with passive, collective movement. In the early twentieth century, the automobile may be the ideal vehicle for asserting individualism and independence; the subway, however, seems to promise that the New York businessman can maintain his usual routines in peace—a less dramatic assertion of individualism, but an assertion nonetheless. Additionally, early imagined responses to the subway like "Would You Live as a Mole?" force us to modify an understanding of technological modernity rooted in novelty, speed, and shock.[14] The subway is novel because it enables the newspaperman to maintain his daily habits; the speed and shock of his movement from midtown to downtown and back are undercut by the ease of it.

The convenience of the subway as a means of travel was understood metonymically through the reference to the city's streets—streets that passengers in the know would no longer have to navigate. "Would You Live as a Mole?" begins with the optimistic lede, "When a man can take luncheon two or three miles from his place of employment without once putting his feet on the pavement, and when a woman can go shopping on a rainy day without taking an umbrella or a cab, modern methods of transit, it would seem, will have reached the top notch of perfection." Here the subway story works in direct opposition to the "intra-urban walking tour" by imagining a form of transportation that is pure movement, avoiding the inconveniences of the sidewalk, though perhaps the picturesque sights as well. Instead, it harks back to the sense of distraction associated with the railroad, where the images outside the window move by at too rapid a rate to be taken in. When Ralph Waldo Emerson rode the train from Boston to Baltimore, he noted that the sights from New York to Philadelphia "make no distinct impression. They are like pictures on a wall. The more, that you can read all the way in the car a French novel" (qtd. in Emerson 219). The subway is the apotheosis of a long line of transit options that minimized visual contact with the outside world.

As with other transportation technologies, the subway redefines the relation between different parts of the city because it connects them more rapidly.[15] The Interborough line's express trains, the first to run on separate tracks, were wildly popular; more passengers rode these trains than the locals. Because expresses ran one-third faster, passengers could live farther away from their jobs without having to spend additional time traveling to them (Hood, *722 Miles* 98). In this respect, the subway quite literally enacted the "time-space compression" theorized by David Harvey (240).[16] Velocity, particularly as experienced on the express trains, distinguishes the New York subway from its predecessors and its peers in other cities. An article that compares New York's train to three other "world subways" suggests that in spite of the "animation and variety" that can be taken in on a streetcar or bus in Manhattan, "the thought of those express trains in the subway is all-conquering!" (Ybarra). The picturesque tradition of New York writing, at its height in the age of the streetcar and elevated train, must come to an end when even artistically minded New Yorkers will give up the varied sights and sounds of the street in order to shave ten minutes off their commute home.

The seamless movement between the subway system and other systems within New York City's transportation regime becomes an important theme in the *New York Times,* one that both exhilarated and worried its writers.[17] Chief among their concerns was the sense of alienation from the outside world that could result when one depended on the subway and other artificial environments for transport and entertainment. A 1910 story considers New York as seen by tourists from Chicago. When they enter the city, "their train will sink out of sight on the Jersey meadows and emerge underground" at Pennsylvania Station; after traveling by subway to shops, shows, hotels, and banks, "they would leave the city truthfully saying that they had never been in the daylight in New York and did not know whether it was hot, cold, stormy, or clear" ("New York's Growth"). The subway brings about the kind of hermetic, artificial environment that both Rosalind Williams and Lewis Mumford see as the epitome of twentieth-century space. Rather than being defined by its subterranean status as such, this kind of self-contained space is defined by circulation: the movement of businessmen between work and home, of tourists between train stations and restaurants, even of goods and services in and out of stores. In 1947 Meyer Berger is still worrying about New Yorkers' unfamiliarity with their wider environment: "When they pop out of the subway kiosks they are blinded to the natural beauties spread before them. When friends come to visit them, they treat them like visiting moles—show them the underground, herd them into cavernous theatres and museums, into smoke-filled rooms and purse-digesting night spots. They seldom walk abroad with them, because walking on the surface is a rare experience for moles" ("Big City"). Paradoxically, the mole becomes a figure not of the natural world but of the artificial, overly civilized world of the urban sophisticate. The mole thus becomes an exemplary animal of modernity.

## Unification

The proliferation of mole imagery reflects the technologically mediated access to increasingly large swaths of the city at the turn of the century. The subway's opening was one of many technological and political processes that led to the unification of New York in this period. The Brooklyn Bridge opened in 1883, followed by the Third Avenue and Willis Avenue bridges to the Bronx (1898, 1901) and the Williamsburg Bridge to Brooklyn in 1903. Just as important as the bridges that made passage between boroughs easier was the passage of the agreement that consolidated them into one entity. In 1898 Manhattan, the Bronx, Brooklyn, Queens, and Staten Island were brought together as Greater New York, centralizing the government of all five boroughs in Manhattan (Lankevich 132–36). Each of these changes brought about a shift in perceptions, requiring New Yorkers to incorporate more square mileage into their mental picture of the city.

The subway system was not easy to imagine as a networked whole in the early days, especially as a result of the isolation of different lines within subway space as it was conceived. The Interborough Rapid Transit and the Brooklyn Rapid Transit companies ran separate subway lines, and even when they worked together to construct new lines in the 1910s, they maintained this separation for structural and economic reasons. They used rolling stock of different sizes and consequently had different requirements for the size of tunnels. Transfers between the two lines were difficult to navigate; as Clifton Hood points out, "neither company wanted to lose any traffic to its rival," so "the planners provided for relatively few connections between their lines, and the handful of passageways that did lead from one company's lines to the others were long, narrow, and inconvenient" (*722 Miles*, 160). In this way, the conceived space of the subway as constructed by separate companies interfered with the ease of passenger movement within the system. Indeed, those connections were effectively invisible on official route maps at least through the 1930s, which showed only those trains that constituted an individual company's lines, though commercial publishers put out maps that included the whole transit system. In *Art and the Subway,* Tracy Fitzpatrick identifies the end point after which all subway maps included a unified system not as 1940, when the subway was unified under city control, but as 1953, when the Transit Authority was established (136–37).

The Interborough Rapid Transit and Brooklyn Rapid Transit corporations may have fought to keep their lines separate, but they also increased the number of possible pathways through the city. After the IRT and BRT signed what were known as the Dual Contracts in 1913, subway line construction expanded exponentially, particularly in the underdeveloped areas of the outer boroughs. This expansion, brokered by the progressive activist and Manhattan borough president George McAneny, doubled the track length and the number of trains that could move along those tracks in an hour (Hood, *722 Miles* 159). The Dual Contracts structured not only the subway system but the logic by which the crowds moved through it as well. The increasing ease with which passengers could transfer underground, at least between lines run by the same company, reinforced the subway's cohesiveness as a network and its self-contained disconnection from the city.

Peter Derrick makes the strong claim that this agreement had a tremendous impact on the spatial organization of New York City, "more than any other project ever built" (1), because it cemented the modern understanding of the city as a radial one, shaped by the regular movement of its inhabitants between center and periphery (246–49). Although much of the rationale for the Dual Contracts had to do with lessening overpopulation in the city's slums, they also brought about more concentrated congestion in the business and entertainment districts; as Lewis Mumford grumpily proclaimed, while new train lines "open up new areas on the outskirts of the city, they but thicken the crowding at the center" (*Culture of Cities* 239). This was the era that saw the development of centralized districts where places of work and entertainment could be found en masse, such as Times Square. From these transit hubs, passengers dispersed to neighborhoods far more distant even than in the era of the elevated trains. A passenger boarding at Times Square could debark at distant locales such as Coney Island in Brooklyn or Van Cortlandt Park in the Bronx without even having to change trains. Because of its extensive reach and affordable fare, the subway is the chief technological force that enables New York to continue what Thomas Bender calls its "paradoxical" development as "at once a concentrated 'slab' city and a dispersed 'spread city' of single-family, duplex, and triplex homes" (xi). Rapid transit thus helps make possible New York's existence as both a concentrated city and a dispersed one, as commuters swarm into business centers in the morning rush hour and return to their own neighborhoods at night. This unification holds true across different spheres of life. For most New Yorkers, the subway bridges the working world of skyscrapers, the family life of brownstones, and the leisure time exemplified by Central Park. As parts of the city are simultaneously divided from and connected to one another, so are the parts of life that they epitomize.

The subway ties into a whole a multiplicity of spaces that were once considered whole unto themselves. Before the boroughs were consolidated into Greater New York, Brooklyn was the third-largest city in America

(Lankevich 117).[18] Along with the bridges, tunnels, and ferries overseen by the Metropolitan Transportation Authority, the subway helps construct a "metropolitan region" that fuses "several metropolitan areas"; the metropolitan region "arises from two intertwined processes: extended decentralization from big cities to adjacent areas and interconnection of pre-existing towns whose territories become integrated by new communication capabilities" (Castells xxxiii). Although the subway functions as a local network that moves the urban masses and not a communication network that allows them to stay in one place, the similarities are otherwise striking. The consolidation of work, leisure, and home life into a closed system for the urban moles of the *New York Times,* then, tells us something about what this newly consolidated city feels like.

As we have seen, before the subway opened, the *Times* imagined its impact on New York life by using the figure of the mole; two years later, one Dr. A. S. Atkinson perpetuates this urban imagery in an article that attests to the "New Senses Developed by Subway Travel," where he asks, "Is the Tunnel Habit Endowing New York Humanity with the Instincts of the Ground Mole?" Atkinson calls upon a developing discourse that considers how passengers orient themselves within subway space. He theorizes that the prototypical New Yorker has learned to calibrate his location constantly within the city as a result of an "unconscious process of reason" that compensates for, and is even in some senses a result of, his physical blindness to his surroundings:

> His mind has had time to adapt itself to the new conditions of travel, and, whether it is a sense of time or a new sense of location which informs him, he invariably closes his paper at the right moment and prepares to leave his station just before reaching it.
>
> What is this sense of location which has been developed? It is not due to the study of landmarks, for there are none except the station which occasionally flashes past the view. It is rather the same instinct which enables the ground mole to find its way under the ground, and without light or landmarks to burrow from one root to another and never lose a sense of position. (Atkinson)

This description of the subway ride evokes many of the central topics in recent discussions of urban modernity, particularly through its analysis of habit and the move from an optic to what we might, using language favored by Walter Benjamin, call a haptic form of perception. While some early accounts invoked medical authority to suggest the dangers of the subway system, this essay uses the ethos of the profession to discuss the subway's normality and contemplate the ways in which it has shaped the human sensorium.[19] Two years after the subway has opened, Atkinson's typical New Yorker has already adapted to underground movement, suggesting the rapid habituation to dramatic spatial shifts that was a central part of modern city life. Yet we can see that this process is still being articulated in a somewhat contradictory manner: the ability to orient oneself in subway space occurs "by way of an unconscious process of reasoning" that is later categorized as instinctual, but Atkinson cannot decide whether this new form of understanding is a "sense of time or a new sense of location." Most important, however, the association of man's "tunnelitis" with the instincts of the mole does not seem to dehumanize him. Instead, it suggests that man's ability to cognitively map his place within the mechanical world is merely an extension of animal adaptation to the natural environment.

By calling upon the idea of cognitive mapping, I wish to bring the work of the geographer Kevin Lynch into dialogue with these early narrative mappings of subway space. Lynch's understanding of the cognitive map, a mental image of the landscape used as a means of orientation, has influenced myriad literary and cultural theorists, especially Fredric Jameson. Here I employ his concept and methodology as a starting point for considering how one might imagine and move through the city with a limited use of the visual faculty. Lynch begins his 1960 book *The Image of the City* with a discussion of how "the apparent clarity or 'legibility' of the cityscape" might be judged (2). Of course, a city is not simply viewed from an external position or read like a text. These qualities should allow a number of different groups to orient themselves within city space and move from one place to another. The image of the city in the mind's eye need not be complete or even to scale; what it should be is useful. The ability to retain the sense of the city as a patterned whole can provide emotional satisfaction as well (4).[20]

The subway serves as a limit case for Lynch's visually centered form of urban development, since external landmarks are at a minimum. How can a passenger locate herself once she, like Elmer Rice, has stopped looking at the tiling? Enda Duffy is critical of Lynch's model of cognitive mapping because it navigates the relation between fixed points on a stable urban map rather than tracing a trajectory. "Lynch's is still a city of spires," Duffy writes, "needing *fixed* landmarks to which the city-navigator-*flaneuse* can raise her eyes to feel confident of her location" (31). He distinguishes Lynch's mode of urban movement from the one described in Jameson's *Postmodernism*, where "the subject is the figure in movement at a new velocity who jettisons the contemplative, cartographic pause" (Duffy 31). The subway, I suggest, unites these two orientations to urban space. The subway system is fixed, with the names of stations providing a landmark for the underground commuter similar to the spires that someone might use at street level. But this is where the similarity ends. Station names are primarily denotative rather than connotative, and they certainly do not receive the adulation that Duffy's city navigator bestows by raising her eyes to the cathedral. Instead, because the subway brings about a visual disconnection from the city, it is the passenger's very blindness to the passing stations that proves her ability to locate herself in underground space.

By 1906 we already see evidence of New Yorkers being able to locate themselves fairly definitively within a mental image of the city as a whole without being able to see where they are in relation to city streets. The subway habit can be understood as a development of the ability to cognitively map one's surroundings while in motion and without reference to external visual landmarks. Even when he or she could look at station names, the typical subway rider is more often than not depicted as distracted by cheap reading material—newspapers for men, pulp paperbacks for women. A 1949 article in *Life* dealing with New York's underground infrastructure concludes with a section on subway manners. "A reasonably human and attractive person aboveground," the article states, "the New Yorker reverts to the burrowing-animal type once he clatters down the subway steps. He develops a mole's blindness to everyone around him, usually insulating himself with a newspaper" ("Underground New York" 90). Curiously, this blindness does not seem to impede movement. As Atkinson points out, even the artificial blinders of a newspaper do not trip up the skilled subway rider. Early subway stories repeatedly explore this paradox, marveling at men and women who seem to move easily through the subway crowd, entering and exiting trains without a glance at the station names.

Passengers who are distracted from their surroundings seem to be more skillful at anticipating the movements of the train and the crowd than those who pay attention. Yet as I showed earlier, some elements of their distraction are unsurprisingly gendered. Men are distracted by newspapers, asserting their allegiance to city, business, or sports team, while women lose themselves in pulp novels, especially ones that suggest transnational romance. A 1929 *New York Times* article titled "Those Who Read in the Subway" sums up the typical working girl's mode of attention while being transported, describing her as

> the girl whose reading in the previous session was interrupted at the point where the desert lover was about to declare his identity as an English nobleman to the fair lady he has rescued from the Arabs. Her book is opened before the train starts, her eyes would be glued to the page except for the shifting of the train; still, she keeps them fixed on the startling words. By some clairvoyance, she places herself above a seated passenger who gets off at the first station, she seats herself without losing a sentence, and remains buried in the book, while others worry about the scarcity of straps. Although she cannot see out of the window to tell when her station has been reached, some instinct seems to guide her here also; for she rises at the right time, and glides off the train in a happy daze.

The reading woman does not ask anything of the space surrounding her, does not jostle other passengers, and indeed seems barely physically present at all. Here the invariable sense of orientation first depicted by Atkinson becomes more pervasive, even allowing the subway reader to find a seat blindly as she enters the car. The anticipatory skill of female subway riders, like the receptivity and passivity of female spiritualists in the nineteenth century, might suggest that women are using their connection to technology as a means of social empowerment (Sconce 27). Because of the female reader's absorption in mass culture, it seems, she can be assimilated more easily into the subway crowd.

We might understand the reader as displacing the subway crush through her choice of reading material. The book this typical working girl reads would have been a best-seller in the early 1920s, one that defined female fantasies of being a powerful modern woman who is overpowered by a more powerful man. The plot point "where the desert lover was about to declare his identity as an English nobleman to the fair lady he has rescued from the Arabs," while typical of the desert romances of the twenties, has its source in E. M. Hull's novel *The Sheik*. Best known for supplying Rudolph Valentino with his most memorable film role, *The Sheik* deals with the capture and "taming" of a modern woman who is vacationing on her own in the Sahara desert. Critics have alternately read the book as reactionary in its rape fantasy and empowering in its displays of female desire.[21] Regardless, the book enables the girl to align her movements and desires with those of the subway crowd. This makes her not only a particularly skillful passenger but also an emblem of the subway's dependence on the incorporation of individual movements into a cohesive, efficient whole (Seiler 25). Riding the subway forces modern New Yorkers to think about how individual agency can function in dialectical relation to the needs of the group rather than existing in direct opposition to it (Seiler 33). The subway, then, can be understood as a place where urban subjects experience the regulation and surveillance of movement known as Taylorism.

The lacing together of horizontal and vertical urban spacesp transformed the whole ensemble of the subway system into a singular machine, one whose efficiency depends on the blind and passive movement of its passengers. In this way, the organization and particularly the reception of the subway system were shaped by the thinking of one of the most influential theorizers of mechanized modernity, Frederick Winslow Taylor (1856–1915). Inspired by the stop-motion photography of Étienne-Jules Marey and Eadweard Muybridge, Taylor's theories of the scientific management of movement revolutionized manufacturing (Tichi 77). Taylor's watchword, "efficiency," reverberated throughout early twentieth-century American culture, from tobacco advertisements to poetics (Tichi 85, 91). It is especially important to note that standardization extends far beyond the assembly line (Lears 303). Rationalized movement became a daily routine for white-collar workers as well as their peers in the factories. Indeed, in this period efficiency and mechanization became more allied with upward mobility and middle-class values.

The era when the subway opened is one in which efficiency becomes a watchword in American households and "machine efficiency becomes a standard for the judgment of virtually every human endeavor" because of Taylor and his work (Tichi 76). Although the efficiency movement takes hold nationwide in the 1910s, signs that the subway was closely allied with ideas of scientific management appeared earlier in the new century. A 1905 advertisement by the Hope clothing company attempted to trade on the currency of Taylor's name by claiming that the company's upcoming sale would provide the customer with "real 'Rapid Transit' selling" and warning that its " 'Taylor' lots" of irregular pants, coats, and vests "will 'go' by 'express' " ("Subway Store" advertisement). The association of the subway with efficiency continued throughout the 1910s: an "efficiency show" at the Grand Central Palace featured a model of the subway that demonstrated its safety features ("Efficiency Show"), and an engineer at the IRT contacted August Belmont about studying the flows of employees at work in order to "evolv[e] some more scientific method for the employment and advancement of men" (Shonts).

Speed and passivity are allied in subway space as a means of increasing efficient movement. C. Wright Mills identifies one consequence of Taylorist efficiency in the office as "the decline of any chance for the employee to see and understand the whole operation" (Mills 212). For the subway rider as well as the office worker, an increase in a system's efficiency meant a decrease in the perceptual involvement of any single person. Garrett Ziegler discusses the lack of agency that continues to define the contemporary subway passenger, noting that "once the doors of the car close, he or she is enmeshed in a spatial flow that nothing can be done to alter" (285–86). The passenger exists as part of a system in motion, and she has little ability to stop that system.

The subway thus demands the surrender of will on the part of its passengers, allowing them to absorb (and become absorbed by) the system that moves them. Underground transit requires a submission to unseen forces, what Joyce Kilmer calls "a blind and beautiful recklessness"; passengers cannot see where they are going, yet they trust that they will arrive at their intended stop ("Great Nickel Adventure" 39). Kilmer highlights the complex play of passivity and activity at the heart of subway speed. The subway grants mobility at the cost of agency. Subway passengers utilize the machine as a means to an end, but aside from perhaps the driver and conductor, they have no power over where it will go.

## Body and System

What we have seen so far in this chapter is a new understanding of the city that moves in two directions: at once more separated from the visual cues of the city street and yet more embodied and intuitive, exemplified by the rider who simply knows when his stop is approaching. Underground movement between distant areas of the city leads to a more segmented conception of the city as a whole. Although the *New York Times* may have worried about the subway ride provincializing its readers by limiting their physical contact with different neighborhoods, later accounts suggest that instead of disappearing altogether, those unseen parts of the city become shrouded in a symbolic haze. Indeed, the historian Thomas Bender suggests that the self-conception of twentieth-century New York was one that viewed public transit as an imaginary mode of linking different parts of the city, much as "civic institutions" did in the eighteenth century and "street life" did in the mid-nineteenth (22). Bender sees the subway, particularly after the expansion of the 1910s, as enacting in fact what consolidation did by law: "The city was unified perceptually and practically on a metropolitan scale for the first time. Subway maps, carried in the minds of New Yorkers, gave definition to the newly unified metropolis" (23). The subway provided a unifying map for its citizens, but this map was "shaped by stations rather than local streets or topography" (23). The subway map thus becomes projected back onto the city itself: it helps define and unify the image of New York, but it does so by flattening out the particularities of individual neighborhoods. How does the subway passenger navigate this newly fabricated image of the city? I turn now to a discussion of both the immediate impact of the subway on riders' habits and its long-term impact on their ability to imagine themselves in the city and in the world.

The modern city may not have had the complexity to transcend human perceptual capacities, but it certainly taxed them; subway stations in New York are most often named after the streets onto which they emerge, enacting a perceptual "tension between surface and subsurface legibility" (Bender 40). In *The Image of the City,* Lynch confirms this difficulty: he describes the stations of the Boston subway system as isolated nodes "strung along their invisible path systems" which passengers found "hard to relate structurally to the ground above them" (74). Even today, passengers in New York subway tunnels cannot be integrated into networks of communication and location that track individuals nearly everywhere else in the city: GPS units work only when trains have emerged from underground, and at this writing only a few stations on the west side of Manhattan are wired for cell phone service (Grynbaum, "Cellphone Service"). For passengers making a long journey beneath the sidewalks of New York, the images of the city in above- and below-ground spaces do not directly correlate. The legibility of subway space, then, depends on a fixed and limited set of elements: stations (designated by name as well as unique tile design in some cases), subway maps, and aural cues.

This suggests quite a different means of mapping the city from that provided by the elevated trains. Most critics describe the elevated view of the city as one that distances the viewer from the crowd below. Writing in 1988, de Certeau, for example, equates "seeing Manhattan from the 110th floor of the World Trade Center" with "be[ing] lifted out of the city's grasp. . . . When one goes up there, he leaves behind the mass that carries off and mixes up in itself any identity of authors or spectators" (91–92). Although this essay was written toward the end of the twentieth century, it belies a mid-nineteenth-century model of urban space in which height necessitates separation from the crowd and depth submersion in it. With the addition of public transportation to the urban landscape, this association of elevation with solitude can no longer be maintained. Rather, elevated trains enact a play of proximity and distance, combining the overhead view of the city with a partial view of the crowd sharing the car.[22]

Many critics of the nineteenth-century city have presented a bifurcated model of urban perception, one that splits the city into an unbroken whole seen from above and a partial view seen from street level or "below," sunk into the crowd. David Pike, for example, divides nineteenth-century representations of the city into the "view from above and the view from below" (*Subterranean Cities* 8), while Douglas Tallack compares "ground-level, everyday, experiential wanderings" and "panoptic overviews," reminding us that one perspective is not inherently more humane and critical than the other (129). In each case the overhead view is totalizing, abstract, and detached, while the ground-level view is partial, embodied, and somewhat dangerous. According to John Kasson, reading the city of New York became increasingly difficult as the nineteenth century passed: construction expanded its borders, and migration and immigration expanded its population. These two models present urban subjects with a means of understanding the city, but at a cost: what Kasson calls "bird's-eye views" lose complexity with their presentation of "various parts subordinated to the whole" (*Rudeness and Civility* 73), while "mole's-eye views" (74) revel in the fragmentation and corruption of the city seen from the ground up.

The subway combines elements of both of these ways of looking at the city. A brief news story from 1927 tells of a runaway child who hid out in the subway. "He went out for food," it says, "but each time he returned and rode again, sometimes switching to the elevated trains of the system, getting a good bird's eye view of Brooklyn and a mole's sense of downtown Manhattan, with a combination of both in Queens" ("Runaway Hid in Subway"). But we might say that subway riders begin to combine the bird's-eye and the mole's-eye views even when they do not get the opportunity to survey the city from an elevated line. Passengers intuitively rise just before their stop, combining the preexisting knowledge of the networked system and unconscious, embodied knowledge felt during each particular ride. The subway rider's immediate, tactile engagement with urban space exists in tension with a more abstract imagining of the body as it moves through a mapped representation of the city.

The distinction that I make between subway ride and subway system carries on de Certeau's distinction between the tour and the map as made in *The Practice of Everyday Life* (119).[23] He borrows these concepts in turn from the linguists Charlotte Linde and William Labov, who analyze and codify the process that New Yorkers engage in when translating the "spatial network" of their apartment into terms that a listener can understand (Linde and Labov 930). Linde and Labov found that 97 percent of the descriptions of New Yorkers' apartments given to them were "tours" (describing the apartment as if walking through it), rather than "maps" (describing the apartment in terms of the relation between the rooms). These results suggest that the lived experience of space is far easier to translate into discourse through the process of embodied movement rather than the overview provided by a map. Maps offer totalizing viewpoints that enable us to see how everything relates to everything else in one image. On a map of Manhattan, the Bronx is up and the Battery's down. Tours, by contrast, organize space sequentially and experientially: first you go in this direction, and then you turn there. This whole is not perceived from above or outside the system. Subway stories alternate between a model of the city shaped by "seeing (the knowledge of an order of places)" and one defined by "going (spatializing actions)" (de Certeau 119). A story appearing in the *New-York Tribune* before the subway opened narrated the experience of "a party of handcar tourists" ("Trip on a Handcar"), spatializing their actions and so familiarizing readers with the sights and sounds of the subway journey. A later *Tribune* story, however, takes the opposite tack, devoting two full paragraphs to listing every station on the Manhattan-Bronx and East Side lines ("Harlem in Twenty?"). Although these lists are narrative, they do not depend on the individual's experience as a motivating force. Instead, their sole purpose is the presentation of places in their proper order.

Spatial theorists have dealt with this distinction between perceptions and representations. Henri Lefebvre suggests how the human experience of space combines the two. In *The Production of Space* he offers a tripartite model of space: as perceived, conceived, and lived. These three terms allow him to consider how different elements of space come to the fore when we highlight its function as physically felt (perceived), abstractly planned (conceived), and creatively imagined (lived) (40). This triad manifests itself in subway space in multiple and overlapping ways: when the "handcar tourists" of the *Tribune* perceive the "cool dryness of the covered tunnel," their immediate sensation is confirmed with the claim that "the engineers have already made comparisons of the temperature inside and outside the tunnel, and a ride through bears out their assertion that it is much warmer in the winter than the streets" ("Trip on a Handcar"). Spatial theorists offer us useful models for thinking about how the technological narratives of this period establish the authority of the body and the authority of the expert as coexisting in subway stories rather than competing, as Carolyn Marvin observes they do in narratives about electricity around this same period (112).

What we begin to see in the popular literature of the 1910s is the falling away of the expert's bird's-eye view in the face of the subway's imperceptibility as a whole. In this way the subway replicates the visuality that Todd Presner ascribes to the railway: "The system as a whole could not be surveyed all at once: there is no transcendental perspective on the railway system such that an observer could know, at any given time, precisely where all the trains were, in what direction they were heading, and at what speed" (64–65). The intuitive and partial perceptions of subway passengers are equally necessary for engineers and planners as well. Isaac Marcosson's 1913 article in *Munsey's Magazine* that posits the New York transit system as "The World's Greatest Traffic Problem" investigates the change in expert views of technology. Invoking the lone figure of the telegraph operator, which is at the center of many of what Lynne Kirby calls "railway rescue" silent films (108), Marcosson says that "the tradition of transportation would dictate that a keen-eyed, alert-faced man sat in a signal-tower somewhere, amid the click of telegraph receivers, with his fingers on the pulse of this mighty traveling drama" (335–36). Rather than a single, heroic engineer figure, the subway system is overseen by "a hundred keepers of time and life" (336). Marcosson undermines the valuation of panoramic perception by suggesting to his readers that it is merely a "romantic illusion" (336). Pulling back the curtain, he invites his readers into one of the offices where traffic is surveyed and controlled, which he designates with alliterative whimsy as a "silent, sleepless sentinel of subway safety" (336). Significantly, this room is hidden rather than panoptically prominent and depends on a mediated image rather than immediate engagement with the scene being surveyed. The figure who most interests the narrator has "his eyes glued on" the box that sits before him, where "a glass chart" displays "the shifting panorama of *part of* the subway" (338, emphasis added). The panoramic view is nevertheless a partial one. The box displays the position of the trains within that segment of the system in a "moving chart." He continues: "Each train is indicated by a red light. As the train speeds on, the light shows its progress. The moment the cars pass a 'block,' a green glow floods the track, indicating that the way is open for the next train. It all makes a fascinating and haunting spectacle, for during the 'rush' hours the chart is a brilliant spectacle of changing color. Every flash of crimson means the swift rush of hurrying hosts; each path of emerald is a brief interval between the pounding cars" (338).

As we see in this description, spectators such as the narrator cannot view the whole subway system from an external, "bird's-eye" perspective; nevertheless, they can still view it as disembodied lights and movement. The bustle of modernity is transformed into a modernist abstraction. The rush hour is much easier to take in as a "fascinating," "haunting," and "brilliant spectacle" when it does not involve the urban crowd. As we'll see in chapter 3, this strategy recurred when modernist poets took on the subway crowd as a subject only to aestheticize it. In the process of presenting this new urban scene, Marcosson proposes an alternative model of the modern scientist that has neither the independence nor the agency of the engineer figure presented in Cecelia Tichi's *Shifting Gears* (97–170). Later in the article, Marcosson describes the subway's chief engineer, Frank Hedley, "sit[ting] at a big desk which is the center of the spider-web of New York traffic" (338). Even Hedley can't see the whole system at once, though; instead he is dependent on the telephone system, which his men use to inform him of any problems. Throughout early popular accounts the subway stands in for and works in concert with other invisible networks of communication and connectivity that are equally difficult to understand. As the city grows in size and complexity, urban subjects find it more and more difficult to cognitively map their place within it. There is always a gap between "the here and now of immediate perception and the imaginative or imaginary sense of the city as an absent totality" (Jameson, "Cognitive Mapping" 283).

Film revealed the gaps between the "immediate perception" and the "absent totality" more clearly than even the best prose account could. The subway might bring together distant spaces, but this sense of connection was distinctly embodied and partial. This is true even in the American Mutoscope and Biograph Company's "actualities," short documentary films that showed the new subway in motion. These films represent the subway metonymically, with the single train or the excavation of a single tunnel standing in for the system as a whole. *Interior N.Y. Subway, 14th St. to 42nd St.* asks us to imagine the whole subway system from the partial vision we are shown. The train moves north underground, with the beginning and endpoints established by the title. This movement structures the film's narrative, with the changes in underground space serving as dramatic interest. As the train rounds a curve leaving the station, the means of filming is briefly revealed: another subway car carrying a huge floodlight runs on the parallel express track. Moments like this show us the apparatus that makes this "actuality" possible. Lit from the side and filmed from behind, the subway car making this journey exposes the hidden work that is necessary to make one subway ride visible. First surrounded by vertical girders, the train moves into a more curvilinear tunnel just before arriving at Forty-second Street. Although the camera's point of view is not associated with a particular person's viewing experience, it is nevertheless "quite dramatically located" because of the mediation of these changing elements of urban infrastructure (Tallack 108).

*Interior N.Y. Subway* betrays a constant tension between the insistent forward movement of the train and the pull of everyday life on the sidelines. Although the subway journey is on the whole one that moves through empty space, it begins and ends in the midst of the urban crowd. At Fourteenth Street passengers wait on the platform; a man crosses on an overhead walkway. The film ends just as it begins, in the midst of New York subway riders. The train pulls into the Forty-second Street station, and for the final forty seconds or so, the frame is static as commuters gawk at the camera. Douglas Tallack claims that in this film the city disappears, that it "transfers movement to the camera" so that we pay attention not to the sights but to the experience of sight in motion (108). This is certainly true of the middle stretches of the film, where we appreciate the move from square girders to rounded tunnels on a purely aesthetic level. The very experience of abstract movement, however, is couched in the embodied particulars of city life. Subway films establish from the start the sense that any totalizing view of the transit system will be undercut by the limitations of the physical.

The understanding of the subway system as a networked space that links discrete parts of city life and that cannot be perceived as a whole takes on increased importance as a concrete analogy for other systems of modernity. Existing both as a coherent system and as an embodied series of rides, the subway enables New York writers of the early twentieth century to interrogate the individual's place in an impersonal and discontinuous social sphere. I conclude this chapter by considering how the subway functions as a synecdoche for modern life; mapping one's location within subway space, as we shall see in the chapters that follow, functions as a more concrete way of provisionally mapping one's cultural, economic, and political position.

## Dreaming of Infrastructure

At this point we have shifted our understanding of the cognitive map, moving from a pragmatic register to an ideological one. Fredric Jameson appropriates Lynch's terminology for precisely that purpose; he sees in the Lynchian cognitive map's imagined relation between an individual and the city a "spatial analogue" to Louis Althusser's "great formulation of ideology itself, as 'the Imaginary relationship of the individual to his or her Real conditions of existence'" ("Cognitive Mapping" 283). New York modernist writers make an analogous claim: by attending to their passive, distracted, and efficient movement through a system that cannot be perceived as a whole, the subway offers its passengers a means of understanding their position within urban, regional, and national systems.

The subway story serves the same purpose within modernist American literature that the travel narrative does in nineteenth-century American literature: both understand mobility as a means of group identification.[24] But as we shall see in the following chapters, that unifying system can be as large as a national identity or as small as an artistic clique. The more we examine modern subway writing, the more we can see how that system is used as a metaphorical structure for understanding how subjectivity is formed through the kind of interplay of social norms and lived experience that Jameson describes. The built environment of New York City thus feeds into the implicit disconnection and overall logic of contemporary discourses from psychoanalysis to bureaucracy and Taylorism, all systems dependent on individuals who cannot conceptualize the whole system in which they participate. It shows how seemingly fragmented and irrational systems operate in highly efficient ways that are invisible to those who move through them. The subway rider's encounter with the urban infrastructure becomes a confirmation of his growing sense that such systems are now so large and complex as to be unimaginable. The subway mediates the individual's relation to other concepts that define the individual's relation to the system such as assimilation and nostalgia, modern ideas that problematize the relationship of part to whole. Cultural representations of the subway system, I argue, attempt to resolve this relationship by insisting on a hidden logic that connects otherwise discrete elements.

Some contemporary critics feared that the acceptance of subway movement as the norm would turn their fellow city dwellers into brainless beasts. Yet in the texts that I discuss, passengers arrive at their clearest understanding of their relation to the systems through which they move in moments of blindness, unconsciousness, or habit. Patricia Yaeger asks, "What is it like to be stuck, night and day, dreaming of infrastructure?" (15). The rest of this book tells the story of the subway as a central figure in the infrastructural dreams of New York modernist literature. Because the subway lies underground, the glimpses of the infrastructure, the flashes of understanding that tell the passenger her relationship to the surrounding city, are brief and impressionistic. Writers and artists use the subway to concretize the larger forces that make modern life possible. Assimilation, migration, urban development, and the poetic tradition are all imagined as underground forces that efficiently move modern subjects. For the poets whom I discuss in chapters 2 and 3, provisional and embodied subway movement provides a modern model for relating to the urban crowd as well as the literary tradition; for the dramatists and fiction writers discussed in chapters 4 and 5, subway movement traces the vexed experience of migrants and immigrants trying to resolve the inconsistencies in their uprooted lives. For writers in the first half of the twentieth century, the subway facilitates a kind of knowledge that cannot be arrived at by walking the streets of New York.

# CHAPTER 2

## HOW THE SUBWAY BECAME SUBLIME

In the previous chapter I discussed the development of habits and mental models that New Yorkers used to navigate subway space. I characterized the experience of the subway passenger as navigation between the immediate—and resolutely partial—ride and the larger, otherwise incomprehensible system. Newspaper articles of the early twentieth century concerned themselves with the novelty of this form of movement, imagining how visitors and residents might understand New York differently as they crossed it underground. Poems in this period took a different approach, imagining the subway in transcendental terms as a vehicle through which one could access the divine in the midst of the crowd. In his essay "The Great Nickel Adventure," Joyce Kilmer discusses the first poem that presented him with this sublime vision of the subway: "Whenever I read Mr. Chester Firkins' excellent poem, 'On a Subway Express,' I am filled with amazement. It is not strange that Mr. Firkins turned the subway into poetry, it is strange that the subway does not turn every one of its passengers into a poet" (38). The poetry that Firkins and Kilmer practice in this period is deeply religious:

the Firkins poem to which Kilmer refers calls his daily commute a "wild ride with God" (181), for example, while Kilmer himself writes a poem in which the subway serves as an object lesson for maintaining one's faith in times of darkness, when "glory comes in transitory gleams" ("Subway" 467). For these poets, the imperceptibility of the subway system from within is a symbol for believers of their inability to see the whole of God's plan.

Between 1908 and 1916, poetry and essays published in magazines imagine the subway system's sublimity in terms of its play between embodied immediacy and boundless immensity. Early twentieth-century magazine verse describes the astonishment of the rider, the terrible noise of the crowds and trains, and the boundless unknowability of the subway system. In doing so, it calls upon the cultural associations of the technological sublime. American studies scholars have long deployed that concept as a means of exploring the wonder, awe, and power that American culture locates in the machine.[1] Although the subway may have been associated with the sublime from the time of its construction, earlier stories and films focus on the engineering skill of the men who built it. These later poets initiate a discourse that associates subway sublimity with a divine rather than a man-made and rational source.

Chester Firkins is a trendsetter in that respect. A minor poet who died young, Firkins was overshadowed even in his lifetime by his older brother Oscar, a writer and critic.[2] His much-anthologized poem "On a Subway Express" first appeared in the *Atlantic Monthly* magazine in February 1908. In this poem Firkins embraces the unstable process of locating oneself within subway space, reading it as an analogue for the ever-evolving, partial, and provisional recognition of the divine. "On a Subway Express" would initiate a wave of poetry in the late 1900s and early 1910s that uses the New York City subway as a figure of technological sublimity. Though focused on underground space, these poems paradoxically elevate the poetic engagement with modernity by positing a link between the seemingly boundless subway system and other systems that cannot be known rationally in full, such as religion. The poems that I discuss in this chapter imagine the subway system as a technology of cultural and moral fusion, one that brings together city districts and city dwellers in a realm as ineffable as that of heaven itself.

This rhetorical strategy constructs a bulwark against the encroaching sense that commercialism defined both urban space and modern poetry.

Georg Simmel's essay "The Metropolis and Mental Life" was first published in 1903, just a year before the New York subway opened and five years before Firkins's poem was published in the *Atlantic Monthly.* "The deepest problems of modern life," writes Simmel, "derive from the claim of the individual to preserve the autonomy and individuality of his existence in the face of overwhelming social forces" (409). He describes how the impersonality of the city and the anonymity of its residents necessitate the dependence on exchange value and external signifiers as a means of gauging personal worth. Subway poets reckon with the forces of commercialization and efficiency by aligning the subway's movement not with the workaday world but with the divine order.

The fear of art being reduced to mere monetary value shaped poetic discourse in this period as well. Verse writers turned to depictions of urban culture as a way of making poetry relevant to contemporary life (Newcomb, *Would Poetry Disappear?* 68–73). Mass-circulation magazines published an increasing, and increasingly sympathetic, number of city poems in the late 1900s and early 1910s, and anthologies of urban verse followed suit in the 1910s and 1920s.[3] Poets could make a decent living selling their works to mass-circulation magazines, but genteel critics worried that the forces of the market might make them gravitate toward fashionable urban subjects instead of more properly poetic ones.

Recent critical work on the early twentieth century has dealt with the popular celebration of the modern city, but that celebration was centralized in mass culture; highbrow commentators still held it at arm's length. City poetry in this period evokes a deep anxiety about the role of the poet in the marketplace, one that was interrogated throughout the decade in popular and avant-garde circles. Joyce Kilmer edited a 1917 collection of essays titled *Literature in the Making, by Some of Its Makers.* In it, the debates continue to rage regarding the impact on American literature of mass media and the modern city. Some essays celebrate modern culture, but the responses tend toward the conservative; John Burroughs's "City Life versus Literature," for instance, sets the two concepts in direct opposition. He dismisses the city as "a place to which one goes to do business," not a place where one can think and write (214). This commercial quality enters into the writing of city dwellers, who produce fiction with what Burroughs calls "a metropolitan quality; it seems made up of showy streets and electric light" (215). Fiction takes on this "metropolitan quality" when it eschews interiority in favor of display, substance in favor of style. With the flashy, even merciless glare of "electric light," Burroughs suggests a number of consequences for writers in the early twentieth century. He evokes the increasing reach of public utilities into the homes of city dwellers, using the metaphor to illustrate the ways that modern writers were connected to mass culture.

These anxieties became more prominent with the rise of mass-circulation magazines in the late nineteenth and early twentieth centuries. *Literature in the Making* warns that the popular taste and the popular press have made it more difficult to produce quality writing. Fannie Hurst mocks the saccharine and insubstantial "'chocolate fudge' fiction" printed in popular magazines (241), and John Burroughs argues that the newspaper has "bad manners" and is "the enemy of all meditation, all privacy, all things that make for great art" (221). George Barr McCutcheon takes up this issue most thoroughly in his conversation with Kilmer, titled "Magazines Cheapen Fiction." He blames the lack of quality in American novels on magazine serialization. English novelists produce better work, he claims, because "they write a novel and not a series of chapters, parts, and instalments" (158). McCutcheon characterizes the composition of a serial novel as a Taylorist process of segmentation, one antithetical to the ideal of a self-contained and internally coherent work of art. Whether the figurative language used by the critics evoked junk food, public gossip, or the factory floor, the more modern a magazine's form was, the worse its content.

The prevalence of early twentieth-century magazine poetry dealing with modern technologies like the subway, the skyscraper, and the Automat could be understood as the verse equivalent to the "chocolate fudge fiction" dismissed by Hurst. Contrarily, critics such as John Timberman Newcomb have suggested that this verse should be understood not in opposition to the modernist experiments of little magazines but as part of a shared poetic project.[4] Throughout this chapter I show how modern city verse in general, and modern subway verse in particular, attempt to forge a new idiom for middlebrow appreciation of technology. The prevalence of the technological sublime as a poetic mode can be understood as a strategy for splitting the difference between highbrow critiques of urban technological modernity and mass-cultural celebrations of them. By staking out this poetic middle ground, poetry of the subway sublime acknowledges its implication in early twentieth-century consumer capitalism while at the same time suggesting that its trendy poetic subject can in fact serve as the vehicle of some transcendental truth.

Poets in the late 1900s and early 1910s depict underground transit in terms of the sublime as a way of elevating their writing's engagement with modernity and making it seem less commodified. The interests in casting the subway as sublime in this era, I suggest, have much to do with the contemporary debates about the depiction of urban life in poetry.

The poetry of the early twentieth-century subway borrows and redefines strategies most often associated with writing about an earlier technology, the railroad. In the nineteenth century, poets describe the train in terms that establish their belief in technological progress and man's control of the machine. John Kasson sees this divide chiefly in terms of class: in this era, those American citizens who control economic and cultural capital see the power of the railroad as a reflection and extension of their own power (*Civilizing the Machine* 183). David Nye distinguishes between two groups who had "imaginative encounters" with the railroad.[5] One consists of what he calls "innocents," those who lacked the language to describe their experience and so "turned to the supernatural: dragons, monsters, or visions of hell" (*American Technological Sublime* 55). The more worldly group, "separated by laughter" from their naïve brethren, saw the machine as a sublime instance of human power (55). For both critics, the cultural interpretation of the machine's power depends on the viewer's position within that culture.

The most canonical American poets of the nineteenth century understand the railroad in sublime terms, but terms nevertheless defined by man's reason and power over it. Walt Whitman celebrates the Pacific Railroad in "A Passage to India," equating the westward expansion of the railroad network with the exploration of the Western world (531–39). Whitman is awed by the machine, but not because it represents something unknowable; instead, his exclamatory passion valorizes the rational drive of the engineers and workers who made such technology possible. "To a Locomotive in Winter" focuses more on the sounds of the train, calling them "metrical" and "lawless music" (583). In "I like to see it lap the Miles," Emily Dickinson addresses both the sound of the train and its compression of space (286). The final stanza plays with sublime imagery, cannily reversing its impact in order to suggest both the railroad's power and her control over it. She compares the train to a star, for example, not because of its blinding light or beauty but because of its "punctual" arrival (286).[6]

The image of the machine does very different cultural work in twentieth-century poetry than it did in the nineteenth century. Writers in the 1910s deemphasize the rationality of subway space and highlight the way it gives passengers direct access to intense feeling. Jonathan Stone's "Song of the Subway," which appeared in *Harper's Weekly* in December 1911, begins with the proclamation, "Here do I call thee, wheeléd work, sublime." For a poem that celebrates technological progress, however, "Song of the Subway" is remarkably backward-looking. The paradox of the subway sublime, as epitomized in Stone's poem, is the sense of irrational, timeless wonder that these poems express in the face of the most modern forms of transportation. Stone's language is intensely old-fashioned, full of "thees" and "thous," inverted sentences, and faux–Old English alliteration, to say nothing of the accent on the last syllable of "wheeléd." The imagery is archaic, from the mythological references of the first stanza to the "dragon, desperate of the lance" to which the subway car is compared.

This poem is not merely old-fashioned, it's practically medieval. More accurately, it seems to find in the subway a venue for the antiquarianism that resurged as part of the late Victorian antimodernist tendencies in American culture and what Michael Saler calls the "medieval modernism" that influenced the design of the London Underground. Confronted with rationalized industrial modernity, many educated Americans around the turn of the century felt a sense of unreality and nagging doubt. They reimagined medieval culture as a way of fulfilling a number of conflicting impulses: "Some wanted simple faith, others spontaneous feeling, others sacred mystery—anything, in other words, except logical order" (Lears 142). The subway provided the vital spark—what Stone calls a "pulse of fire and death" (22)—that gives modern life its novel sense of adventure. When Stone imagines the train's headlights transforming from "ruby orbs" like dragon's eyes to "seraph-torches," we should understand it not as a naïve response but as one that seeks the innocence of earlier responses to technological innovation. The desire to understand the subway as a space of mystery suggests a desire to unify the urban population's attitude toward the machine by an appeal to emotion rather than reason. Although other poets characterize the subway in less archaic terms, they all share a vocabulary of affective power. In the following section we see how the subway sublime borrows rhetorical strategies less from the railroad poetry of the nineteenth century than from the didactic sublimity of the Fireside Poets.

## Naturalizing the Subway Sublime

As the decade wore on, other verse writers of the 1910s joined Chester Firkins and Joyce Kilmer in singing the subway. They did so in spite of the fact that this technological turn was not universally welcomed. Contemporary debates foreground the city's commercialization and noise as antithetical to poetry, criticizing modernity through the fruits of its labor. Arguments against city poetry were almost universally made by writers who opposed what Georg Simmel and later critics have seen as the constitutive elements of the metropolis and its mental life: a focus on novelty, an increase in commodification (of the self as well as the surrounding environment), an overwhelming number of sensory stimuli, and an alienation from the natural world.

The enemies of cityscape poetry responded to the presumed commercialization of the metropolis by identifying (and even inventing) a pastoral tradition in nineteenth-century American poetry. Critics of city poetry could have asked "What's the Subway to Me?" as Henry David Thoreau asked "What's the Railroad to Me?" Thoreau's poem suggests that the novelty of the train cannot compare with the richer sources of poetic material just outside his door. Indeed, the construction of the railroad makes the natural world seem more alive:

> It fills a few hollows,
> And makes banks for the swallows,
> It sets the sand a-blowing,
> And the blackberries a-growing . . . (Thoreau 6)

The belief that the city dehumanized and the country individuated was so strong that it led to some seemingly nonsensical claims. In 1917, when Walt Whitman had become all but canonical, John Burroughs states that Whitman's "way of writing wasn't metropolitan, you know; you might say he treated the city by a country method" (217). An anonymous editor of *The Independent* also holds the genteel assumption that poetry should serve as a source of moral elevation in the way that the verse of the Fireside Poets had. These predecessors eschewed the crowd and the marketplace as subjects for their writing even as they benefited from the "modern commodification of the literary work" (Newcomb, *Would Poetry Disappear?* 24). The editorialist claims that poets like Bryant and Lowell "satisfy our aspirations and better appetites even as we toil among the sordid and oppressing objects which the newer school of city poets is at such pains to reproduce" ("Editorial: City

Poets" 396). They did so by glorifying village life and the more direct relationship to nature that was presumed to be available away from the city. In poems such as "To a Waterfowl" and "The Prairies," for example, William Cullen Bryant presents archetypal scenes of "moralized sublimity" through his depictions of a "piously domesticated wildness" (Wilson, *American Sublime* 122). That the city might offer images of moral elevation seemed ridiculous.

René Laidlaw maintains the moral distinction between city and country in *The Century* in 1912 with an article titled "On Gutter Verse: From an Unsympathetic Country Gentleman to His Town Cousin, Who Writes for Magazines." From its subtitle onwards, Laidlaw's essay uses the persona of the "country gentleman" to mock the popular magazines, setting their ephemerality in sharp contrast to the stability and permanence of his library filled with the works of François Villon and Robert Browning. One of the "open letters" regularly featured in the magazine, the signed first-person piece describes the contemporary trend of urban poetry with an ironic distance that might evoke Addison and Steele's Mr. Spectator. Laidlaw does so in order to check what he sees as the versifiers' celebration of modern urban content as an intrinsic good in their writing. He describes these writers as "amusing" but "complacent" since they found their source material so close to home (634). Much of what Laidlaw's open letter criticizes is the compulsive novelty of cityscape poems. This goes hand in hand with their authors' lack of knowledge about the tradition to which they contribute: he assumes "that very few modern magazinists (which is the newest neologism, I believe) read anything in French literature earlier than Zola" (634). With cheeky alliteration, Laidlaw addresses the practitioners by the "newest neologism," emphasizing at once the desperate trendiness and the redundancy of their poetic project. In a reminder of the messiness inherent in periodization, this essay was published in 1912, the year that Ezra Pound, Richard Aldington, and H.D. decided on the literary principles of imagism (Pound, *Early Writings* xii). "On Gutter Verse" reminds us that not everyone was so eager to "make it new."

In the first stanza of "On a Subway Express," Firkins addresses both the novelty and the presumed lack of moral elevation in an urban setting. He begins his poem by acknowledging the abandonment of the natural world that comes with living in the big city:

> I, who have lost the stars, the sod,
> For chilling pave and cheerless light,

> Have made my meeting-place with God
> A new and nether Night. (181)

Firkins allows for then-contemporary assumptions that the country serves as a better setting for religious faith to blossom; both the rootedness to the soil implied by "the sod" and the evidence of heaven in the "stars" are "lost" in the city. The rest of the poem, however, makes an argument that the subway replaces (and in some senses surpasses) the natural world as a setting through which God could be better understood. We might read Firkins, then, as responding to the version of the American poetic sublime modeled by the Fireside Poets: "You that 'neath country skies can pray, / Scoff not at me—the city clod" (181). Even before the rise of the antiurban sentiment expressed in the articles that I've presented, the poet senses the transgressive character of a claim that the subway, not nature, can serve as a place of repose and contemplation.

City poetry establishes a new vocabulary of the sublime, one in which bridges supplant mountains and thunderous streets overtake thunderous falls as images of the unimaginable. The editorial in *The Independent* pursues this comparison: "The East River with its ferries and bridges mountain-high takes the place of Rhine and blue Danube; the 'cascading thunder' of city streets takes the place of Niagara Falls; the recreation park crowds out the 'glimmering landscape'; lamp-posts replace the sentinels of the forest" ("Editorial: City Poets" 396). As Lisa Gitelman reminds us, new media tend to progress through a transitional phase when they are understood according to the established functions of older ones; we might understand the conservative impulse in poetry of the 1910s as a literary means of testing new technologies against old ways of representing the city. Concerned with the business interests of the real estate developers and hoteliers of the period, the *New York Times* made the subway seem less scary; concerned with the continuing relevance of their craft in a commercialized urban sphere, magazine poets reconcile the city to poetry. The East River may not have the patina of tradition that the Rhine and the Danube do, but its "mountain-high" bridges and ferries add to its natural grandeur rather than reducing it. That the noise of the streets could equal the thunderous churning of Niagara Falls suggests that one of the nineteenth century's key settings for understanding the sublimity of the wilderness has been surpassed by a setting in the built environment.

By 1916, the ideal of the subway sublime had become enough of a middlebrow commonplace that it could be parodied in verse. It was that year when "On First Looking into a Subway Excavation" appeared in the pages of *The Century*, the same periodical where René Laidlaw had railed against "gutter verse" some five years prior. Written by Christopher Morley, this sonnet is of course structured after Keats's "On First Looking into Chapman's Homer," and its many humorous parallels depend on the loss of seriousness from the former to the latter. "Much have I travelled in the realms of gold / And many goodly states and kingdoms seen" transforms into "Much have I travelled, a commuter bold, / And many goodly excavations seen" (Morley 796).[7] Morley's verse gives us perhaps the best example of the feeling of loss that characterized critiques of the subway sublime. Compared to the heights reached by British Romantic poets, the sights seen by the "commuter bold" seem paltry indeed.

Although Morley's chief intent is to ironize the poetic trends of his day, he also gives us a clear sense of the forces of urban development at work in the period when this poetic trope was fashionable. Max Page characterizes the first decades of the twentieth century as a period of "creative destruction" for the city (*Creative Destruction of Manhattan* 5). The boroughs consolidated, and transit systems tied them even more closely together; real estate boomed. All of this construction, however, could endanger passers-by. It was utterly within the realm of possibility for a pedestrian to pass by pits being dynamited and have to watch for "flying rocks" that "would lay him stiff and cold" (Morley 796). Like Morley, the poets who recorded the subway sublime to sincere ends did so in ways that placed the subway within larger systems of circulation. This too suggests how the subway served as a synecdoche for the measureless expansion of modern systems of transit.

## A Divine System

The sublime is a concept that, at its core, unites opposing feelings and attitudes in its confrontation with unimaginable immensity. In his theory of the psychological processes that motivate the continental Romantic sublime, Thomas Weiskel suggests that "the very indeterminacy" of the relation between the passenger and the subway system "is taken as symbolizing the mind's relation to a transcendent order" (24). We can understand the hazy descriptive terms in this stanza as an attempt to minimize the anxiety evoked by the shocks of an increasingly mechanized everyday life by casting it as part of an ineffable, benevolent pattern.

Why would poets in this era be so invested in discussing a man-made technology in terms that suggest its place within a divine order? They wish to present a poetic alternative to the subway as a vehicle that makes possible the metropolis's continuing role as "the seat of the money economy" (Simmel 411). The poems naturalize that infinitely extending circulation in order to counteract the sense that passengers are mere parcels moving from one point to another. This anxiety is a manifestation of the era's mixed attitudes toward the increasingly complex circulation of people, goods, and ideas. Circulation is a particularly important concept for theorists of technology in the late nineteenth and early twentieth centuries. Wolfgang Schivelbusch brings his analysis of the railroad passenger's "panoramic" perspective into dialogue with the attitude of the modern department store customer in late nineteenth-century France: "The customer was kept in motion; he traveled through the department store as a train passenger traveled through the landscape. In their totality, the goods impressed him as an ensemble of objects and price tags fused into a pointillistic overall view" (191). The relation of a subway passenger to the landscape is far different, as I have discussed; the "overall view" has to be imagined or represented, since it cannot be experienced firsthand. The provisional separation of the subway system from the street means that the subway offers an escape from the cycles of production and consumption that go on aboveground.

The poetic diction of "On a Subway Express" elides the subway's involvement in the urban economic system: Firkins describes a passenger who uses the subway not to commute from home to work and back, but to pray. Throughout this era we can see poems sublimate the role of the subway as an economic engine. For poets of the period, the subway does not repeat the experience of the working world above; instead, it offers the "only respite of the Day" (Firkins 181). The discourse of the technological sublime enables early twentieth-century poets to acknowledge the role of the subway as a system that enables the circulation of goods within the city while simultaneously elevating it above other mere vehicles of modern capitalism. Firkins and poets like him suggest that subway riding and subway writing are part of a divine order rather than the man-made order of the modern city.

Poems of this period establish the transcendent meaning of the subway by connecting it with a number of other systems, through a suggestion of either similarity or contiguity. In doing so, they extend the power of the subway as a sublime system by connecting it with other systems, suggesting the infinite extension of the grid plan in urban design. They do so, I suggest, as part of a two-step process: connecting the subway's circulation with that of the rest of the city, and connecting those intertwined forms of traffic with more eternal systems of meaning. One of the most common ways of metaphorizing the subway was imagining it as a human circulatory system. Describing a later visit to New York, Salvador Dalí proclaimed feverishly: "The poetry of New York is not serene esthetics; it is seething biology. . . . And the subways of New York do not run on iron rails; they run on rails of calves' lungs!" (134). Dalí's embodied metaphors were taken up earlier (and in a more stately way) by Joseph Clarke:

> Deep in thy vitals the dynamos whirring
> Are feeding thy nerves that are wires,
> Thy tunnels, thy veins,
> Stretch out as the human tide swerves,
> And thy hidden fires
> With the breath of thy bosom stirring
> Make life in the dark for thy lightning trains. (16)

Clarke's subway is a part of a city that he addresses as an embodied being. Although the subway is a hidden part of Manhattan, it circulates people throughout the city as nerves circulate sensations and veins blood. In this way the poem naturalizes the city and its residents: commuters are not merely going to work; they're bringing oxygen to different neighborhoods.

Not all subway poems humanize the city. Indeed, "On a Subway Express" attempts to link the subway to extraterrestrial systems. In an extended metaphor, it describes other passing cars as celestial bodies in deep space:

> In this dim firmament, the stars
> Whirl by in blazing files and tiers;
> Kin meteors graze our flying bars
> Amid the spinning spheres. (181)

This stanza betrays a tension between order and chaos. The system seems to operate according to some invisible plan—the stars move in "files" and "tiers"—yet the confusion of "whirling" and "spinning" keeps the reader from assuming too comfortable a position while viewing this scene. Indeed,

Firkins suggests a near-collision between subway cars with the line "Kin meteors graze our flying bars." Only a fairly seasoned subway rider would be able to translate this line into a typical visual experience, one evoking the parallel movements of an express and local train with the "flying bars" of pillars passing between them. His defamiliarizing language emphasizes the difficulty of locating oneself in a stable world. But we should not read this instability negatively; the poem uses opaque metaphors to transform an uncomfortable ride into a mysterious encounter with the divine and the fantastic. Contemplating the subway system from his position, usually within the subway car, the speaker-passenger experiences the feeling that Thomas Weiskel calls "an immediate intuition of a disconcerting disproportion between inner and outer" (23–24). The speaker minimizes himself in the third stanza as a mere "figment," while the action outside the car seems threateningly substantial, with "stars" that "whirl by" his windows and "meteors" that "graze" the outside of the vehicle. Indeed, this poem seems to reverse the terms in Schivelbusch's conception of the railroad as a vehicle of "panoramic perception" (64): it is the viewer, rather than the view, that is flattened and dematerialized. Here, the fact that the subway cannot be perceived as a whole serves not to detract from its sublimity but to amplify it; because the subway system can be perceived only through the individual experience of the rider, its boundlessness becomes a central attribute. Firkins uses this breakdown of boundaries between nature and culture, underground and outer space, as evidence that the subway is a "wild ride with God!"

Poets in this era imagine the subway in relation to metaphorical systems that equal its complexity but differ radically from it in scale, such as the body and the cosmos. They also imagine it connecting to and echoing other forms of transit, extending the scope of the subway system even further than the eventual Dual Contracts construction would. In this era of urban development, poets convey a sense of the technological sublime through their depiction of "ever wider and larger infrastructure networks" (Graham and Marvin 45). In her poem "The Subway," Ruth Shepard Phelps situates the train within a matrix of many simultaneous forms of transportation. She describes a city where

> Barks are riding on the sea
> Air-ships skim the blue:
> Iron chariots carry me
> These dim caverns through. (23)

The city is envisioned as an organic whole crisscrossed by people in motion at every level. In this stanza Phelps moves from one level of transit to another in a way that connects and even transposes their locations. By calling zeppelins "air-ships" and the sky "the blue" in the second line, she suggests that their elevated movement is similar to that of the barges on the water. The line break between the "iron chariots" and the caverns through which they move also brings them back to ground level, at least for a moment. The location of public transit within the city becomes relational rather than absolute. Even though the subway seems to be moving in a straight line underground, it demands a constant recalibration in order to keep track of where the passenger is in relation to the rest of the city.[8]

In this way, the Progressive Era depiction of the subway offers a counter-example to the current understanding of the American technological sublime. Rather than presenting "the sublime object" as "itself a manifestation of reason" (Tapper 157), magazine poets of this era appeal to a sense of the reality beyond human reason. Joyce Kilmer's sonnet "The Subway; 96th Street to 137th Street" unites underground and elevated transit with their moral equivalents. The title refers to stations on Manhattan's Upper West Side, where the subway runs up Broadway past Columbia University and toward the City College of New York. The West Side IRT line—now the 1 train—runs underground for three stops, emerges on an elevated platform, and then returns underground.[9] The elevated 125th Street stop provides a transition from the octave that focuses the literal subway ride to the sestet that imagines its metaphorical resonance. We see

> A glance of daylight at Manhattan street,
> The rest all gloom. That is our life, it seems.
> Thru sunless ways go our reluctant feet,
> The glory comes in transitory gleams. (467)

As a Catholic author, Kilmer uses the brief emergence of the subway into city space as a metaphor for human encounters with the divine. The internal rhymes of "glory" and "transitory," and the alliteration of "glory" and "gleams," suggest that the heavenly plan echoes the subway plan. His later essay "The Great Nickel Adventure" expands on these ideas, proposing that the brief loss of natural light and human conversation during the "daily disciplinary ride" (43) makes passengers appreciate these things all the more when they return to street level.

In his poem Kilmer transforms the crowd from an ensemble of urban types to a collective "we" experiencing this divine revelation together. Yet in doing so, he mystifies the particularities of urban experience that nineteenth-century writers celebrated. Chester Firkins both blesses the crowd and reduces its impact in "On a Subway Express" when he writes,

> Life throbs about me, yet I stand
> Outgazing on majestic Power;
> Death rides with me, on either hand,
> In my communion hour. (181)

Acknowledging the material presence of the crowd surrounding the speaker with the opening clause, this stanza nevertheless turns away from the immediate concerns of the commuting crowd. A focus on the lives of the passengers surrounding him would grant too much power to their mortal, ephemeral view of the city. "On a Subway Express" refocuses our gaze out of the subway car and into the abyss. As we will see in the next section, a wide array of public culture in this period did similar work in either turning away from or aestheticizing the crowd as a way of managing anxiety about the loss of self-determination in the busy turn-of-the-century city.

## The Subway Crowd

For Fireside Poets, sublimity is encountered in the natural world and experienced in isolation. For the poets of the 1910s, however, the divine could be encountered not only alone in nature but in the midst of the crowd as well. Since Joyce Kilmer is one of the best-known modern Catholic writers in the United States, we might understand this as a Catholic version of the sublime, one in which the mediation of other people and devices does not reduce the strength of the narrator's feelings.[10] The subway poetry of this period thus elides Jeffrey Schnapp's distinction between "thrill-based" and "commodity-based" forms of transportation (8); rather than finding the sublime in the pure agency of the open road, these poets experience it in the submission to a larger force.

By thinking about the subway crowd being drawn together in a sublime moment, early twentieth-century poets elide realities of class difference in the city above in order to emphasize the transcendent quality of modern mass transit. The rhetorical moves that bring disparate passengers together into a symbolic whole have a long history, one that extends from the railroad poetry of the nineteenth century to the public arts outreach campaigns of the late twentieth and early twenty-first. From its inception, the New York subway has been celebrated as a democratic space, one where rich and poor pay for the same experience. Kilmer's essay "The Great Nickel Adventure" exults in the democracy of a space where "the ragged bootblack does not kneel at the broker's feet, he sits close beside him, or perhaps, comfortably at rest, watches the broker clutch a strap and struggle to keep his footing" (41). In this way, the subway follows the example of the American railroad, where passengers of different classes traveled together instead of dividing into first-, second-, and third-class cars as in England. John Godfrey Saxe's popular "Rhyme of the Rail," first published in *Knickerbocker Magazine,* observes that the

> Men of different "stations"
> In the eye of Fame
> Here are very quickly
> Coming to the same.
> High and lowly people,
> Birds of every feather,
> On a common level
> Travelling together! (55)

Saxe then goes on to describe different types with whom he shares the car, subjecting the "high and lowly people" to his humorous gaze. Though his fellow passengers may be strangely dressed or overly paranoid, the narrator observes them all with equanimity as evidence that it "is pleasant / Riding on the Rail!" (58). Critics of subway verse tend to use the Fireside Poets as a counterexample to the technologically minded writers of the early twentieth century, but even these forefathers found the railroad to be a useful background for their poetic lessons. James Russell Lowell in "An Incident in a Railroad Car" imagines a workman reading Robert Burns to his "rude and rough" comrades; though the setting is not mentioned except in the title, it still casts the action in a more dynamic and modern light (92).

The subway crowd combines the didactic diversity of railroad crowds with the sublimity of those found on the nineteenth-century street. William James famously remarks of Walt Whitman, "He felt the human crowd as rapturously as Wordsworth felt the mountains, felt it as an overpoweringly significant presence" (248). Baudelaire and Whitman both modeled a lyric voice that reflected on and interacted with the passers-by on city sidewalks. Recent criticism may have exhausted the possibilities for discussing them as flâneurs, spectators of city life. Their positive attitude toward the urban throng would nevertheless have influenced American city poets around the turn of the century, particularly as it offered a more attractive alternative to the pathologizing of the crowd in work by Gustave Le Bon and Gabriel Tarde. Baudelaire imagined the "painter of modern life" as "a mirror as vast as the crowd itself" (10); Whitman mirrored the diversity of the crowd and foregrounded the poet himself as part of that mass.[11]

The appropriate relation of the poet to the masses and to mass transportation becomes a central concern both in city poetry and in essays criticizing it. Choosing an urban setting requires that artists accurately describe its population, a call that Carl Sandburg makes in earnest in his 1916 "Halsted Street Car." René Laidlaw, however, conveys a palpable distaste for poems of the subway that take as part of their mission "cataloguing all the unpleasant types, male and female, who brush against you in the stage-coach of the underworld" (634). This dismissal refers specifically to Joyce Kilmer's sonnet "The Subway; 96th Street to 137th Street," which appeared in *The Independent* in 1910. The first two lines of Kilmer's sonnet are repeatedly invoked in essays opposed to urban poetry as shorthand for the cityscape poet's unhealthy attachment to the unsavory city crowd. Kilmer's sonnet illustrates the move from picturesque classification to collective identification. Its first two lines anatomize the crowd surrounding him as types: "Tired clerks, pale girls, street-cleaners, business men / Boys, priests and harlots, drunkards, students, thieves" (Kilmer, "Subway" 467). The next two lines continue to hold the narrator apart from this crowd: Kilmer observes how "each one" feels pleasure escaping from his workday and animalizes these people by saying "they mingle" in a "pen." His narrator seems to enter into the subway car itself in the following line. From that point onward, the poem describes the collective experiences of a "we" that moves together through the darkness, ascends at 125th Street, and returns underground. Kilmer revised his own lines when self-citing in "The Great Nickel Adventure": " 'Tired clerks, pale girls, street-cleaners, business men, boys, priests and sailors, drunkards, students, thieves'—all gain a new sincerity" (41). Notably, he eliminates the "harlots" of the first version in favor of "sailors," writing out the passengers who most explicitly sell themselves in favor of a group that emphasizes the subway as a venue of mobility and adventure. Nevertheless, in both cases the narrator becomes part of the group. Why does this catalogue serve as a synecdoche for the poem itself across a number of essays? It does so, I suggest, because it communicates the emergent understanding that all subway passengers, regardless of status, are goods in circulation. Other critics associate the crowd and the commercial more directly: *The Independent,* for example, calls the subway passengers of Kilmer's poem "freight" ("Editorial: City Poets" 395), downgrading them from unpleasant but typical subjects to mere cargo.

American magazine poems set in the midst of the subway-riding populace unnerved genteel critics, who found representations of the crowds both distasteful and derivative. "You are imitators," Laidlaw says, "of one another, and of greater, naughtier predecessors" (635). Not only is the new trend less transgressive than its practitioners imagine, but also it is less new. This sense of city poetry's derivativeness was a common critique in magazine editorials. Curiously, the problem seems to have inspired somewhat staid writers to their most punning and playful: *The Independent* bemoaned "contemporaries bent on out-bawling Baudelaire and out-whizzing Whitman" ("Editorial: City Poets" 395), while *Scribner's* diagnosed an outbreak of "Baudelirium" ("Point of View" 408). This playfulness contrasts to the high seriousness that ought to be the purview of poetry. Only onomatopoeia and portmanteau words can accurately convey the ridiculousness of the new verse. One might also note the disorder at the heart of each neologism: the imitators of these nineteenth-century city poets seem like crying babies or members of a mob, their poems like carnival rides.

Although the crowd may have served a sublime function in nineteenth-century poetry, turn-of-the-century critics suggests that writers should focus on interiority, normally understood to be a characteristic of modernist poetry. Indeed, the invocation to "know thyself" serves as a kind of bulwark against the foreign masses. Laidlaw insists that the poets of the city "should strive for" self-knowledge and what he calls "larger sincerity"; "let them understand themselves," he prescribes, "before they try to interpret the Babel of all their fellow-citizens" (635). This admonition suggests an understanding of the lyric subject as eminently singular as well as white, male, and English-speaking. The language of the interior self needs to be understood in poetry, but it does not need to be "interpreted," as does the foreign "Babel" of the multiple voices heard on the city street. For all his ironic bantering, Laidlaw expresses the same sentiment that Andreas Huyssen locates in the modernist rejection of the feminized masses, a fear that mass cultural success is synonymous with being devoured by the crowd ("Mass Culture as Woman" 47).

The presence of crowds and noise in this setting works against the still dominant Romantic ideal of the writer in solitary meditation. "I don't see how literature can be produced in the city," says John Burroughs. "Literature must have repose, and there is no repose in New York so far as I can see" (215). The city is an antipoetic environment because it prevents the poet from experiencing the silence and distance from one's surroundings that are necessary prerequisites for contemplation. Though Burroughs shows an antimodernist horror toward the crowds and noise of the modern city, he begrudgingly admits the possibility that others may enjoy it. Yet even this discussion seems to agitate him, as he exclaims: "Some people can find repose in the city—I can't. I hear that people write on trains, on the omnibus, and in the Subway—I don't see how they do it!" (215). Burroughs maintains a mindset that places technology and repose in opposition to each other. What we see in subway poetry of the 1910s, however, is the nascent understanding that machines provide a kind of mental escape for city dwellers. Margaret French Patton, a distant relative of the general with the same surname, published magazine verse throughout the 1910s with quietly religious and political themes. "On the Subway Train," a poem that appeared in *Harper's Weekly* in January 1913, is written in the voice of a working-class figure who finds the subway to be the most peaceful environment in his or her daily routine:[12]

> The children quarrel when I'm home,
> The factory blurs my brain,
> So back and forth from work I like
> The quiet of the Subway train. (21)

The subway suspends the speaker between the functionality of a work role and the expectations faced at home. Because it is an in-between space, passengers have no assigned duties and are subject to no expectations. They can simply find "A quiet central place of peace, / Where God sits in a silence bound" (21). As Firkins does, Patton imagines the subway ride as a respite where the passenger's escape from the instrumentality of the factory and the demands of the family give her time to pray. Here we begin to see how subway versifiers respond to the common misconceptions about the city. In the process, they refigure the understanding of the urban crowd that had been inherited from the picturesque discourse of nineteenth-century newspaper and magazine writing. Rather than seeking color and interest in the sights of the city, the narrator admits that there's already too much stimulation from which one needs respite. For Patton and Firkins, the subway serves as the best emblem of their position in the Christian cosmos.

Early subway poetry marks the beginning of a dramatic shift in American literary representations of the urban crowd. When passengers of all classes and backgrounds share the same crowded subway car, it no longer makes sense to talk about "a split between those who understand and control machines and those who do not" (Nye, *American Technological Sublime* 60). Even the educated passengers who "understand" the subway more fully—whether because they are engineers or because they have read Dante—have precisely the same amount of control over their trajectory as the less informed passengers. What educated passengers can do, however, is imagine their position within the subway as it maps onto their position in other systems, from the temporal to the economic to the social. This emergent form of perception had become the norm by the end of the nineteenth century, when "the capitalist world's recomposition on the basis of modern traffic had been completed. From then on, traffic determined what belonged where" (Schivelbusch 194). If we understand the turn-of-the-century city as one recomposed "on the basis of modern traffic" (194), then this recomposition affects the knowledgeable and the uneducated alike.

Recent work on the visual and theatrical culture of turn-of-the-century New York City has articulated two important ways that circulation should be understood in this local context. First, we should remember that culture of this period explores urban circulation as a site both of freedom and of restriction. Kristin Whissel discusses this tension as it is enacted in the seminal narrative film *Traffic in Souls* (1913): "At the heart of the film's articulation of technological modernity is a contradiction specific to the experience of being absorbed into traffic: when one merges into the mobilized mass of bodies and machines, one constitutes traffic by acting as a single unit of its broader movement; yet, at the same time that one *constitutes* traffic, one is *constituted* by it—that is, defined by and subordinated to an already-determined path of twists and turns, forward propulsions, and arbitrary stops" (167). The urban subject makes circulation happen; without any people, there would presumably be no traffic. Yet one cannot make any kind of circulation happen, since the pathways are predefined and the movement regulated. Subway passengers are both freely engaging in Kilmer's "blind and beautiful recklessness" and being blindly herded into the cars like cattle.

Indeed, the modern belief in the imperceptible logic by which one is moved through the subway becomes the modern analogue for religious belief. "The Great Nickel Adventure" shows Joyce Kilmer celebrating the idea that even the most rational man will "give himself up to the subway with a sweet and child-like faith" (40). The idea that riding the subway means submitting to larger forces recurs throughout New York subway literature. In the first half of the twentieth century, at least, this loss of control seems to have its benefits. Earlier in Kilmer's essay, this straw man ("a man of uncompromising practicality, a stern rationalist" [39]) expresses his cartoonish contempt for blind acceptance. By paying his fare, however, he blindly enters into the system with little concern that it will take him home quickly and efficiently. "When he started for home in the evening," Kilmer writes, "he read the words 'Dyckman Street' on the car window with a *mediaeval* simplicity. And on the guarantee of these printed words, placed there by minions of the capitalist class, he gave up the privilege of directing his course" (40, emphasis added). Here the trope of medieval faith in the face of modern technology is made explicit. Just how different is unquestioning acceptance of the signs on a subway train from unquestioning acceptance of, say, the Gospel? Of course, Kilmer's tongue is firmly in his cheek; "minions of the capitalist class" sounds ripped from the socialist broadsides. Even so, he foregrounds the rapid acceptance of this technology and the loss of agency that goes with it. Tamed by transit, the modern skeptic becomes "as a little child" (44). This childlike devotion in turn becomes a positive sign of modern man's simplicity and faith rather than a negative sign of his loss of self-control. Embracing the loss of agency experienced by the system's passengers, poets of the subway sublime cast one of the presumably negative experiences of modernity in morally positive terms. The modern city dweller may have lost control over her own circulation through the city, but she still maintains a capacity to trust in the public good.

We should remember that the depiction of urban mobility in the period does not directly reflect the physical experience of those spaces. By casting this new experience of passivity as one experienced in relation to a divine agency, poems of the period accommodate a new and unfamiliar urban habit to preestablished aesthetic ideals. In describing the subway in sublime terms, they both reflect ideological norms of the day and enable a commonly unpleasant experience to be felt as a pleasure. Whereas newspapers complained about the "subway crush," for example, popular songs imagined the movement of the crowd as a dance. City dwellers were "fascinated by the potential unsettling aspects of circulation," yet it is important to remember that "what makes the delight in traffic possible—and what transforms travel as an adjunct to work into travel as pleasure—is the filmic mediation itself" (Haenni 27, 28). Genteel subway versifiers render the most unpleasant aspects of travel as pleasure by emphasizing the transcendence of the system in which their passivity plays only a small part.

The cityscape poem circulates within the modern metropolis. As a result, it directs its attention toward the heterogeneous urban crowd, both as a subject and as a possible reading public. When the subway system can symbolize and connect with an infinite number of other systems, the passengers are connected in an equally depersonalized way. Poets of the New York subway thus share the aim (if not the optimism) of those designers in London who imagined that art in the Underground could provide "an organizing framework" for a fragmented society just as the cathedral had done for medieval cities (Saler 92). The rhetoric of the technological sublime has the effect of unifying its audience, either in a shared appreciation for man's dominance or in a shared sense of national pride. By ascribing a transcendental meaning to the subway system, city poets attempted to forge an urban subjectivity that participated equally in genteel tradition and cosmopolitan modernity. Understanding the technological sublime within the context of a metropolitan area means understanding how the imaginary connectivity can operate on a local level as well as a national one.

Of course, this desire for a technologically mediated form of connection suggests an increasing sense of fragmentation. In this chapter I have considered how the anxieties about literary production and consumption, epitomized by the increased influence of mass-distribution magazines, can be understood as the anxiety animating the description of the subway as a poetic vehicle of sublime communion. The transcontinental railroad can overcome regionalism and draw the Union together, but the subway presents the city crowd as already atomized. For Kilmer, the crowd can be united into a collective "we," but only for the duration of the ride; for Patton, the shared experience of the crowd comes only in the recognition of an isolating, if meditative, moment reflected across the car. Only when "the train stops suddenly" (Patton 21) does the poem's speaker notice the other people in the car and wonder if they too are experiencing the same divinely sanctioned silence. Instead of being a technology that unifies its passengers, the subway turns everyone's attention in the same direction, isolating them even further because of it. Although Nye insists that the American technological sublime is often experienced in a crowd (*American Technological Sublime* 277), the subway sublime is felt while one is alone in a crowd.

Genteel subway poets react to "the trauma of Taylorization" in quite a different way from those in the same period who celebrated the freedom of travel by automobile. While the loss of a sense of individualism may have "necessitated the ideological production of a new, compensatory subjectivity," as Cotten Seiler argues, the work that I've discussed in this chapter does not offer a subject "characterized by self-determination" (Seiler 29). Instead, the poems compensated for these new historical forces by offering a humbled urban subject, set on the same level as the rest of the crowd, thrilled by the same machinery and worried by the same everyday problems. It's no wonder this attitude didn't take hold; it flies in the face of most commonplaces about modernity, modernism, and American character as a whole. This group of minor American poets gives us a sense of what lay between the celebratory mass cultural representations of the subway and the dismissive high-cultural ones. And this in-between attitude, I suggest, persists in the Manhattan Transit Authority's public art programs like Arts for Transit and Poetry in Motion.

## Poetry in Motion

Like all images of the American technological sublime, the subway sublime had a short shelf life.[13] Ridership increased throughout the subway's first decades, both in overall numbers and in frequency. Consequently, the wonder associated with the subway decreased. Nye discusses the tendency of each new invention to subsume earlier versions of the technological sublime, but he uses the language of generations: "Machines that arouse awe and admiration in one generation soon cease to seem remarkable and the next generation demands something larger, faster, or more complex" (*American Technological Sublime* 60). In the case of the subway, sublimity becomes much less prominent in representations of the technology within a decade or so after its initial opening. Yet the defining characteristics of the subway sublime continue to influence reception of the space. I conclude this chapter by considering the afterlife of this brief movement in subway poetry, suggesting that its vision of the subway sublime echoes through the system to the present day.

The poetry of Kilmer, Firkins, Stone, Patton, and other middlebrow city writers fell out of fashion once modernist verse came into the mainstream. Nowadays, subway poetry is the domain of Ezra Pound, William Carlos Williams, and Hart Crane—the subjects of the next chapter. Magazine poets of the subway's first decade nevertheless should be understood as important and underexamined precursors for later poets who think about the subway in religious terms. From Allen Tate's tunnel that serves as a realm of "angry worship" (105) to Muriel Rukeyser's swaying passengers described as "tense and semi-crucified things" (53) to the prayers offered in Molly Peacock's "Subway Vespers," the subway continues to be understood as a realm that encompasses both the everyday and the transcendent. These later iterations most often invoke the sublime in service of an argument about urban alienation; the subway is sublime not because it unifies the city but because it is so resolutely separate from it. Though Tate shares these earlier poets' Catholic faith, he cannot share their belief that the subway reflects a divine coherence imperceptible to individual believers: the underground portion of the subway demands an "angry worship" that is unearned, and the sight of the heavens from the elevated tracks leave him reeling like a "blind astronomer" or an "idiot" (448). Even the two parts of his sonnet, "Subway," seem disconnected from each other, like parts of a city that cannot be resolved into a coherent system. Louis Zukofsky's poem "Mantis" seems equally pessimistic, with that insect's abandonment in the subway serving as the central image for imagining clashes of nature and culture, the poor and the wealthy.

But this poetry's importance extends beyond the literary realm to the domain of everyday life. Whereas earlier technologies facilitated an image of the technological sublime that was visual, extensive, and active, the subway system's spatial organization leads to an experience of the technological sublime that is sonic and tactile, imaginative, and passive. Passengers experiencing velocity, extensiveness, and obscurity from within feel quite differently about it than do passengers gazing on it from without. By focusing on the sublime as a force that can be experienced while in transit, subway poets show how it can be acclimated into the commercialized world in much the same way that a cigarette break might be incorporated into a workday. In "The Politics of the Third Rail" Garrett Ziegler sees a resistance to the conceived space of the subway in the poetic visions of the early twentieth century. He notes that "the safe and smooth planned space of the functionalist city is undermined by its reassembly as a devouring force" (290). Nevertheless, the terror inspired by the subway in the poetry of the 1910s tends to the brief and fantastic, balanced with wonder at its speed and connective power. Additionally, the transformative power of the subway on its poetic passengers occurs at the same time that it continues on its scheduled path. It seems too utopian to call this "a discursive space in which the subway does not function according to plan, where it disrupts subjectivity to the point of spiritual obeisance" (Ziegler 291). To present an urban space that "disrupts subjectivity" without disrupting service is less "an oblique politics of resistance" than an assimilation of the subway system into previous systems of morality.

The idea that poetry might jolt subway passengers into a new frame of mind while they continue to move smoothly through the system lies at the heart of Poetry in Motion, a program of the Poetry Society of America through which lyric poems were posted in subways and buses, taking their place alongside advertisements and transit company notices. The program has run in a number of cities across the United States, from Boise to New Orleans ("Poetry in Motion"). The first and best-known version, however, was the eighteen-year collaboration with the Metropolitan Transportation Authority of New York City. It began in 1992 with poems by Emily Dickinson, Walt Whitman, William Butler Yeats, and Lucille Clifton. In this period the subway is still associated with graffiti and crime; at its best, it is a necessary evil. The story told by the founders from the beginning of the New York program to its end in 2008, however, leans heavily on the language of epiphany, respite, and "uplift" found in the subway poetry of a century before (Grynbaum, "Literary Quotations"). A "Talk of the Town" article in the *New Yorker* narrates "a startling experience" that MTA president Alan F. Kiepper has "as a consequence of his own program," an epiphany that he had when reading the Emily Dickinson poem " 'Hope' is the Thing with Feathers" on a Brooklyn-bound subway (Cohen 57). Rather than giving them lightning flashes of revelation, Kiepper describes the program as one that creates a peaceful environment for passengers in the subway, "a serene pause from the din and confusion of the daily urban life" (qtd. in Nadell 41). The subway no longer serves as the exemplary space of urban sublimity, but it continues to provide the respite and perspective that Progressive Era poets found underground.

Although the subway evoked a far different response from passengers in the early 1990s, Poetry in Motion still imagines its separation from the city as an opportunity to turn away from the commercial values of the street. The Poetry Society of America website quotes one rider's testimonial about the program: "Reading the poems while I am in transit helps me to realize and remember that there is so much more to life than just earning money" ("Poetry in Motion"). In this way it provides an important counterpoint to the advertisements that take up the most space on the walls of subway cars and buses. Martha Nadell suggests that the line between poetry and advertisement is blurred when these poems are posted in the same space, but she nevertheless acknowledges that the commodity being sold is the lure of escape from the disquieting workaday world (41). We can understand the poets of the subway's first decade, then, as the first wave of intervention that gives New Yorkers the language and imagery to read the subway as a sublime poetic experience rather than an alienating commercial one.

Literature and public outreach exist along a continuum of interventions that try to shape the reception of technology and the behavior and attitude of its users. This vision of the subway as a poetic space, both in the poetry of the 1910s and in the public program of the 1990s, asks riders to gaze mentally outside the confines of the subway car. Except for an extract from "Crossing Brooklyn Ferry," the texts of Poetry in Motion do not deal with transportation directly: the poems are mostly brief, philosophical lyrics, though nature poems and extracts from Shakespeare's plays are also featured. Poetry of the 1910s values the subway as a space of private transcendence; similarly, the Poetry in Motion program suggests that passengers pay attention to the poetry of Walt Whitman instead of the "face to face" encounters he celebrates in "Crossing Brooklyn Ferry," one factor that "serves to dismantle public experience by constructing a private space for reading within it" (Nadell 43). Mystifying the subway as a venue for private reflection impedes passengers' ability to imagine it as a space for public encounters with diverse fellow passengers on their own terms. Magazine poets and public art programs both participate in the long history of downplaying the subway crowd's collective experience in favor of the subway rider's private experience.

# CHAPTER 3

# MINDING THE GAPS IN MODERNIST POETRY

In the verse of Joyce Kilmer, Chester Firkins, and the other poets invested in the ideal of the subway sublime, the passenger's orientation to the system parallels the believer's relation to the divine: although neither person can perceive its object, each experiences flashes of wonder and peace that confirm its coherence. These middlebrow Catholic poets see the subway as a vehicle that counteracts the irreligious rationalism of their age; with its underground tunnels and complex pathways, the subway can be understood only through parallels and metaphors. By eschewing the transparency of the gear-and-girder world, the subway's form nearly demands that educated passengers trade their expertise for an almost medieval faith in a sublime system.

Although the chaos of the early twentieth-century city may suggest that ideals of order, beauty, and truth have fallen by the wayside, the magazinists discussed in chapter 2 propose that this view is merely a failure of imagination on the part of the city dweller. The city replicates the universe in miniature, and the view afforded by public transportation helps us see the mysteries of both. What happens to this model of coherence, then, when the sublime becomes routine? Avant-garde poetry of the 1910s and 1920s offers an alternate solution to the problem of technology as a medium for reading the city. Coherence is not presumed but rather hard-won from the buildup of knowledge gained through the everyday experiences of public transportation. Hart Crane, along with other modernist poets of this period, finds in the Babel of the subway crowd and repetition of commuting habits an alternative to transcendental meaning. Unlike the middlebrow verse writers of the 1910s, who glossed over the class differences of the subway crowd, Crane is particularly interested in examining the physical fragmentation experienced by working-class riders; his interest, however, is less political than formal. The broken repetitions seen in the movements and heard in the language of his fellow passengers model a form of engagement with literary predecessors that Crane carries out in his poem "The Tunnel."[1]

In order to understand Hart Crane's view of technology, one must begin with the body. Crane resists sublimity when discussing the relationship between technology and verse in his much-cited essay "Modern Poetry":

> Contrary to general prejudice, the wonderment experienced in watching nose dives is of less immediate creative promise to poetry than the familiar gesture of a motorist in the modest act of shifting gears. I mean to say that mere romantic speculation on the power and beauty of machinery keeps it at a continual remove; it can not act creatively in our lives until, like the unconscious nervous responses of our bodies, its connotations emanate from within—forming as spontaneous a terminology of poetic reference as the bucolic world of pasture, plow, and barn. (171–72)

Unlike his peers who have replaced the subway with the airplane as the technologically sublime vehicle of the day, Crane insists that the subway can function as a poetic subject only after it has been incorporated fully into everyday life. In early subway verse the machine itself is indeed kept at a "continual remove"; poetry of the 1920s, by contrast, abandons the "wonderment" in favor of a focus on the "familiar gestures" associated with subway riding: dropping a nickel into a turnstile, squeezing into a crowded car, swinging on a strap. This suggests that the meaning of the subway becomes visible in the "unconscious nervous responses" of passengers accommodated to its mechanical routines. New York modernists can no longer separate themselves from the subway they write about, so deeply associated with urban space and culture has it become. Rather they consider how it has formed "a terminology of poetic reference" and shaped "the unconscious nervous responses of our bodies." The understanding of the subway system, like the understanding of American poetry itself, moves away from a dependence on transcendental truths to provide coherence. Instead we see the subway deployed in service to a model of coherence like that of a collage or a cinematic montage, one in which the beholder must fill in the blanks and mind the gaps.

Modernist poetry models the cognitive efforts of subway riders in a search for innovative means of expressing gaps between knowledge and feeling. In a period when psychoanalysis was becoming part of the popular culture, the subway served as a resonant figure for the unconscious mind: while its submerged structure is completely determined by outside forces, it nevertheless enables a multiplicity of creative pathways and surprising connections. Although a few earlier critics have dealt with subway poetry as a genre, they tend to discuss it in terms of content rather than form.[2] Modernist subway poems certainly deal with issues of modernity, creating "microcosm[s] of modern urban life" (Balestra 90), but this claim does not tell us how poems differ from other genres of writing about the same space. When modernist poets deal with subterranean transit, they also tend to deal with subterranean connections, exploring less obvious and less direct paths in their poetic construction. By focusing on "The Tunnel," I show how the minor modern genre of the subway poem enabled New York writers like Crane to theorize increasingly complex poetic structures. By asserting the subway's spatial coherence in terms of its self-sufficiency as a system, this poetry argues for its own formal coherence on similar terms. The underground connections enabled by the subway system, in effect, model the underground connections made by the reader. This writing thus breaks from the literary tradition that encompasses earlier representations of subway space.

Modernist subway poetry of the 1920s shares a formal interest in collage as well as a thematic interest in understanding and incorporating the heteroglossia of the subway crowd. Texts oscillate between embodiment and abstraction; perspective shifts dramatically from one moment to the next. These formal characteristics reveal an interest not only in fragmentation but also in figuring out what kinds of structures can hold fragments together without imposing a false coherence. An underlying logic gives shape to subway movement, though it is impossible to perceive it while one is in the midst of the ride.

Modernist subway poems by the likes of Ezra Pound, Maxwell Bodenheim, William Carlos Williams, and Hart Crane use the subway as a kind of modern laboratory for the atomization and reconnection of urban imagery. In some instances these reconnections are successful; in others, the center fails to hold. For Hart Crane in particular, the partial and resolutely physical sensations of the subway present a new model for poetry seeking a more complex orientation to the urban crowd and to the literary past.

The relation between poetic parts and wholes animates Crane's 1926 subway poem "The Tunnel." I focus on the Crane poem both as it enters into dialogue with other subway poems and as it functions as a section of his larger work *The Bridge*. This stands to reason, since the poem was initially published in T. S. Eliot's magazine *The Criterion* in November 1927 (Fisher, *Hart Crane* 354), then as a part of the book-length epic poem in 1930. In a letter to his friend the critic Waldo Frank, Crane describes the composition process as "rather ghastly, almost surgery—and, oddly, almost all from the notes and stitches I have written while swinging on the strap at late midnights going home" (Crane 484). Crane tries to combine his "notes and stitches" into a whole poem, but the process is complicated, even "ghastly." Habituated to the subway ride, he can jot down bits of poetry or overheard conversation while "swinging on the strap"; he struggles only at the point of reconstruction, when trying to make sense of these pieces in a larger system. "The Tunnel" foregrounds the subway as a technology through which the regular experience of fragmented and partial rides provides a provisional sense of the subway as system. This building up of embodied knowledge through repeated, piecemeal observations, the "notes and stitches" of Crane's letter, offers a particularly useful process for understanding how technology mediates the modern subject's relationship to his surroundings and the modernist poet's relationship to the literary past.

As I have previously discussed, the subway troubles the coherence of urban cognitive maps. "The Tunnel," then, can be thought of as an exploration of an important facet of the fragmentation of city space in this period, as described by the geographer Kevin Lynch: "The buried paths of the

Boston subway could not be related to the rest of the environment except when they come up for air, as in crossing the river. The surface entrances of the stations may be strategic nodes in the city, but they are related along invisible conceptual linkages. The subway is a disconnected nether world, and it is intriguing to speculate what means might be used to mesh it into the structure of the whole" (57). Here Lynch describes the subway as a form of transportation that makes imagining the city as a spatial whole nearly impossible. Although his remarks are concerned with Boston's subway, they reflect remarkably well the view of the subway articulated in "The Tunnel." The poem begins in Times Square and ends beneath the Brooklyn Bridge, both readily recognizable New York locations. The bulk of the poem, however, takes place in a "disconnected netherworld," one that relates to its starting and stopping points psychologically but does not mimic a possible aboveground path. The end of the poem even "come[s] up for air," offering a clearer and more coherent view of the self's relation to the city as it gazes over the East River. Yet there the similarities end, for Lynch considers the subway's relation to the geographical "whole" of the city, while Crane attempts to mesh its disconnected perceptual world into the larger narrative structure of his poetry.

*The Bridge*'s central unifying image is of course the Brooklyn Bridge, which connects American history to present-day concerns as it connects Manhattan to Brooklyn. The subway in "The Tunnel" has long been read as the evil twin to the Brooklyn Bridge, one whose underground path and disjointed surroundings are a necessary precondition for the rapturous union of the poem's conclusion, "Atlantis." Critics of "The Tunnel," like many critics of subway writing in general, tend to ignore the actuality of the subway as a part of city life; they leap too quickly to a metaphoric reading of the subway as underworld or hell, instead of first considering the setting as a culturally, historically, and spatially located environment. Brian Reed has characterized the poem as the retelling of "an infernal subway ride" (*Hart Crane* 128), and Gordon Tapper has called it "nightmarish" (138). In this way, readings of the subway in "The Tunnel" are not that different from those in other poetry of the period: Kristiaan Versluys says that modernist subway poetry is defined by its "topophobia" (329–30), and Gianfranca Balestra notes that it "tends to be represented as a sort of epitome of the city as mechanized hell" (97). While I would not commit the interpretive violence required to call Crane's depiction of the subway a totally positive one, I feel it necessary to balance out the gruesome readings by focusing on the subway as habit, one that modern subjects use to get to know the city. The subway in "The Tunnel" is a vehicle by which even frightening sights can be made sense of through repeated physical encounters.

Subway poetry of the 1920s uses its underground setting to interrogate how isolated sensual data come together into a coherent mental image. This concern took root in perhaps the most famous subway poem, Ezra Pound's brief lyric "In a Station of the Metro," which first appeared in *Poetry* magazine in 1913. With his focus on juxtaposed images with little to no explanatory connection between them, Pound set the stage for avant-garde writers of the 1920s. In one of several accounts of the poem's composition he writes:

> The "one image poem" is a form of super-position, that is to say, one idea set on top of another. I found it useful in getting out of the impasse in which I had been left by my metro emotion: I wrote a thirty-line poem, and destroyed it because it was what we call work "of second intensity." Six months later I made a poem of half that length; a year later, I made the following *hokku*-like sentence:—
>
> "The apparition of these faces in the crowd:
> Petals on a wet, black bough." (*Early Writings* 286)

This poem sets the faces in the subway station next to the wet petals. As countless commentators have observed before me, this suggests a relationship between the two images, one that the reader must work out for herself. Although Pound disavows cinematic poetry (Early Writings 287), "In a Station of the Metro" resembles an Eisensteinian montage. The first line is realistic, albeit from a subjective perspective; the colon (or semicolon in later versions) provides a grammatical "cut"; and the second image puts an impressionistic cast on the gritty urban setting. In the first version of the poem that appeared in *Poetry,* gaps separate six clusters of images; in this version Pound has closed the gaps within each line, but the relation between the two remains unresolved.[3] Pound's process depends on condensation: he moves from thirty-six lines to eighteen to two (three including the title). Even the most radical abridgment cannot fully bring together the first line and the second. The reader, then, must resolve the tension between the first and second lines by constructing a mental link between them. The paths are multiple and overdetermined: the petals are like faces; the dark bough is like the dark subway station; apparitions and wet petal both appear translucent. The list could go on. Subway poetry of the 1920s similarly asks its readers to construct the relationship between the given images.

Maxwell Bodenheim's "Summer Evening: New York Subway Station" (1922), William Carlos William's "Rapid Transit" (1923), and Claude McKay's "Subway Wind" (1922) all follow Pound's lead. In modernist poetry, a move into subway space signals a poetic leap, a transition from one diegetic level to another. The difference is one of intensity rather than kind. Although the texts discussed in chapter 1 present the subway as a system that parallels others—the ocean, the galaxy—they do so chiefly in order to confirm that urban circulation is as natural as that of fish or planets. While situated within the literal boundaries of New York City, the spaces that the subway traverses are more often figurative ones—grounded, one might say, by the materiality of the movement being described. Subway poems foreground the modernist poetic movement from one linguistic register to another and from one temporality to another. The logic of forward motion unites otherwise unrelated sounds and images, suggesting that the underground journey came to serve as an increasingly useful aggregative tool.

Hart Crane reconstitutes his "notes and stitches" in a way that portrays the subway as a system while acknowledging its existence as an amalgamation of individual rides. The tension between transcendent wholes and awkward, piecemeal parts animates much of the contemporary critical conversation about Crane's poetry. Brian Reed in "Hand in Hand" reads Crane through the work of Jasper Johns, connecting the "separate yet conjoined canvases" of Johns's 1962 painting *Diver* to the poetic logic of "conjunctive disjunction" between sections of *The Bridge* (32).[4] I find "conjunctive disjunction" to be a constitutive element of "The Tunnel," and indeed of modernist subway poetry in the wake of Pound's subterranean haiku. Reading "The Tunnel" as an example of modernist subway poetry shows that this difficulty of constructing a poem out of individual perceptions has important antecedents in urban life of the period. The subway serves as a central model for "conjunctive disjunction" both as a way of moving through underground space and as a poetic process.

The sense of divided connection among city neighborhoods becomes part of New Yorkers' daily life in the era of the subway. "The Tunnel" plays a unique role in *The Bridge* because it pays extended attention to everyday technology and its repeated use. Crane's narrator walks across the Brooklyn Bridge, but it remains an otherworldly symbol in the proem and "Atlantis"; the ships in the section titled "Cutty Sark" and the airplane in the following section, "Cape Hatteras," are described rapturously because they make journeys on a more dramatic scale. By contrast, "The Tunnel" closely heeds all the details of the subway ride—not just how it parallels an epic descent to the underworld, but even what quotidian sounds it makes when the doors close. Many technological spectacles in *The Bridge* can be understood within the frame of the technological sublime—particularly the pilot soaring and crashing his plane in "Cape Hatteras." The subway in "The Tunnel" is not simply triumphant or terrifying. Crane's shifts in tone, diction, and perspective throughout "The Tunnel" attempt to register both the subway's sublimity and its mundanity. Crane repeatedly embraces the repetitions of the regular subway ride as a means of smoothing over, and even embracing, the fragmentation of modern life. The in-betweenness of subway space and the regularity of subway routine make this reconciliation possible.

The subway enables urban subjects to envision the underground connections taking place in the process of their commute without denying their inherently fragmented view of the city. This capacity for making sense of disjunctive reality is applicable even in regard to the initially terrifying image of Edgar Allan Poe, whose disembodied head we encounter mid-poem. The narrator asks:

> Whose head is swinging from the swollen strap?
> Whose body smokes along the bitten rails,
> Bursts from a smoldering bundle far behind
> In back forks of the chasms of the brain,—
> Puffs from a riven stump far out behind
> In interborough fissures of the mind?
>
> And why do I often meet your visage here,
> Your eyes like agate lanterns—on and on
> Below the toothpaste and the dandruff ads? (Crane 69)

Poe's head swinging from a strap ominously conflates commuting and lynching; his eyes shine like ghostly lanterns. This disembodied head is normalized by its placement in an utterly prosaic location, "below the toothpaste and the dandruff ads," where riders might see other disembodied heads.[5] This perhaps accounts for the narrator's acclimation to the head in this second stanza, where we discover that he "often" meets it while riding the train.[6] The singular vision has become a regular encounter, and the sublime has become routine.

Rather than finding them deadening, Crane finds routines to be hypnotic, empathy-inducing, even—in a word appropriate to the subway—transportive. Michael Taussig locates the magical quality of modern perception in "a certain tactility growing out of distracted vision" (143). It is precisely this tactility that Crane discovers in "The Tunnel," as if the blind movement of the subway necessitated that passengers feel their way through the city. Before the passing sensations are registered as symbolic, the poet and the reader experience them as tactile fragments. Functioning as the shadow side to the bridge's panoramic promise, the subway in "The Tunnel" connects the boroughs invisibly. Like other subway poems of this period (and standing in stark contrast to many British modernist poems set on the London Underground), "The Tunnel" deemphasizes vision as a means of orientation in the modern city.[7] In the wake of Pound's (admittedly visual) poetic image, subway poetry of the 1920s takes on an increasingly sonic and tactile character, troubling the centrality of the visual image in our understanding of modernist representational strategies.

In the next section I compare the role of physicality in other subway poems to its role in "The Tunnel." Unlike other poets of the period, Crane engages with the fragmented physicality of the crowd and imagines his narrator as subject to the same forces as the laborers who surround him. The narrator's submission to crowded, mechanized space allows Crane to reimagine a relationship to the American poetic tradition and, finally, to imagine the subway ride of "The Tunnel" as part of *The Bridge*'s larger system of meaning. The separation of subway space enables riders to skim over the shocks of modern life, uniting geographically distant spaces and temporally distant experiences.

## "Someday by heart you'll learn each famous sight"

Reed's "conjunctive disjunction" can be seen throughout modernist writing on the subway, yet in "The Tunnel" it takes on a different cast—one that is distinctly embodied. The "ghastly" quality and the feeling that he is engaging in "surgery" foreground Crane's sense that the individual pieces that he is suturing together into a whole poem are body parts. It is telling that Crane calls the process of composition "almost surgery" in the letter quoted at the beginning of this chapter, for it suggests that the pieces of the poem he is grafting are almost but not quite corporeal. In his essay "Blood on the Cutting Room Floor," the poet-critic Charles Bernstein uses a similarly qualified metaphor, calling writing "a kind of psychic surgery" (351). He later calls this new possible relationship between parts of a poem "dysraphism," a medical term for the "congenital misseaming of embryonic parts" (359). This violently physicalized term helps Bernstein imagine a mode of composition in which the differences between disparate source materials are not resolved out of existence—in which the scars are still visible even when the poetic body is whole (359). "The Tunnel" finds in the subway an ideal location for dysraphic poetry. Crane presents impressions, sensations, and fragments of conversation that are physicalized and unresolved, lines that never quite come together into a complete work.

"The Tunnel" calls into question the poem's ability to record the shifting urban landscape accurately. Indeed, the beginning of the poem interrogates the legibility of the city itself. The first stanza introduces us to a spectator struggling to make sense of the "performances, assortments," and "résumés" as he (or the crowds that he watches) moves "Up Times Square to Columbus Circle." The faces in the crowd are "refractions of the thousand theatres" that surround them, transmuting their stories into a different medium. "The Tunnel" describes these visions as "mysterious kitchens," suggesting both their everydayness and their impenetrability (Crane 67). The first five lines of the poem are almost entirely constituted of nouns in apposition, as are the two lines of "In a Station of the Metro." Crane's lines are far more abstract than Pound's, however, and no relationship is suggested between them; they are paratactic rather than syntactic. The endpoints of Times Square and Columbus Circle tell us that we are most likely on Broadway, but the "performances, assortments, [and] résumés" may be taking place in Broadway theaters or on the street itself. The confusion is heightened by the poem's spatial order: whereas Pound asserts connection between the two clauses of his poem with a single punctuation mark, Crane peppers his first five lines with commas, dashes, and ellipses, suggesting interruption as well as connection. Something's cooking in these "mysterious kitchens," but we can't even read the menu.

Even this perplexing onslaught of sights and sounds can be reduced to a comprehensible spectacle, Crane suggests. A caesura follows the "Mysterious kitchens," as if the narrator has paused in thought. The second-person address becomes mocking:

> You shall search them all
> Someday by heart you'll learn each famous sight
> And watch the curtain lift in hell's despite;
> You'll find the garden in the third act dead,
> Finger your knees—and wish yourself in bed
> With tabloid crime-sheets perched in easy sight. (67)

Unlike in the first four lines, here the protagonist is a bored theatergoer, removed from the drama he observes. The ineffable impressions of the city have been fixed in the language of trashy newspapers. Crane presents a deadened sense of shock as the eventual end to picturesque spectatorship. Even the regularity of these poetic lines and the exactness of each couplet's rhymes evoke the formulaic quality of his vision of the city. If the poet is going to consume mass culture passively, Crane suggests with Eliotic irony (as well as a similar rhyme and syntax), he might as well do so in the comfort of his own home. The repetition of the word "sight" also suggests its association with the kind of perception Crane does not want to explore. In his essay "General Aims and Theories," he mocks the mere "retinal registration" of the city presented by "impressionists" like e. e. cummings (162). Similarly, Pound's condensation removes the physicality and everydayness of the subway commute, turning it into an aesthetic event which the narrator can observe from outside. In Crane's view, being a city dweller, and particularly being a city poet, is exciting only when you take advantage of embodied urban perception. Unlike the nineteenth-century urban flâneur, Crane values vision from within the crowd over detached observation of it.

In this way, "The Tunnel" offers a substantially different model of urban interpersonal relations than that of other subway poetry. Pound, Williams, and Bodenheim acknowledge the difficulty of reading the city and the implied threat posed by the crowd. Like the British imagist poets discussed by Andrew Thacker, these American writers "subdue the terrors of urban disorientation" (*Moving through Modernity* 106). Unlike Crane's, their response to this threat is a withdrawal from the physical space of the subway station. "In a Station of the Metro" presents its implied narrator as an external voice, not subject to the subway space in the same way as the crowd that he observes. Thacker's "Imagist Travels in Modernist Space" describes one account Pound gives of the epiphany that led to the poem's composition. When Pound "refers to being jostled by the departing passengers," Thacker writes, "touch is thus replaced in the poem by the detachment of the gaze" (*Moving through Modernity* 100).

The "detachment" of the poetic voice in relation to the underground landscape hints at a connection to models of urban movement more often associated with automobility in this period. Crane's poem stands out in a genre that is more concerned with independence because it understands the subway as an eminently interdependent and relational space. While the "subway crush" might represent the strain of collective movement in the Progressive Era, the narrators in subway poems are seldom jostled in the same way as the figures they describe. Instead, they perform their agency within a faceless crowd through a transformational aesthetic reading of the urban surroundings. Indeed, we might understand the modernist investment in novelty and unique style as a response to the normalizing forces of modernity like the subway.

Modern American poetry betrays an anxiety about being part of the crowd, and particularly about the loss of physical control that arises from this movement into anonymity.[8] William Carlos Williams's poem "Rapid Transit," included in his 1923 volume *Spring and All*, retreats from the embodied experience into the verbal representation of it, from the physical jostling within a crowded car to what Barry Ahearn calls "a series of verbal jostlings" (96). The poem begins by engaging with the possibility of physical destruction on a statistical and personal level:

> Somebody dies every four minutes
> in New York State—
>
> To hell with you and your poetry—
> You will rot and be blown
>
> through the next solar system
> with the rest of the gases—
>
> What the hell do you know about it?
>
> (Williams, *Collected Poems* 231–32)

The eponymous example of what Cecelia Tichi calls his "rapid transit" poetics concerns itself less with the isolated visions seen from a moving vehicle than with making sense of the assault going on within the subway car (248). The couplets, with their suturing dashes, enact an underground connection between the disparate images, snatches of speech, and advertisements. The angry question in line 7 marks the last appearance of anything approximating an individual speaker in the poem. The deep fear of becoming a statistic is suppressed throughout the rest of the poem, replaced with "AXIOMS" (232). Still, the subway ride never entirely disappears: the movement of the subway train toward a destination echoes and underscores the logic of the poem's movement toward the final line, "Interborough Rapid Transit Co." (232). Barry Ahearn reads "Rapid Transit" as a poem that "proceeds from the private quarrel of poet and critic [lines 3–7] to the language of corporate or political entity" (96). Although we have been presented decontextualized advertisements, images, and insult, all of the disparate elements of language are united as utterances within the purview of the company that runs the subway.

By constructing a subway ride through voices and advertisements alone, "Rapid Transit" brackets the urban crowd, instead substituting a crowd of linguistic detritus for our poetic consideration.[9] We see an amplification of this anxiety in the preceding and succeeding texts of *Spring and All*: an essay on the poetics of Marianne Moore leads into "Rapid Transit," and it is followed by another poem called "At the Ballgame." In the essay, Williams insists on the distinctness of Moore's lines: "Marianne's words remain separate, each unwilling to group with the others except as they move in the one direction" (*Collected Poems* 231). With this emphasis on the interplay between individuality and union toward a common goal, Williams gives a different gloss on the relation between the individual experience of a ride and the collective experience of the subway system pursued in "The Tunnel." "At the Ballgame" engages directly with the conformity, power, and appeal of the urban crowd. The crowd in the stands is "moved uniformly // by a spirit of uselessness / which delights them" (233). Although the crowd is beautiful "in detail," it is also "deadly, terrifying," and "without thought" (233, 234). In this way, "Rapid Transit" itself serves as a hidden means of linking Marianne Moore's citational poetics with the collage of voices that make up the experience of urban life.

Even subway poems that attempt to master the urban crowd through verbal description acknowledge the difficulties they face. Maxwell Bodenheim's "Summer Evening: New York Subway-Station" renders the chaotic setting with a kind of provisional coherence that the narrator himself seems not to believe. The reconnection of atomized images into a system seems to be a never-ending battle: "The scene consists of mosaics / Jerkily pieced together and blown apart" (51). The second half of the poem focuses on two waiting passengers, a poor young girl and an old man. They do not interact with each other in any way, and their stories seem not to intersect. Descriptions of each figure put them into a kind of aesthetic dialogue, however: the girl's face is "loosened" by weariness, and the old man's is sweaty and wrinkled; both wear black hats that appear disconnected from their heads. The poem ends with a couplet separated from this description that calls them "Two figures on a subway-platform, / Pieced together by an old complaint" (51). It is only the poem, then, that pieces them together into an image of urban suffering by noticing the formal parallels between them. Their coherence within an aesthetic system seems a hollow echo of an urban community.

Crane moves away from the typical modernist attempts at mastering the urban spectacle. Instead he foregrounds the narrator's equivalent sense of fragmentation within the scene. We initially see this concern in "For the Marriage of Faustus and Helen," a longer poem near the end of his first collection, *White Buildings*. In "General Aims and Theories," Crane describes his intention in this poem as finding "a contemporary approximation to an ancient human culture," elaborating, "So I found 'Helen' sitting in a street car; the Dionysian revels of her court and her seduction were transferred to a Metropolitan roof garden with a jazz orchestra" (160). The narrator comes across "Helen" through the vicissitudes of city life, and he depicts their meeting in appropriately conditional terms:

> And yet, suppose some evening I forgot
> The fare and transfer, yet got by that way
> Without recall,—lost yet poised in traffic.
> Then I might find your eyes across an aisle,
> Still flickering with those prefigurations—
> Prodigal, yet uncontested now,
> Half-riant before the jerky window frame. (20)

Unlike the "mobile urban observers" (Zurier 91) seen in other city poetry of the period, Crane's narrator cannot easily navigate the urban infrastructure. He boards the streetcar with no fare, no transfer, seemingly no memory of how he even got there. He performs this lack of mastery in a graceful manner, however, being "lost yet poised in traffic." This lack of mastery leads him to the "Helen" of the poem. Her eyes never fully meet his: they "flicker" with visions, wander in a "prodigal" manner, and may be laughing at him.[10] This visual desire is quickly transformed into a desire for a physical connection, but that desire just as quickly feeds back into a description of the city: "There is some way, I think, to touch / Those hands of yours that count the nights / Stippled with pink and green advertisements" (20). Here the advertisements serve as a lovely counterpoint to the sights within the streetcar, evoked by the painterly word "stippled" along with a palette of natural colors. The passivity of Crane's narrator in "For the Marriage of Faustus and Helen" does not prevent him from making meaning or making connections. Indeed, the very instability of his status seems to open him up to chance encounters.

"Faustus and Helen" establishes Crane's interest in the chance meetings made possible by public transportation.[11] As Michael Trask and other recent critics have described, Crane's poetry explores how anonymous interactions are inflected by the settings and relationships of modernity. Queer theory readings of Crane have been the most attuned to the physicality of his poetry as well as its engagement with city space.[12] In the next section we see how the physicality specifically associated with the working class offers a model for modern subjectivity along with modern poetic form. In "The Tunnel," the background of labor and the pressures of capitalism fragment the figures being described as well. Crane does not suggest that working-class figures are *more* broken, however; instead his narrator embraces the brokenness that these figures exemplify.

## "Just my body dragging me home"

From overheard conversation to the sight of shoes ascending an escalator, the physicality of the commuter in "The Tunnel" establishes the perspective from which the city is perceived. And this perspective is constantly attuned to the relationship between the body and the urban infrastructure into which it is placed. This translates to a depiction of all passengers, including the central narrator, as self-reflexively considering the forces at work on their own bodies. Crane portrays the initial entrance into the subway, for example, as an involuntary accommodation of the self to the system. A reflexive and passive verb phrase describes the body unconsciously taking on the appropriate positions: "You find yourself / Preparing penguin flexions of the arms" (67). Those "penguin flexions" are not just an isolated flight of fancy. Other New York modernist writers also compare subway passengers to animals, suggesting a pervasive sense that subway movement broke down the boundaries between human and inhuman.[13] The image of the penguin and the sputteringly alliterative "p" sounds give the commuter's arm movements a jerky feel; additionally, "flexions" are movements specific to muscles, a choice of words that indicates Crane is breaking actions down into their smallest component parts. The rush of images slows down as the commuter enters the subway, defamiliarizing each element of the common gesture. In this way Crane's poetry examines heretofore invisible detail with the same penetrating attention that Walter Benjamin locates in the cinema's slow-motion and close-up shots (232–34). Crane's poetic breakdown of movement into its component parts allies his poem with new forms of capitalist temporality in the early twentieth century, the era of Taylor and Ford.[14] The syntax proceeds as if Crane were presenting a Muybridge time-and-motion study of a horse galloping or a man running.

In "The Tunnel," Crane participates in a larger modernist discourse on commuting, characterized by an estrangement between the body performing urban habits and the mind observing and recording them. I fully agree with Michael Trask's assertion that "the hand of the laborer" needs to be recovered as a metonym that "helped shape the world of modernism and modernity" (110). Trask reminds us that the lack of bodily coherence associated with the working class extends beyond the field and the factory floor. And Crane's modernist engagement with the subway as a space of bodily fragmentation is just one of many descriptions from a broad cross-section of modern writers. Factory worker Mildred Kuhn wrote a poem at the Bryn Mawr summer school for working women that ends with the line "Just my body dragging me home" (qtd. in Hollis 108). Cornelia Stratton Parker, the author of *Working with the Working Woman,* describes her first trip home from the factory in a similar way: "I am no aggressive feminist, and I am no old-fashioned clinging vine, but I surely do hate, hate, hate every man in that Subway who sits back in comfort (and most of them look as if they had been sitting all day) while *I and my feet* stand up" (16, emphasis added).[15] Indeed, in "The Tunnel" Crane foregrounds the relationship between the commuting body and the demands of the city as a way of fostering cross-class identification. In this way he participates in and revises the kind of physicalized empathy central to what Eric Schocket calls the "class transvestite narrative." Schocket notes that this genre reduces the experience of poverty to a set of physical experiences that the narrator embodies and thus contains (109). In "The Tunnel," by contrast, working-class physicality spreads throughout the subway car and indeed through the urban population as a whole.

Crane's critics have made much of his affiliation with sailors, boxers, factory workers, and other exemplars of working-class masculinity.[16] This strong connection has generally and rightfully been read in the context of same-sex desire, but the working-class characters in "The Tunnel" are just as often designated female as male. In Crane's descriptions we see a provisional, questioning attempt at understanding the female laborer's situation. Crane's speaker apostrophizes an Italian American washerwoman:

> And does the Daemon take you home, also,
> Wop washerwoman, with the bandaged hair?
> And after the corridors are swept, the cuspidors—
> The gaunt sky-barracks cleanly now, and bare,
> O Genoese, do you bring mother eyes and hands
> Back home to children and to golden hair? (70)

With her "bandaged hair," presumably a reference to her headscarf, this figure displays a body visibly broken by her work cleaning "corridors" and "cuspidors." The reflexive construction in Crane's description—bringing her own eyes and hands home—shows one worker relating to her own body as an object. The enforced passivity of the subway commute gives laborers the time to pay attention to (and sometimes even articulate) their alienated physicality. The subway setting brings about the cross-class contact that gives Crane's narrator the chance even to ask such questions. The questions in turn allow Crane to imagine "a queer community of the interstices, where those whose bodies are regulated by an unjust economic and sex-gender system can discover common cause" (Reed, *Hart Crane* 165). Situated between work and home, the subway is an interstitial space; as such, it functions as a point of contact between subcultural communities that would otherwise have little reason to encounter one another.

"The Tunnel" takes place in the middle space of urban transit, the free fall between selves like the one that we see in the proem, where "elevators drop us from our day" (Crane 33). Many sections of *The Bridge* depict people on this threshold: Columbus returns to Spain in "Ave Maria," Rip Van Winkle hurries to his job, the son in "Indiana" leaves home to strike it rich in Mexico. Crane depicts the voices and bodies of commuters coming home from work in "The Tunnel" in a way that acknowledges this liminality on a psychological level as well as a poetic one. Subjectivity is defined by the spaces in which it takes place, and the identities of characters appearing in "The Tunnel" are indeterminate, in flux. His description of the Italian washerwoman, for example, moves from the dehumanizing to the reverent as the subway crosses into Brooklyn: in the same stanza, the racist epithet "wop washerwoman" and the apostrophe "O Genoese" both refer to her. Crane imagines a subway rider beholden to wildly differing expectations at either end of the train ride.

As we see throughout "The Tunnel," the urban subject experiences an "interborough fissure" between work self and home self because the subway separated the two locations by a considerably longer distance than had previously existed. As I discuss throughout this chapter, and particularly in the next, spatial estrangement from the city's centers of power was radically exacerbated by public transportation's patterns of development.[17] The underground commute divides work from home not only in space but also, even more palpably, by time. Crane underscores this distancing with language that takes on characteristics of the geographical path it traces, moving from the harshness of Manhattan to the gentle nostalgia associated with the other boroughs:

> "Let's have a pencil Jimmy—living now
> at Floral Park
> Flatbush—on the fourth of July—
> like a pigeon's muddy dream—potatoes
> to dig in the field—travlin the town—too
> night after night—the Culver line—the
> girls all shaping up—it used to be—." (68)[18]

Crane's use of overheard voices has been compared to that of William Carlos Williams, and the first line of this stanza is reminiscent of Williams's "Shoot it Jimmy!" in *Spring and All* (Paul 266). Surprisingly, Crane records voices as local as those in Williams: this stanza seems to invoke pastoral activities of a distant past, but Floral Park and Flatbush, the places evoked so nostalgically, are neighborhoods in Queens and Brooklyn. Originally owned by the Long Island Railroad, the "Culver line" connected central Brooklyn to Coney Island in the late nineteenth century and was annexed by Brooklyn Rapid Transit Company during the expansion of the subways in the 1920s (Feinman et al.). There is a tension in this subway reverie, a tension between evocative part and fragmented whole. As we see throughout the twentieth century, the outer boroughs are associated with the past as well as the countryside. The pastoral and the urban are not set in opposition to each other in this passage, however, and their intersection is not ironic or tragic, as it is in "Quaker Hill." This section's fractured pastoral reminds us that city and country interpenetrate, and that our divisions between those spaces are merely fantasy (Marx 31–32), or as Crane formulates it, a "pigeon's muddy dream." Here we can understand Crane's poem as participating in the larger social discourse that situates the outer boroughs in the past as a means of masking or celebrating the uneven development along different stretches of the subway.

The city has simply incorporated everything, albeit without uniting the pieces into some greater whole. New York City's loose conglomeration of disparate parts serves as a model for Crane's incorporation of overheard conversations. Critics most often address the conversations of "The Tunnel" in relation to T. S. Eliot's poetry.[19] As with most American modernists, Crane was writing in opposition to Eliot as much as he was writing in thrall to him. In particular, Crane responds to Eliot's ethnographic anxieties, presenting what would seem to be the most culturally authentic utterances—such as those of his Brooklynites—in a more visually, aurally, and spatially fragmented manner than those of the modern, alienated subway passengers. In this stanza, dashes segment lines in odd places, literalizing the gaps between one phrase and another. Brian Reed notes the physicalized quality of Crane's lyrics, arguing that all of his poems can be read as "a maimed piece of an absent, ungraspable whole" (*Hart Crane* 121). Heard in their chopped-up state, the voices of these subway passengers are no longer signs of presence. Instead they allow the narrator (and the reader) to imagine the absent, ungraspable whole self in which conversations and habits play only a part. Like his questioning of the washerwoman, the conversations he presents do not allow absolute access into the minds of fellow riders; rather they offer up those maimed pieces as the only possible representation of the city.

"The Tunnel" addresses a more explicit form of transitory urban encounter with an oblique reference that has generated much critical discussion:

Crane delves into the unconscious, repetitive experience of subway space when he cryptically states, "The phonographs of Hades in the brain / Are tunnels that re-wind themselves, and love / A burnt match skating in a urinal—" (68).[20] The match in the urinal is commonly read as a metonym for a homosexual encounter in a subway restroom, one that has been tossed away after lighting a postcoital cigarette. Underground movement enables this erotic frisson of anonymous sexual contact: willing partners lock eyes in the rush hour crowds, the subway bathrooms provide a space both public and private, and the trains allow for an easy departure. He again emphasizes the possible failure to read the signs of the city, though, with this opaque and dense cluster of lines. Following Crane's opaque poetic syntax, however, we can theorize that the tunnels and the match are not just tenors in parallel metaphors (phonographs are tunnels, love is a burnt match). They are also connected images of the urban body compelled to engage repeatedly in anonymous encounters with and within city space. Since the "phonographs of Hades" are in "*the* brain," rather than "your brain" (or mine, or ours), Crane seems to imagine habitual processes hard-wired into the urban mind through repetition rather than consciously undertaken by heroic effort. The lines reinforce knowledge of the subway system on a bodily level, with the circling match in the toilet echoing the circling of the tunnel. An illicit encounter by a urinal is just one manifestation of the ephemeral contact with fellow city dwellers that the subway makes possible.

But there is a libidinal aspect to the repeated subway rides Crane depicts in "The Tunnel" even when they do not include same-sex cruising. Repetition brings into focus the machine's erotic qualities. The fragmented sights and sounds of the subway carry the narrator through the underground space in the same way that the movement of the line carries the reader through the poem. Once the narrator has boarded the subway train, we can see and hear this rhythm being established:

> In the car
> the overtone of motion
> underground, the monotone
> of motion is the sound
> of other faces, also underground—. (68)

Enjambment lends a dynamic quality to Crane's description, since it both cuts off the regularity of the rhythm and reinforces the eventual rhymes between "overtone" and "monotone," "underground" and "sound." This poetic movement echoes the movement of the train, suggesting an "overtone of motion." This stanza exists in a spatially impossible landscape, or at least one that combines sight and hearing so that an "overtone" can be heard "underground." Here the spatial disorientation present throughout the poem results in a generative synesthesia. The boredom of the subway ride is productive as well: although the train's movement is monotonous, it allows the narrator to hear the "sound / of other faces."

The enforced routine gives the narrator many chances to piece together fellow passengers' fleeting emotions and fragmented conversations. By embracing routinization, Crane's narrator turns it into an aesthetic problem rather than a metaphysical one. Reed suggests that Crane "finds 'euphoria' in contemplating the loss of self as mechanical processes supplant, or rend, the integrity of the individual" (*Hart Crane* 109). But mechanical routines do not merely fracture the possibility of integrity; instead, the hypnotic and erotic rhythm of mechanized routine allows Crane's narrator to empathize with the other passengers sharing the subway car. Regular movement transports the narrator beyond normal perceptual capabilities and into a mechanically induced fusion of the senses.[21] Crane's narrator does not minimize the discreteness of the individual lines, phrases, and fragments that he records along his journey. Instead, he emphasizes the various ways in which the urban sensorium operates. When logical ways of making sense fall through, the brain and body keep moving, finding echoes and connections on other levels.

In "The Tunnel" the subway rider and the poet share this sense of the difficulty of fusing isolated views of modern life; in both cases, only the repetitions of physical habits allow them to envision the system as a whole. The poem certainly lingers on the mental and physical experiences of subway passengers: the habits that carry one's body to the station unconsciously, the claustrophobic encounters with crowds, the melancholy overheard conversations. Rather than considering "The Tunnel" as a source of data about modern subway riding practices, we can consider how it employs these practices as a mode of textual organization. Crane suggests an answer to Kevin Lynch's concern about the relationship between underground nodes and the cities of which they are a part, examining how the "invisible conceptual linkages" made by the body hold crowds together in a provisional way.

Fragmented physicality lies at the heart of the poem's perception not only of fellow passengers but also of fellow writers. Working-class and ethnic figures present the immediate model by which "The Tunnel" imagines its relationship to the literary past. In the case of Edgar Allan Poe, this physical state is taken to an extreme, in the reproduction of both his body and his words. While his lack of bodily coherence makes him a less imposing literary ancestor, the complex spatiality of his tales maps onto subway space a more complex model of literary ancestry.

## "Whose head is swinging from the swollen strap?"

Throughout *The Bridge*, Crane connects literary innovators with technological innovation. "Cape Hatteras" pairs the airplane and Walt Whitman, while "Cutty Sark" features a sailor thought to be Herman Melville. In part this is a strategic break from the past, since embracing technology helped American modernists envision a tradition not beholden to Europe (Tashjian 230). The figure of Walt Whitman, unsurprisingly, is the most celebrated.[22] Even the drunk, nostalgic sailor in "Cutty Sark" seems to be a noble ancestor figure, with his paeans to the sea and his memories of working on the Panama Canal (Crane 51–52). Though presented in a far less admirable light as a character in the poem, Edgar Allan Poe is the writer of the city who looms largest in "The Tunnel." Poe's story "The Man of the Crowd" dissects the urban spectacle and takes its protagonist on an apparently fruitless journey, as does Crane's poem. Poe's tales—particularly "The Fall of the House of Usher"—imagine a deep connection between literal and psychological spaces. Even the repetitions of "The Raven" echo through "The Tunnel." American modernists of the 1920s imagined Poe as a forefather to their poetic experimentation because he offered a local point of origin, an alternative to the Eurocentric citation of greatest hits and lesser works in "The Waste Land."[23] As a writer focused on materiality and partiality, Poe functions as an early model for the poetic strategy most often associated with modernism: the poetic collage.

Poe's appearance in "The Tunnel" is hardly heroic: silent and broken, his head swings from a strap inside the car while his "body smokes along the bitten rails" (69). Why would Crane present *The Bridge*'s final representative of American literary history in this way? By reviving Poe's corpse and his corpus in a strategically piecemeal manner, Crane suggests that the passivity and lack of mastery that I have described throughout this chapter is not a burden but a benefit to the modern poet. In "The Tunnel," Poe exists in two worlds. His severed head swinging on a strap, Poe connects literary labor to that of the other fragmented commuters surrounding him. His body, however, lies outside the car on the "bitten rails," making him part of the system as well as subject to it. Both as a character in the poem and as a historical figure, the Poe of "The Tunnel" models a modernist form of coherence whereby citations refer to and acknowledge the disintegration of the literary tradition.

William Carlos Williams and Hart Crane both engage with Edgar Allan Poe as a means of bringing the received history of the American past into dialogue with the present. Poe appears in the penultimate chapter of *In the American Grain* (1925), Williams's collection of historical essays that spans the Viking exploration of North America and Abraham Lincoln's assassination. After reading *In the American Grain,* Crane noted that Williams "puts Poe and his 'character' in the same position as I had *symbolized* for him in the 'Tunnel' section" (498). Like *The Bridge, In the American Grain* reexamines the American landscape through a poetic lens. In fact, Crane worried that their books would be *too* similar. In a letter to Yvor Winters on November 12, 1926, he explains, "I don't want to read *In the American Grain* until I get through with *Bridge* because I hesitate to complicate the organization of a work which, from what I've heard of his chronicle, is on such similar subject matter" (494). By November 21, however, he had apparently overcome that anxiety, writing to Waldo Frank that "Williams'—*American Grain* is an achievement that I'd be proud of. A most important and *sincere* book. I'm very enthusiastic—I put off reading it, you know, until I felt my own way cleared beyond chance of confusions incident to reading a book so intimate to my theme" (498). Some of Crane's language suggests that the two poets shared a similar vision of Poe. Williams describes Poe's avoidance of influence throughout and characterizes his critical essays as "a movement, first and last to clear the GROUND" (*In the American Grain* 216). The relation to the past in both books, like Crane's relation to his literary contemporary, is both anxious and appropriative.

Their books share themes and sources: both use the diaries of Christopher Columbus and the same history of Pocahontas, as well as the same line from Poe's poem "The City in the Sea" (Gregory 239). Most parallel, however, is their strategic use of recontextualized historical language that allows the quoted material to enter into partial dialogue with the present while retaining its material and partial connection with the past. Williams celebrates Poe for his dismissal of past forms as much as he does for literary innovation. He imagines—and becomes critically invested in—a particularly modernist understanding of Poe as an author who asserts his own originality through the act of repurposing mass cultural materials and the work of earlier writers (Elmer 32–37). Williams, like Crane, sees Poe as an exemplar of new ways to deal with old materials. He reads Poe as a writer immediately concerned with issues of form, one who avoided poetic language "hung by usage with associations, the pleasing wraiths of former masteries" (*In the American Grain* 221). Here Williams distinguishes Poe from the Fireside Poets, whose words activate sentimental associations without communicating anything direct. These older poets cheat their readers by using poetry to short-circuit historical consciousness, sending them through a "sentimental trap-door to beginnings" (221) instead of rationally considering the relationship between past and present. Instead of covering up the "old language," Poe strips it down to its barest denotation in order to make it new (221). The kind of fragmentation that happens in the subway space of "The Tunnel" can be understood not as a loss of wholeness but as an unsentimental streamlining of language, one that Poe also undertook.

Unsurprisingly, Williams praises Poe for a skill that Williams himself developed throughout his poetic career. "The rose is obsolete," a poem in *Spring and All* that offers a proliferation of roses as an attempt to rid that flower of its literary associations, is perhaps the best example (*Collected Poems* 195). He locates a similar ability in the work of Marianne Moore. In an essay discussing her work which precedes "Rapid Transit," Williams posits, "Poetry liberates the words from their emotional implications" (*Collected Poems* 230). in another essay on Moore, Williams emphasizes the ways that her poetic language is eminently material: "With Miss Moore a word is a word most when separated out by science, treated with acid to remove the smudges, washed, dried and placed right side up on a clean surface. Now one may say that this is a word. Now it may be used, and how?" (Williams, *Imaginations* 318). Williams reads Moore as a poet who removes her language from cultural context. Her frequent quoting appears less a desire to evoke the quotation's source than a wish to repurpose it entirely.

Considering the relationship between Williams and Moore as exemplified in "Rapid Transit," we see a careful navigation of poetic authority through quoting practices. Williams does seem to be paying homage to Moore by following an essay about her writing with a poem that imitates her highly citational poetic form (Kinnahan 220). Williams abdicates authority as the source for his poetry, instead taking on the role of arranger of language that comes from elsewhere. Yet the poem is not merely homage. One might even read the poem's third line, "To hell with you and your poetry—," as being somewhat combative toward the poet he had been discussing three lines earlier. Additionally, the language he uses in the poem is *not* completely decontextualized from its original sources, since all of the quotations can be understood as coming from the subway itself—either advertisements seen in the car or overheard conversations of fellow passengers.[24] By bringing Moore's poetic technique into the subway car, I suggest, Williams acknowledges and undercuts her authority. He renders her quoting techniques all the more material by allowing the fragments of advertisements to exist both as fragments and as evocations of the forward momentum of the ride.

Crane engages in a similarly conflicted form of appropriation. He repeats Poe's poetry in a more commonplace context: "Eyes like agate lanterns" suggest the "agate lamp" in Poe's "To Helen," but we see them "below the toothpaste and the dandruff ads." In Poe's poem, Helen is physically separated from the narrator, who exclaims: "Lo! In yon brilliant window-niche / How statue-like I see thee stand, / The agate lamp within thy hand!" (68). There is a vital difference between Poe's and Crane's attitude toward the transportive sights they describe. Unlike the figure presented in "To Helen," Poe's head cannot be kept at a poetic distance. He appears in a darkened space near the speaker rather than a framing window niche; instead of being a statue-like, aestheticized body holding a lamp, he is bodiless. Crane brings the vision he describes much closer to the spectator and reveals it as a fragment, not a synecdoche.

Staging Poe's reappearance in "The Tunnel," Crane takes on a similar role to that of the child in the famous "fort-da" game Freud describes in *Beyond the Pleasure Principle.* The child copes with his sense of parental abandonment by pretending to throw away a wooden toy and then pulling it back, taking pleasure in both its disappearance and its return. Freud gives two possible interpretations of this game: that the repetition of an experience of passivity and discomfort gives the person repeating it a sense of control, or that this repeated game satisfies a suppressed wish (*Beyond the Pleasure Principle* 14–15). Both of these interpretations can be applied to Crane and his relationship to his poetic forefathers. Crane shakes off Poe's influence by forcing him to appear, denuded and fragmented, in this modern space; Crane also repeats and revises Poe's words and his mistakes, deploying the language of brokenness and submission as aesthetic choices.

"The Tunnel" literalizes issues of descent that are central to Crane's poetic practice—and, indeed, to American poetic tradition. The poem complicates the presumed authority and coherence of American literary ancestry through its extended attention to Poe's physical fragmentation and his violent death.[25] An early biographer of Poe describes "the fixed belief of the Baltimoreans" regarding his demise: that local party hacks kept him locked up, plied him with alcohol and opium, and then forced him to vote the Whig ticket at polling stations (Ingram 427). Of this horrific, though most likely fictional, occurrence, Crane's narrator asks:

> And when they dragged your retching flesh,
> Your trembling hands that night through Baltimore—
> That last night on the ballot rounds, did you
> Shaking, did you deny the ticket, Poe? (69)

Poe's body is not merely fragmented here, it is actively abject: "retching," "trembling," and "shaking." The act of voting described in this stanza is a parody of democracy, with Poe's lack of self-will over his body's movements echoed in his lack of political control. But this form of surrender is not placed in the past, since Poe's movement is connected to that of the subway commuter through the word that unites politics and transportation: "ticket" (Giles 93). To pursue this comparison: self-determined democracy is replaced by enforced engagement with the political machine, and self-determined movement through open space is replaced by enforced transportation through preestablished underground pathways. In this sense Poe's experience parallels the submission of the subway rider much more closely than the active, optimistic engagement with machines described by other modernists, the "wonderment experienced in watching nose dives" that Crane critiques in "Modern Poetry" (171). Poe's acuity in predicting central concerns of the modern condition was another factor that led early twentieth-century poets to embrace him. Waldo Frank writes, "Only Poe [of all early American authors] guessed the transfiguring effect of the Machine upon the form of human life, upon the very concept of the person" (130).

Crane sees in Poe's enforced movement an early expression of the modern sense of being transported against one's will by larger forces. It is only by imagining a more conscious means of submission that Crane finally escapes Poe's terrible fate. When submission is inevitable, Crane suggests that we should embrace its capacity for transport.

The passivity of the subway passenger, what Andrew Thacker calls "a kind of paralysed subject position," is "the normal reaction to surrounding social space" ("Uncompleted Life" 115). "The Tunnel" implies that it may be the normal reaction to the literary tradition as well. Instead of anxiously struggling against its own belatedness, Crane's poem surrenders to the subway crush of poetic influence. For all this talk of Poe, it should be noted that he does not play the same role in this poem that other authors do in other sections of *The Bridge*. "The Tunnel" is not a poem about Poe in the same way "Cape Hatteras" is a poem about Whitman: Whitman's appearances neatly bookend that poem, and his language is present throughout. In "The Tunnel," by contrast, Poe appears halfway through a text that begins with a Blake epigraph and borrows many techniques from T. S. Eliot and William Carlos Williams. In the couplet "—And did their riding eyes right through your side, / And did their eyes like unwashed platters ride?" (69), Poe's severed head and the "unwashed platters" suggest Eliot's sheepish John the Baptist in "The Love Song of J. Alfred Prufrock." The rhythm and syntax of the lines also echo the rhetorical question that begins William Blake's poem "And did those feet in ancient time," also known as "Jerusalem" (Blake 161). Even Poe's insistent and influential presence is refracted through Crane's other influences, all of whom question the possibilities of urban life. The eyes of the silent observers parallel the lurking silent influences in the poem. As we can see in this stanza, "be[ing] minimum" (Crane 67) is not just a question of deemphasizing one's physical presence on the subway. Crane minimizes his own interpretive voice here, presenting an underground of poetic influence where there is no single guide, no Virgil or Rousseau—only an echo chamber of fragmented forebears. The American poetic tradition is as crowded as a rush hour subway car, and the path it follows is far more complex and modern than that of a family tree.

Of course, Poe's legacy was not that of a great poet but that of a great tale teller. Crane's idea of descent and influence is engaged with Poe's tales as much as with his poems. The idea of the fissure in particular connects and separates Crane's complex subterranean space from the uncanny locations of many of Poe's tales. In "The Fall of the House of Usher," the first foreshadowing of the house's imminent destruction comes when the narrator notices a "barely perceptible fissure" running down the length of its façade, and "fissure" is repeated twice when the narrator describes the house's collapse (141). For Poe, the fissure is what eventually leads to the house's destruction; because of the cracks in the foundation, the house collapses into the tarn and the water closes over it. In contrast, Crane's interborough fissures span *and* separate. Because the subway ride is a routine rather than a unique, grotesque event, the water regularly closes over Crane's commuter, but also parts for him just as often.

"The Tunnel" envisions a new model of descent and influence, in which Poe exists on one of myriad possible paths through American literary history. The spatial complexity of the subway is an improvement on the model of transmission in Poe's tale: Usher's line of descent is a single stem with no branches, wherein direct transmission from father to son is the only model of inheritance (Poe 140). When Crane locates Poe in the "back forks of the chasms of the brain" and "interborough fissures of the mind" (69), he imagines a more complex form of descent and influence. The construction of the first spatial metaphor branches off into one prepositional phrase and then another, suggesting both the subway system and the nervous system. Subway space, with its back forks and fissures, offers multiple paths for the poetic commuter to follow; it also eliminates the suggestions of stunted growth and inbreeding that come with straight lines of descent like those of Roderick Usher. Repetition forges connections that value the literary past only as it coheres with the distracted modern present. And the complex space of the subway is an appropriate technological structure for understanding the lines of descent in American poetry. Instead of a single, direct line over centuries, we see a tradition that is fractured, fragmented, and glimpsed in passing.

"The Tunnel" continues to make use of the poetic past, but these fragments are not representative of larger problems of urban life (as in "The Waste Land") or even representative material arising from the landscape (as in *Paterson*). The past no longer needs to be slavishly known as a whole; instead, citations seem to be equivalents to Poe's fractured body, appearing when he is present in the tunnel and then passing on as the speaker moves to another station. In this way, Poe plays the role of fragmented predecessor that Crane himself has continued to play for a number of modern and contemporary poets.[26] Jacques Khalip analyzes "the compulsion to produce Crane as a corpse-like figure" in elegies by poets such as Allen Tate, Robert Lowell, and Philip Levine (67). The recurrence of the poet as a corpse suggests that Crane's influence is spectral and yet resolutely material: he persists, in pieces.

## "Here at the water's edge"

The spatial complexity of the subway offers a model of descent and a model of poetic structuring. Subway movement enables Crane to short-circuit literary lineage imaginatively. "The Tunnel," however, does not conclude in this complex underground space. Instead, it moves toward the celebratory connectivity of *The Bridge*'s final poem, "Atlantis." Poe's head shows us the sublime becoming routine; these final stanzas show us the routine becoming sublime. The conclusion of "The Tunnel" turns abstract and Romantic as the narrator ascends into Brooklyn, ending with the kind of visionary language much more common in the celebratory nineteenth-century accounts of man-made technologies (Nye, *American Technological Sublime* 55): a hand reaching for a nickel becomes a "Hand of Fire" (71); the overheard words of passengers become "some Word that will not die" (70). With this celebratory conclusion, one might rightfully ask what distinguishes "The Tunnel" from its proto-modernist predecessors. The poetry of the 1910s often uses the subway as a figure for leaping from the prosaic to the divine, and that is in part what occurs in the final stanzas of "The Tunnel." How does Crane's conclusion differ from that of Chester Firkins, who in 1908 declared his time "On a Subway Express" to be a "wild ride with God" (181)? Is Crane merely echoing the Catholic sentiments of Joyce Kilmer, whereby the "darkness" of the subway makes the divine "light more sweet" ("Subway" 467)? While I do think that the poem's conclusion activates the associations present in such poems, Crane's narrator tries to account for the divine and the mundane aspects of underground movement, though the "conjunctive disjunction" of the subway car works against resolving disparate views.

He does so in part by describing the subway with phrases that foreground its contradictions. "And does the Daemon take you home, also[?]" (70), Crane's narrator asks of the Genoese cleaning lady with whom he shares a newly empty subway car traveling beneath the East River to Brooklyn. A daemonic subway system could be a guardian spirit of new forms of urban perception or a devil trapping city dwellers in inescapable routines (and most likely both). Similar to the Brooklyn Bridge and the Mississippi River in other sections of *The Bridge,* the subway sweeps up individuals caught in its wake. Although David Nye characterizes the technological sublime as "a celebration of the power of human reason" (*American Technological Sublime* 60), the subway's sublimity is certainly irrational—as is the narrator's attempt to make sense of it. In the next stanza the daemonic repetition of the daily subway ride is conveyed through its contradictory status as a conveyance of death and birth. Even the "yawn" that describes the subway throughout this poem becomes a "demurring and eventful yawn" (70), both the yawn of boredom or fatigue and the yawn of eternity. The subway system "cruelly inoculate[s]" the dawn by ferrying passengers into Manhattan "toward worlds that glow and sink," suggesting figures rising and falling in the stock market (70). It "spoon[s] us out" to Brooklyn once again as the stars are dimly perceived at dusk (70). Like the "interborough fissures" earlier in the poem, the subway has an "umbilical" quality (70) that emphasizes the division of Brooklyn passengers from their workday identities in Manhattan even as it connects them to the island that provides the lifeblood of the city. The subway serves as a vehicle perpetually shuttling between opposite states.

Crane thus echoes the work of prior subway poets who imagine subway space containing its pastoral opposite. "The Subway" by Ruth Comfort Mitchell (1916), a poem in three parts, concludes each section on the oppressive commute with an italicized coda that offers a contrasting landscape—a house in Maine, a prairie, and "a sanctuary, inviolate and still" (56). This strategy continues through the 1920s. In his 1922 book *Harlem Shadows,* Claude McKay sets the "captive wind" of the rushing subway train in contrast to the "fresh and free" trade winds of the Caribbean, linking the two locales in order to suggest how migrants like him might feel in such a cold urban environment (54). He does so with a line that brings together the two opposing forces nearly at the center of the sixteen-line poem "Subway Wind." McKay says of the children riding the train who seek the breeze from open windows and doors between cars, "Their laugh is swallowed in the deafening roar / Of captive wind that moans for fields and seas." The embodied individual experience of the subway ride is overcome by the mechanized wind—wind brought about by the movement of the train through the tunnel. This "captive wind," however, transforms immediately back into an outward sign of an interior affective state like that of the children's laughter: the wind itself "moans for fields and seas." The dividing line between inside and outside, between human and machine, is repeatedly broken down in this liminal space.

Crane does not represent the moment of emergence from the eponymous tunnel; instead, he cuts it off mid-experience. In this way he forecloses any possibility of resolution between the two worlds. He aspires to feel the subway's emergence into Brooklyn as a kind of rebirth, "—A sound of waters bending astride the sky / Unceasing with some Word that will not die . . . !" (70). Description ceases at precisely the point where tunnel and bridge might meet: the waters bend astride the sky, articulating some divine word that might register as a coherent connection between the world above and the one below. This process concludes with ellipses and an exclamation point, paradoxically trailing off while expressing enthusiasm. His point of view is then further cut off from the narrative through a shift in perspective marked by a section break.

Crane complicates the symbolic resonance of the subway's geography by considering it on a horizontal axis (moving from Manhattan to the outer boroughs) as well as a vertical one (moving from street level to underground to above). As the poem concludes, the narrator has emerged from the subway in the same place where he ended the first poem in *The Bridge,* gazing at the East River from the piers beneath the Brooklyn Bridge. Ascent and elevation are commonly described as positions that turn the urban spectator into a visionary, both removing him from the scene and allowing him to see more of it. Michel de Certeau depicted the view from the 110th floor of the World Trade Center as one that "makes the complexity of the city readable, and immobilizes its opaque mobility in a transparent text" (92). The "opaque mobility" of the subway system is in fact rendered invisible in the poem's final stanzas. Crane's verse makes that break textually visible, showing that the seemingly transparent text of the city can remain opaque even when looked at from above. The final stanzas of "The Tunnel" mark an obvious point of intro- and retrospection, but its conclusions are murky at best: the river that the speaker has "driven under" is an "oily" black "abyss." It also seems to mark a dividing line between one form of subjectivity and another by stating that "at the waters' edge the hands drop memory" (70). "The Tunnel" does not end in the same liminal realm; instead, it suggests that the subway makes connection between realms possible without eliding the geographical, social, and political differences between them.

The final section of "The Tunnel" is decidedly separate from the rest of the poem, a separation that is performed (by asterisks marking the break) but not narrated or explained. To return to Kevin Lynch's geographical analysis, the poem does not offer a point where the underground paths of the subway "come up for air" (57); instead, it concludes at an edge, a "boundar[y] between two kinds of areas" (62) that has "disruptive power" (64). Here we might think of Robert Park's meditation on the distinct formation of Chicago's neighborhoods and the implicit boundary lines dividing them: "Not only transportation and communication but the segregation of the urban population tends to facilitate the mobility of the individual man. The processes of segregation establish moral distances which make the city a mosaic of little worlds which touch but do not interpenetrate" ("The City" 40). The social formation of New York City's discrete yet adjoining ethnic enclaves—Little Italy and Chinatown, for example—certainly predates the building of the subway, yet the underground connection of neighborhoods only exacerbates the process. Repeated, embodied engagement with the city does not resolve the differences between its distinct districts: the "purgatory" of the subway and the "open sky" of "Atlantis" cannot be synthesized into a coherent whole (Crane 441). Indeed, the working-class commuters whom Crane takes as his models might themselves be understood as "mosaic[s] of little worlds," embodying different personality traits, expectations, and habits that come with each piece of the mosaic.

While modernist poets used the elevated rhetoric of their medium to soften their sociological observations, dramatists and fiction writers use the techniques of modernism to highlight the diversity of the city's "mosaic of little worlds" and the ways that the subway both enables and undercuts the segregation between them. The subway has long served as an image of the melting pot for New Yorkers, but this utopian image has masked a complex interplay of acceptance, assimilation, and aggression. The subway often appears as a miniature melting pot in nationalistic discourse of this period; city dwellers of every background civilly share the ride. In the following two chapters I consider texts that situate migrant figures in subway space in order to materialize the physical feeling of displacement that came with disparate regional and cultural identifications.

# CHAPTER 4

# UNDERGROUND ASSIMILATION IN ETHNIC DRAMA

....

*The Bridge* ends with a retrospective look at the Brooklyn Bridge, imagining that the interborough icon unifies the poem and, Hart Crane suggests, the country's history. In order to gain that syncretic perspective, the poem has to abandon the subway car and the habit-driven working-class physicality that it found there. The fantasies of cultural connectivity that the poem locates in the Brooklyn Bridge were commonly ascribed to other nineteenth-century innovations like the telegraph and the long-distance telephone. According to Carolyn Marvin, scientific experts at the turn of the century believed that new media could bridge cultures without decentering them (192). We might understand the extension of the subway under the Dual Contracts system in the same way: immigrants who had previously lived in overcrowded slums could now rent spacious apartments in Brooklyn and the Bronx while maintaining their (now technologically mediated) connection to the center of the city, Manhattan.

The cultural rhetoric of the modern New York subway calls upon the ideals of cultural pluralism while maintaining the implicit hierarchy between (American) center and (ethnic) periphery. The subway has long been understood as a miniature version of the melting pot. Editorial cartoons of the 1920s, woodcuts of the New Deal era, even action films of the 1970s like *The Taking of Pelham One Two Three* (Sargent) depend on the common understanding of the New York City subway crowd as a cross-section of the city as a whole. The trope of the subway as melting pot implicitly congratulates the city for its openness to different cultures and suggests that the shared experience of the subway ride forges common identity among them. The counterargument to this claim suggests that the only common identity is a shared sense of isolation. In a 1917 article in which he claims to go, as the title puts it, "In Search of the American Soul," Joseph McCabe declares that "the fires of the great melting pot are too clement" (231). He uses the multiplicity of ethnic newspapers as evidence that Americanization isn't working: "As I sit in the subway, I read, to right and left of me, journals in Yiddish, Italian, Greek, German, French, Hungarian, and Spanish; and over each journal broods the familiar face of each country, alien and inflexible" (231). The assimilation of races into an American whole will never take place, McCabe implies, when even their reading materials maintain staunch divides from one another. Although his language is nativist in tone, it evokes a model of cultural pluralism and cultural isolation that is maintained on the subway to this day.

We can see this process at work in a similar way in the best-known visual emblem of the subway as a provisional amalgamator of ethnic difference, Reginald Marsh's "Subway Sunbeams" cartoon titled "The Melting Pot," which was published in the *New York Daily News* in 1923 (fig. 1).[1] What we see in Marsh's sketch is a group that strikes a tenuous balance between ethnic differentiation and the power of a unified crowd. From the fashionable white flapper standing at the left edge of the panel, to the shawled immigrant woman holding onto the pole, to the bowler-wearing African American man on the right, the image compresses a wide range of typical New Yorkers into its narrow frame. Though the passengers face in different directions, each head wears a hat, and each face is easily legible as a signifier of an urban type, whether ethnic, racial, or class based. There is no "melting" going on here. Instead, it is at the level of the crowd's bodies that we see amalgamation among riders, as well as between riders and the subway itself. Only the three passengers who stand in the foreground of the image have visibly delineated bodies: the shawled woman, a short woman who clutches a purse with one hand, and the wriggling child she clutches with the other. Even those two women blend together, with their draping white sleeves furrowed by cross-hatching. The flapper blends into the subway itself, with her upward-curving arm echoed by a downward-sloping pole. Signifiers of ethnicity and gender operate in tension with Marsh's loose, sketchy line, which seems to imply that regardless of background, these New Yorkers are cut from the same cloth. Although the caricatures separate the subway crowd into types, their physical proximity suggests that they will move en masse when rounding a corner or stopping short at a station. Their heads are distinct; their bodies are part of the crowd.

The melting pot is of course the most popular metaphor for the process of Americanization in the first half of the twentieth century. In his 1908 play of the same name, the British author Israel Zangwill imagines the formation of American culture as a mystical process, one that takes place with no small amount of toil. His visionary hero David Quixano concludes the play with a monologue imagining the process of acculturation within a "crucible"; there "the Great Alchemist melts and fuses" the individuated races that constitute America, binding them into a magnificent alloy "with his purging flame!" (185). The idea of the melting pot has been put to a number of uses in the ensuing decades, many of them politically conservative calls to abandon cultural differences entirely in favor of a monolithic American identity.[2]

In this chapter I discuss a play penned by another Jewish author, one that transferred that melting, fusing, and purging process of Americanization from an alchemic crucible to a sweltering subway car. My focus is the Russian American playwright Osip Dymov's comedic fantasy *Bronx Express. Bronx Express* is not an unknown play: often cited in histories of American Yiddish theater, it was published in Nahma Sandrow's 1999 anthology *God, Man, and Devil: Yiddish Plays in Translation.* From 1919 to 1925, productions of *Bronx Express* trace a circuitous route through New York City, from Madison Square to Broadway to the Bronx.[3] The play opened in 1919 as part of the debut season of Jacob Ben-Ami's Jewish Art Theater (or *Naye Teater*), with Dymov directing; it was translated into English and opened on Broadway in 1922 to mixed reviews (fig. 2).[4] *Bronx Express* merits further study not only as a Yiddish play of acculturation but also as an early consideration of the subway's problematic role as a vehicle for advancing that process—perhaps the earliest. The protagonist, Khatskl Hungerproud, is a Jewish button maker who runs into an Americanized friend, Jake (formerly

Figure 1. Reginald Marsh. "Subway Sunbeams: The Melting Pot." *New York Daily News,* June 26, 1923. Photo Jim Frank. © 2013 Estate of Reginald Marsh / Art Students League, New York/ Artists Rights Society (ARS), New York.

Figure 2. A promotional still for the 1922 Broadway opening of *Bronx Express*. White Studio / © Billy Rose Theatre Division, The New York Public Library for the Performing Arts.

Yankl) Flames, on the subway ride home to the Bronx. Dymov's protagonist has worked in America for twenty-five years while changing little: according to a critic of the Broadway production, "[he] has been bold enough to leap from Russia into the melting pot and then finds to his despair that nothing much has happened to him. He does not melt" (Broun). The rest of the play shows Hungerproud pursuing an exaggerated version of assimilation, only to abandon it in favor of life as it was.

At first the issue seems of little concern to him: in the version that ran on Broadway, when Flames chides his friend for reading a Yiddish newspaper on his commute home instead of one written in English, Hungerproud replies: "It's all right. On my way home when I want a little nap, I open the paper and turn to the editorial page, where it says about the melting pot—it can thunder and lightning—children can scream—I sleep from Fourteenth Street to One Hundred and Tenth Street! And sometimes all the way to Prospect Avenue" (Dymow P-5). By 1919, when *Bronx Express* debuted in Yiddish, the melting pot was still an issue subject to debate by Jewish intellectuals, but it had been rehearsed so often that it could put workingmen to sleep. Dymov cannily plays on the tiredness of this issue, staging the rest of *Bronx Express* as a dream encounter with the mixed cultures and conflicted desires of the modern city.

I focus here on the intervention of subway culture into conversations about ethnicity at the time. Michael Brooks and Tracy Fitzpatrick both engage in lively critical discussions of how race and gender inflect the embodied experience of subway ridership, but ethnicity has not been explored as thoroughly. This is a surprising omission, since issues of assimilation were resonant in what John Higham calls the "Tribal Twenties" (264). After World War I, nativist pride and the desire for "100 percent Americans" resurged. Writers from the period repeatedly mention objects that emphasize the ethnic difference of fellow subway riders, from the multilingual newspapers of unassimilated New Yorkers mentioned by McCabe to the misshapen bundles and shopping bags of a shawled and kerchiefed "East Side matron" (Grey, "Characters in the Cars" 257). McCabe's anxiety and Marsh's ironic gaze are both directed at the subway because it is a quintessential space of cross-cultural encounter.

Although Cotten Seiler rightly points out the ways that mobility has been limited for Americans without the full privileges of citizenship accorded to white Anglo-Saxon Protestant men, the subway functions as a kind of underground marketplace where "lesser" Americans prove that they too deserve to be mobile (23). This is true of the films, novels, and comic strips of the 1910s and 1920s in which young workingwomen imagine the subway as a vehicle of social climbing through marriage (Brooks 174–75).[5] It is equally true of Hungerproud's interaction with advertising trademark characters, in which he uses his cultural knowledge of Jewish workers to help them maximize their corporations' profits. In this way we can understand the subway as a problematic urban space where both workingwomen and ethnic minorities take advantage of the subway's ability to connect them with people of higher status, facilitating upward mobility.

Hungerproud falls asleep as the prologue ends; though we do not know it until the epilogue begins, *Bronx Express* is literally and figuratively a play about an American dream. Hungerproud's adventures in the play's three main acts involve his family and Flames, as well the brand mascots that surround him on the train as they come to life and take part in a meeting of millionaires which Hungerproud crashes. He befriends the characters, first by pretending to be a millionaire himself and then by convincing them that they can make more money by forcing Jews to work on Yom Kippur. Successful but unhappy, he vacations in Atlantic City but longs for his home in the Bronx. He finally wakes up at the end of the subway line, just as his children are returning home from Bronx Park. They board the subway with him for the return trip as the play ends.

Here I should point out that Dymov's play is best understood as an example of American expressionist drama.[6] A theatrical movement of the 1920s as practiced by Eugene O'Neill, Elmer Rice, Sophie Treadwell, Susan Glaspell, and John Howard Lawson, expressionism eschews realistic dialogue and sets in favor of those that create an overall mood.[7] Characters in these plays tend to be types rather than individuals, while the incidents taking place onstage represent the forces of modernity. American expressionist drama gravitates to the subway because it is a setting that emphasizes the mental isolation of city life. Like their German predecessors, American expressionist playwrights used theatrical space to externalize the emotions being experienced by their central characters. O'Neill's Emperor Jones doesn't just feel "little formless fears"; we see them enacted onstage with him (O'Neill 1045). In a realist drama, Hungerproud might discuss the pressures of assimilation represented by the advertising trademarks on the subway; in expressionist drama, however, he argues directly with the figures themselves. In this way expressionist drama turns the subway inside out, revealing the active dream life of its passive passengers. Later plays that follow this pattern include *The Subway* by Elmer Rice (1929), *Subway Circus* by William Saroyan (1940), and *The Owl Answers* (1963) by Adrienne Kennedy. Like Dymov, each of these playwrights comes from an ethnic or racial minority and uses the subway to highlight the sense of separation experienced by its passengers. These plays differ markedly in tone, but they all utilize the subway to explore the difficulties of cultural hybridity.

*Bronx Express* deals with some of the most common issues in the canon of American Jewish literature, yet the play's ethnic modernist style and multilingual origin have kept it from being fully assimilated (and I choose that word consciously) into either the Yiddish or the modern American dramatic canon. *Bronx Express* is a nearly unclassifiable play because it incorporates multiple languages and ethnic theatrical traditions in its examination of Jewish intraurban migration. This linguistic complexity arises in part because of Dymov's background. Born Joseph Perlman in Bialystok, Russia (now Poland), Dymov took his pen name from a character in Anton Chekhov's short story "The Grasshopper." He emigrated to the United States in 1913 but continued to write most of his plays in Russian and, according to the *Lexicon of the Yiddish Theater,* "translated them into Yiddish with the help of friends" (Zylbercweig 560, trans. Beatrice Smedley). The subway thus becomes a figure not only of physical circulation but of linguistic circulation as well. The Yiddish dramatic tradition within which *Bronx Express* first appears is "a resolutely impure cultural form" (Freedman 18), one that combines a number of genres and conventions.

In this way both *The Melting Pot* and *Bronx Express* can be understood in Sarah Wilson's terms as "melting-pot modernist texts," plays with "polyglot formal effects" that embody the diversity of turn-of-the-century America rather than merely describing it (10). *Bronx Express* shares with *The Melting Pot* not only a mixed linguistic pedigree but also a heterogeneous style that highlights the ambivalence of their protagonists to the process of assimilation. Both plays encompass a broad and often contradictory set of theatrical principles, including ethnic naturalism, vaudeville comedy, and Shavian drama of ideas. *Bronx Express* adds to this list the expressionism of German playwrights such as Ernst Toller and Georg Kaiser.

In his reception history, Joe Kraus explains that *The Melting Pot* was criticized for its "formal messiness" and its attempt to combine the sentimental and the conceptual (3). Indeed, one of the reviews quoted by Kraus sounds remarkably like a review of *Bronx Express:* the critic for *The Nation* calls it "an unstable compound of melodrama, farce, burlesque, and rhetoric" ("Drama and Music" 240). *Bronx Express* was all the more unstable a compound for having gone through multiple translations before its Broadway debut. Written in Russian and translated into Yiddish for its stage debut, the play was then translated into English by Samuel Golding and adapted for the Broadway stage by Owen Davis, who was best known as the author of spectacular melodramas such as *Nellie the Beautiful Cloak-Model.* A review by Weed Dickinson makes a joke of the play's mixed provenance, suggesting that no one involved could have had any direct contact with the experiences being presented in the play. Dickinson gives credit as follows: "fantasm by Ossip [*sic*] Dymow, translation by Samuel R. Golding, adaptation by Owen Davis, geographical jokes not credited on the program." He then admits, "It is rather difficult to imagine a self-confessed 'fantastic comedy' of Bronx life, written by a Russian, translated by somebody else and adapted by a melodramatist, however excellent" (*Bronx Express* Clippings

Folder). These plays may have failed to adhere to modern drama's tenets of formal consistency—exemplified by David Belasco around the turn of the century and Eugene O'Neill in the 1920s—but they nevertheless reflected the *inconsistency* of the immigrants whose lives they depicted, from their linguistic code switching to their encounters with highly mixed messages about American culture.

As I show throughout this chapter, *Bronx Express* reflects a common tension in modern writing about ethnic ridership on the New York subway. Newspaper writers and cartoonists, dramatists, and average New Yorkers oscillate between an understanding of the subway as a vehicle of ethnic isolation and one that imagines it as a place where the process of melting into an American alloy must inevitably occur. In this way, *Bronx Express* continues to explore concerns that were central to earlier American drama, bringing the role of technology to the fore. As Joyce Flynn notes in her seminal article "Melting Plots," "A considerable number of nineteenth-century American plays focused on racial and ethnic relations and examined the new social arrangements potentially created by ethnic combinations and/or ethnic coexistence" (420). She classifies those plays in terms of their final spatial and social placement of these discrete ethnic groups: "The dramas arrange themselves on a continuum from plots of ethnic absorption and mingling of the melting-pot sort to separate-but-somewhat-equal stage groupings" (Flynn 420). The subway plays an important role in modernist versions of this dramatic concern, since it exacerbates both the "mingling" of ethnic groups and their "separate-but-somewhat-equal" status, whereby every ethnic group has a neighborhood and a newspaper of its own. In the next section I describe the increasing separation of Jewish neighborhoods brought about by the subway expansion; I then consider how *Bronx Express* reimagines the melting pot of national identity as one based in consumption. Spatial distance from and formal similarity to the white Anglo-Saxon American ideal go hand in hand in the 1920s and 1930s. As the Second World War approaches, however, we see an emergent understanding of the subway as a space of resistance to capitalist pressures. The subway evolves as a space of isolation and ethnic pluralism in art of the 1930s and 1940s such as William Saroyan's play *Subway Circus* and Walker Evans's series of subway photographs, *Many Are Called.* Dymov and Saroyan, then, are two ethnic dramatists whose work on technology has a considerably wider resonance than has been previously understood. I conclude by discussing how subway art and drama of this era cement an understanding of the New York City subway that persists to this day in film and television.

The subway's role in ethnic American drama is a mediating one. It puts New Yorkers from different backgrounds into contact with one another, though that contact is generally silent and distracted. This is the tension that is pursued throughout the multiple considerations of the subway as a space of ethnic performance. American drama stages a subway rife with cultural codes that separate passengers into discrete ethnic groups: language, whether spoken or read, becomes a means of asserting difference in an anonymous crowd. Consider Hungerproud's accessory that transcends ethnic divisions: the newspaper. Cultural critics of the period invoke the newspaper-reading subway rider as a sign of rudeness or apathy, as we saw in chapter 1; they also use the wide availability of foreign-language newspapers in New York as a figure of the city's cultural diversity, often using negative, nativist language.[8] Of course the newspaper is not merely a sign of ethnic difference, since Hungerproud's paper places him in conversation with the myriad other businessmen who use the same kind of reading material to avoid contact with their fellow New Yorkers on the way home from work. The fact that it is a *Yiddish* paper marks him as an outsider to that group, however. Rather than functioning as an everyday reminder of the "simultaneity" of his experience with that of the broader community of New Yorkers and Americans, Hungerproud's paper "continually reassure[s] him" of his Jewishness (Anderson 35). The subway thus supports other technologies, such as newspapers, in reshaping the ways that Americanization takes place: it brings ethnic groups into close physical contact with one another for the duration of the ride while simultaneously estranging them from one another geographically and culturally.[9]

## Migrating by Subway

In the era when *Bronx Express* made its debut, certain New York subway lines were popularly understood as Jewish spaces, and particularly as Jewish theatrical spaces. In his review of *Awake and Sing!*—Clifford Odets's seminal drama of American Jewish family life—Walter Winchell calls the play "as non-Aryan as a Bronx Express and as swift" (Smith, *Real Life Drama* 208).[10] Alison Smith agreed that the subway epitomized Jewish life in the Bronx, writing in her review of the Broadway adaptation that the Bronx Express was "as appropriate a background for a Jewish folk-drama as the Whispering Well or the Old Homestead," alluding to then current plays about British weavers and Yankee farmers (*Bronx Express* Clippings Folder). This comparison suggests an understanding of Jewishness as intimately allied with technology. The "Whispering Well" and the "Old Homestead" were distant, timeless spaces; the subway ridden by millions of New Yorkers of all faiths is proposed as an equally useful setting for a drama about Jewishness. At least for New York theater critics of the period, folklife and modern transportation were complementary rather than contradictory.

Ethnic studies scholars, particularly those who focus on Jewish and African American studies, have felt an increasing sense that transportation technology plays a part in this process of acculturation, since it opens up possible places of settlement, shuts down others, and structures the modes of contact between areas. Recent criticism has begun to unpack the complex and conflicted relationship of Jewish literature to the railroad, for example: the train car becomes a "Judaized" space in German- and Yiddish-language modernist literature (Garrett 19), both because of the prominent presence of Jewish passengers and because of the structural relationship of those passengers to the state through which they move. Todd Presner sees the railroad as a technology that decenters the Jewish subject by situating him within a larger and more abstract network of affiliation, "the dialectical and disaggregated network of the railway" (27). In Sholem Aleichem's *Railroad Stories* in particular, Jewish conversation fills the third-class cars, but it is constantly interrupted by passenger departures and haunted by the humiliations of life in the Pale of Settlement. Theories of movement, exile, and diaspora have of course long played a part in Jewish studies. These new perspectives highlight how those ideas take shape in relation to the technological innovations of what Presner calls "mobile modernity." For European Jewish literature before World War II, railroads embody a number of cultural tensions. They suspend their passengers in a liminal space between tradition and modernity, free movement and restriction, ethnic and national identity. These suspensions, however, take place in the context of travel within a nation or across its borders. With my focus on *Bronx Express,* I hope to show how the movement between boroughs of a city can be felt as a similarly complex movement between worlds, one not unique to Jewish New Yorkers.

The ship and the railroad may be central figures of international Jewish mobility, but the subway serves as their local counterpart.[11] It is rivaled only by the Manhattan Bridge, gateway from the Lower East Side to Williamsburg, Brooklyn, as the formative transit technology for first- and second-generation Jewish immigrants to New York in the early twentieth century. In *At Home in America*, her influential history of second-generation Jews in New York City, Deborah Dash Moore argues that "transportation unlocked the door to urban expansion" (33). The Interborough Rapid Transit Company unveiled New York City's first subway line in 1904, leading to a redistribution of the urban population from overcrowded Manhattan to the then pastoral outer boroughs. By 1920 the system had more than doubled its initial track length and the number of trains it could provide in an hour (Hood, *722 Miles* 159). Because of this increase in service, the population of the Bronx grew by 150 percent in this period; 75 percent of the population of this borough in 1920 was made up of first- or second-generation immigrants, and many of those were German and Russian Jews (Hood, *722 Miles* 111). By 1930, nearly one-third of New York's Jewish population lived in the Bronx (Moore 23).[12]

*Bronx Express* does not merely document the historic impact of this migration, though it does that too: Hungerproud invites his friend to Sabbath dinner, telling him that he lives "in the Bronx, Prospect Avenue. Five blocks from the station" (Dymov 271). The subway structures ethnic neighborhoods in such a way that they are associated with discrete subway stops. For Dymov, this leads to an understanding of urban experience that uses the logic of parataxis, juxtaposing different spheres and different populations without suggesting precisely how they are connected. The subway opens up more of the city to Jewish New Yorkers, but it creates a newly abstract relationship between those realms. In this way we can see how the subway functions as a miniature version of the railroad imagined by Garrett and Presner. Both critics understand the railroad as a vehicle that disrupts prior models of space and time: it brings the shtetl and the city into closer proximity, along with the values associated with each location.[13] The subway serves as an equally liminal space in *Bronx Express,* juxtaposing the observant Judaism of the Bronx with the consumerism of Manhattan as an element of Hungerproud's daily commute.

Paradoxically, increased contact between ethnic groups within the liminal space of the subway took place precisely because ethnic populations had moved farther away from the center of Manhattan. Throughout the subway's early decades, the nickel fare prevented the truly destitute from riding; additionally, "the ridership appears to have been weighted toward the upper middle class before World War I," though the demographics of the subway-riding population became more diverse in the following decade (Hood, *722 Miles* 180). Working-class ethnic New Yorkers, the population who had previously lived below Fourteenth Street, dispersed to the outer boroughs in the late 1910s and into the 1920s. They could no longer walk to work, so they rode. Many of the rhetorical gestures of modernist subway writing can be imagined as a means of restoring the kind of geographic proximity between classes and ethnicities that was no longer possible in the day-to-day life of modern city dwellers.

Later Jewish writers such as Alfred Kazin emphasize the ways in which the subway opens up access to the city outside immigrant neighborhoods (*Walker in the City* 93–95). In this play, however, we see that the subway streamlines immigrant life by allowing passengers to bypass any unnecessary encounters with "American" culture. The subway moves Hungerproud more efficiently from his job at a button-making factory on the Lower East Side to his home in the Bronx, connecting one Jewish ghetto to another. When they encounter each other in the play's prologue, Flames dismissively asks him: "What do you know about America? Between 14th Street and Harlem 160th is exactly where America is. You've been sleeping through America, and under America, your entire life" (Dymov 272). Hungerproud's commute is a typical one for men of his background at the time, starting from the button "shop on Canal Street" where he has worked for twenty-five years (269) and ending at Bronx Park (304). If we assume that he boarded the 6 train at Canal and Lafayette streets and switched to the express at Fourteenth Street, the stop where the play begins, Hungerproud's subway ride covers approximately eleven miles and today would take around forty-five minutes.

As Jack Flames charges, this long ride that takes place mostly underground is concrete proof of Hungerproud's cultural estrangement from real Americans. In Flames's exaggerated language, there is an astute understanding of the new Jewish American relationship to the city made possible by the subway's expansion: the farther you move from the centers of power and industry, the more alienated from them you become. The kind of spatial separation that Dymov depicts is not the same as living on the Lower East Side. Previously, Jewish immigrants had been separated from the "America" of "14th Street to Harlem 160th" by culture and language, but not absolutely by geography. With the subway's expansion and the subsequent movement of Jewish New Yorkers to the Bronx, this separation becomes an absolute one.[14]

Yet if the subway cuts off immigrant neighborhoods from sites of power and prestige, it also reconnects those who can afford it. The distance between the Bronx and Manhattan is both extended and made bridgeable by the subway; the subway thus bypasses conventional routes of social access. After Hungerproud returns home to his Sabbath dinner, he slaps his shy prospective son-in-law and leaves his house to go find "a Broadway millionaire" to marry his daughter instead (283). He boards the train again, asks the conductor where the "big shots" get off, and pays a nickel when he leaves (after also, presumably, paying a nickel when he got on). "Pay and pay is all they know," says Hungerproud bitterly (283). Dropping a nickel into the turnstile is a habit, but it is also a ritual gesture of entrance into modern American life. The subway takes a toll in more senses than one, however: Hungerproud expresses a psychic resistance to assimilation, a deep resentment of his situation and its cyclical, never-ending nature. Even in his dreams, he senses that his only way to reconnect with the world of "the Americans" in Manhattan is through financial success. The subway estranges Jewish New Yorkers from Manhattan, ensuring that their assimilation takes place on a narrowly defined, mechanized, and monetized path.

Transit technologies play an important role in New York's cultural imaginary during this period of interborough expansion, and the subway comes to be understood as the vehicle most representative of Jewish migration within the city. At the same time, the subway appears not only in *Bronx Express* but throughout the culture of its time as a metonym for industrial capitalism. These two issues come together in Dymov's exploration of Hungerproud's success among the millionaires. As his sleeping body is carried closer to his home in the Bronx, his mind takes him further afield in the cartoonish realms of assimilated and commercialized American modernity. By the end of the play, the subway setting has literalized the pleasures and dangers of mobility, leaving its audience with a sense that the system may be inescapable. With Hungerproud's predicament, Dymov gives us a concrete infrastructural model of New York Jewish immigrant culture's relation to that of modern New York City. Hungerproud is on the fringes but can quickly move to the center, though this movement is dependent on access to money and technology and takes place beneath the obvious sites of power. Ted Merwin, one of the few contemporary critics to discuss *Bronx Express* extensively, characterizes its central theme as "the contest between traditional Jewish values and assimilated American 'capitalist' values" (97). This contest is figured throughout the play by the image of the New York subway that suspends its protagonist in the unresolved position between these opposed sets of values, represented by different neighborhoods within the city.[15]

*Bronx Express* explores how melting pot culture changes when the element uniting the diverse strains of American culture is not nationalism but capitalism. The subway becomes an important vehicle of assimilation not because it shows passengers how to take on new American traits but because it shows them how to consume at properly American rates. In *Adapting to Abundance,* Andrew Heinze notes that phrases from advertisements were among the English terms that made their way most rapidly into American Yiddish; similarly, advertisements for American products appeared with increasing frequency in Yiddish newspapers (149). As we will see in the next section, the "car cards" that appeared in subway cars can be understood as a vehicle of assimilation for the immigrant workers who ride the train daily. But in *Bronx Express,* Dymov understands advertising as far from a benevolent force. His choice of Mr. Pluto, a devil figure, as the leader of the trademark characters suggests the nefarious quality of this mode of acculturation.

## Assimilation and the Marketplace

If *The Melting Pot* imagines ethnic differences overcome by love, *Bronx Express* sees them overcome by money. Like other Yiddish-language writing of the period, *Bronx Express* dealt with the subway crowd as a microcosm of a money-crazed city and nation.[16] The play's prologue begins with anonymous passengers making conversation out of dollars and cents, ironically followed by strains of the patriotic song "America" (Dymov 268). The clearest way that the subway focuses an otherwise disparate crowd on the business of Americanization, however, is through the advertisements displayed there. As a site of commuters' fantasy, the subway advertisement, or "car card," as it was called, exploits both the immigrant's dream of assimilation and his extended subway ride that confirmed his separation from the cultural mainstream. The play's focus on the advertising trademarks underscores the way in which the subway acclimates the Jewish immigrant to American capitalism. The subway separates immigrants from the city, but subway ads reconnect them to the pleasures the city affords.

Modern transit ads first appeared in nineteenth-century streetcars. It was not until the turn of the century that advertisers took advantage of this environment to its fullest extent through the use of advertising trademarks that gave their products a "face." The trademarks that become central characters in *Bronx Express,* including the Red Devil on Pluto laxative water and the Turkish girl on Murad cigarettes, played an important role in reshaping the understanding of advertising in this period. *Fame,* the trade magazine published by car card impresario Artemas Ward, offered a number of arguments in favor of transit ads—many of them in verse. The magazine's light verse addressed white-collar businessmen, making the subway an object of shared enjoyment among those sophisticated enough to appreciate it as a new venue for advertising to the masses. A 1917 poem by John S. Grey characterizes the trademark figures in advertisements as "traveling companions":

> I need no introduction to the people I have named
> For, better than the riders, their identity is famed.
> I seek no conversation with the passengers or guards—
> My traveling companions are the advertising cards! (167)

In gravitating to the New York subway, expressionist playwrights highlight its dependence on the interior focus of its riders. Not wishing to interact with one another, these passengers look for a place to direct their attention. Car cards offer a solution to this problem.

In the subway in particular, the faces of advertising characters function as an alternate crowd, friendly and familiar, that hovers above the impersonal, abstracted, and too-close bodies of fellow city dwellers. Susan Buck-Morss calls this personal quality "a new dissimulating aura [that was] injected into the commodity, easing its passage into the dream world of the private consumer. . . . Advertising images attempt to 'humanize' products in order to deny their commodity character" (184). What better place to test the humanity of the car cards than in the subway, where people were constantly looking for evidence that they were not commodities themselves?

In *Bronx Express,* Flames literalizes this process, animating the brand mascots with the motivations of the capitalist structures that make them possible. There are "millionaires right over your head," he tells Hungerproud, and lists the net worth of the advertising characters:

> FLAMES: Do you have any idea what's going on with the Americans? Nestlé? That baby? Two hundred million. And chewing gum, Wrigley's, three hundred million. And Smith Brothers Cough Drops, three hundred fifty million.
>
> HUNGERPROUD: Both brothers together?
>
> FLAMES: Each brother separately. Both together, five hundred. (273)

The faces in advertisements invite Jewish immigrants into the American business culture, where personal value and monetary value are synonymous. Hungerproud, Flames insists, doesn't "have any idea what's going on with the Americans" even though they are trying to tell him. But the rest of the play shows us that the reverse is true: Hungerproud knows the names and faces of all the American advertising figures, which have had a presence in his work life for twenty-five years (293). The permeability of the boundary between interior self and exterior world means that the fantasy life of subway passengers has been rapidly colonized by the omnipresence of advertising.

In one sense, the fantasy enacted in *Bronx Express* is not the fantasy of wealth and fame but the fantasy of being able to talk back to the images of consumerism embodied by the subway advertising characters. At the millionaires' meeting Hungerproud is offered a cigarette, which he refuses because Jews are forbidden to smoke on the Sabbath. This causes the millionaires to rant about how Jews "spoil [the] business" by refusing to consume at the rate that good Americans do (292). Hungerproud retorts: "I hid from you under the ground. I needed peace from your yelling and from the hard work that I do for you. For you, not for myself. But you found me and dragged me out, you tear at me and yell: 'Buy! Buy! More! Money! Don't spoil the business.' Some fine bunch you are" (293). Here Hungerproud's speech suggests the inevitability of assimilation through technology. He has tried to hide from consumer culture "under the ground," but ads have invaded even the space of the subway, dragging him into American culture just when he wants to avoid it.

Particularly at the play's climax, we have the sense that even the most permanent traditions are negotiable. Hungerproud finally capitulates to the demands that follow him home. He achieves success as one of the millionaires only when he reveals his big idea, the ultimate gambit to force assimilation: paying Jews overtime if they work on Yom Kippur. In the Broadway version of *Bronx Express,* the loss of Yom Kippur is seen as equivalent to losing Saint Patrick's Day, Columbus Day, or some other holiday that celebrates ethnic pride (Dymow 2–39). Hungerproud's identification with other marginalized groups comes only in response to the most combative assimilationist rhetoric.

At one of the tensest moments in an otherwise comic story, Dymov becomes intensely citational. First he evokes Faust, imbuing Goethe's tale with the added burden of ethnic betrayal. Hungerproud has literally sold his soul to the devil, a fact underscored by a thunderclap in the stage directions (294). He explains the consequences of his action in cartoonish but ominous language:

> Yom Kippur breaks down, everything breaks down. No holidays, no religion, no tradition. Everything one pot of schmaltz. Everyone cooked in the same pot. The iron grinder grinds them all up together, with the Poles, Italians, Chinese, Japanese, Negroes—everyone thrown in the iron wheels. Wheels and people—a machine with no holidays, no language, no traditions—a great mass of workers that works and buys, works and buys, and eats and chews, and swallows. Two for a quarter, five for a dozen. The nicest, the best, delicious, you need it. Historical process, capital and labor. (295)

Between the assimilative vision of the Progressive Era and its post–World War I counterpart, the marketplace intervenes. David Quixano in *The Melting Pot* feels conflicted about his cultural inheritance, yet he has no doubts about its persistence in the contemporary American landscape; as the play ends, his mother's Irish maid has put on a false nose for Purim and speaks a number of Yiddish phrases (Shumsky 31). *Bronx Express* is far less optimistic about the bidirectional nature of assimilation: Jew and Gentile are "cooked in the same pot," a conflation of assimilationist ideals and the cannibalistic drives of the marketplace. The result seems terrifying: different ethnic groups are ground together, becoming a mass of workers that is half-man, half-machine, and all-consuming. When ethnic groups abandon their distinctiveness in order to join the wider consumer culture, they lose not only their cultural difference but their very humanity as well.

The melting pot presented here is a bitter parody of what Werner Sollors calls America's culture of consent.[17] Rather than becoming a part of the nation by their own volition, immigrants do so in order to feed their families. Their culture, their religion, all traditions that make them unique are lost in the process of making money. In this monologue Hungerproud suggests that there is no middle ground between ethnic diversity and a bland cultural sameness. The rhetoric of the melting pot no longer causes Hungerproud to fall asleep; instead it wakes him up to the dangers of assimilation.

This monologue formally echoes its own content, breaking down into a modernist collage of advertising slogans and Marxist phrases. Before it does so, however, it presents an unmistakable parody of David Quixano's visionary monologue that concludes *The Melting Pot.* That Jewish dramatic hero gazes out onto New York Harbor and imagines the "Celt and Latin, Slav and Teuton, Greek and Syrian—black and yellow" immigrants pouring in (Zangwill 184). "How the Great Alchemist melts and fuses them with his purging flame!" he marvels (185). No longer an alchemical crucible, the melting pot is described by Dymov in more homey Yiddish terms as one for rendering chicken fat. He thus explores the paradox of assimilation with an ethnically marked image of cultural homogenization. Even more important is the shift away from an international vision of America's diversity to one that is as claustrophobic as a rush hour subway car. In Zangwill's vision, ships provide the exogenous contributions to American culture, which are nobly fused together into an even stronger alloy; in Dymov's, the subway provides an endless cycle of endogenous workers, both migrant and immigrant, who are ground together into a kind of cultural sausage. The subway comes to represent the melting pot not because it unites a diverse group of New Yorkers with common purpose, then, but because it renders them equally subject to the advertisements that surround them.

In the play's final act, the subway car becomes a site of hellish rootlessness for everyone in Hungerproud's family. The subway had separated work in Manhattan from home in the Bronx, but the two are now irretrievably mixed. Hungerproud has married Miss Murad, the cigarette trademark, and they have taken the adopted Nestlé baby with them on a honeymoon to Atlantic City. In Rudolph Schildkraut's production of *Bronx Express* in 1925, the Atlantic City set retained a row of subway ads across the top (fig. 3),

Figure 3. A promotional still for the 1925 Yiddish-language production of *Bronx Express.* Museum of the City of New York.

reinforcing the spatial confusion along with the confusion of identity. His family members keep appearing throughout the vacation as menial workers: a respected teacher has been forced to take a job as a messenger boy; Hungerproud's son shines shoes and whistles jazz tunes; and his daughter hopes to make a good match with one of the Smith Brothers. Whether through desire or necessity, everyone in Hungerproud's extended family—and, Dymov suggests, everyone in the city—finally submits to the system represented by the subway. Hungerproud is grief-stricken and nearly crazy, bitterly joking that this is "the last stage of Americanization" (303). If the intraurban migration to the Bronx at first allowed the Hungerprouds to keep American culture at arm's length, it has now completely overwhelmed the Jewish part of their lives.

We see the dangers of nativist ideology come to the fore when the play deals with that most typical of ethnic folkways, food. When a homesick Hungerproud encounters his "former" wife, Sara, now a cook in a restaurant, he asks her to make some Jewish-style food for him; Miss Murad discovers that her new husband remains married to both of them. Unlike the Swedish immigrant who calls Sweden his "mother" and America his "bride" in Werner Sollors's *Beyond Ethnicity,* Hungerproud tries to accommodate both Jewish and American elements of his identity in the same position and endangers his relationship to each (154).

When the advertising figures learn he is a bigamist, they threaten to lynch him and actually tie a rope around his neck (303–4). More commonly associated with African Americans in the post-Reconstruction South, death by lynching calls into question both Hungerproud's personal identity and his geographical location. The best-known lynching of a Jew was that of Leo Frank, the manager of a pencil factory in Atlanta, who was hanged by a mob in 1915 after being convicted of the murder of Mary Phagan, a young white woman who worked in his factory (Jacobson 62–68). The trial fueled public anti-Semitism and renewed interest in the Ku Klux Klan; it also led to the founding of the Anti-Defamation League. This frightening conclusion to act 3 suggests the perilous consequences of Americanization. Nativist violence may be the only way of cutting through the haze of consumerism presented in the subway.[18]

*Bronx Express* emphasizes the underlying violence in an increasingly business-oriented culture that renders Americanization synonymous with consumerism. Beginning with the resentful conversation among the trademarks in act 2 about observance of the Jewish Sabbath spoiling their business, we see the suspicion of cultural difference that interferes with the profit margin. This logic is played out in the conclusion to act 3: although Hungerproud is threatened with lynching for committing bigamy, he also seems to be guilty of preferring a home-cooked meal over a lavish hotel feast. Here we are reminded that the 1920s were a decade not only of increasing consumerism but also of increasingly virulent anti-immigrant sentiment. Indeed, in the six years between the Yiddish debut of *Bronx Express* and its Bronx revival in 1925, American immigration had been irrevocably altered, first with the establishment of temporary quotas for different ethnic groups in 1921, and then with the passage of the Johnson-Reed Act in 1924. Eastern European immigrants like Hungerproud now had a much slimmer chance of making the same journey. In *Bronx Express,* cross-cultural identification occurs in response to the implicit violence of demands for assimilation, both in the multiethnic content of Hungerproud's nightmarish melting pot and in the regional and racial confusion of his imagined lynching. The pluralism of Dymov's theatrical styles begins to seem like a protest not only against stylistic purity but against national purity as well.[19]

Contemporaries of *Bronx Express* such as *The Jazz Singer* and *Abie's Irish Rose* assuage cultural anxieties about ethnic diversity with a generational logic: the parents who immigrated to America hold on to their old culture, while the native-born children gravitate to the new. *Bronx Express* is particularly remarkable because it works against that trend. Hungerproud betrays his role as the patriarch of the family in order to become a successful American millionaire, while his children offer a positive mix of traditional Jewish and Americanized traits. Striking that balance, Dymov suggests, seems to be the best way to avoid the most onerous complications of a hybrid identity. This explains why Hungerproud calls out to his son as the third act ends. He pleads, "My son, help your father" and "Children, help me" (304), suggesting that only they can resolve the tensions between the old and new world that have gotten him into trouble. At the end of *Bronx Express,* as at the end of a melodrama, Hungerproud is reunited with his children in the subway car. They have come from Bronx Park, where they had been picking flowers to celebrate their father's twenty-five years in the button-making factory. The reunion with the children suggests that perhaps in time New York Jewish families will be able to strike a balance between the values of Manhattan and those of the Bronx. After all, Hungerproud's children are not the ones running off with dancing girls: his son reads Sholem Aleichem and is preparing for his bar mitzvah, and his daughter is in love with a shy, scholarly Zionist. Nevertheless, *Bronx Express* raises some cultural anxieties about the fate of the immigrant family that its happy ending cannot overcome. For one thing, Hungerproud's family is not fully restored: his wife is absent, presumably cooking at home. Even more suggestively, the picture of Miss Murad still hangs among the car cards (305). Hungerproud spits at it and sets off for his appropriate station, but the possibility of submitting to the seductions of consumer culture still lurks in the subway with him.

Subway expansion enabled families like the Hungerprouds to move into a more spacious apartment in a pastoral neighborhood, yet it also offered constant reminders of the other choices they might have made. In the next section I historicize the experience of Hungerproud's subway ride, suggesting how it stands in for a wider experience of technologically mediated assimilation in this period. The subway develops as a figure of the melting pot in the popular imagination, I suggest, precisely because it suspends immigrants between sections of the city that represent different interpretations of what it means to be a New Yorker and an American.

The idea of the subway as melting pot evolves from the 1920s into the 1930s and 1940s. While the market-driven focus of the subway space seems to suppress cultural differences between workers, it also creates imaginative bonds that transcend religious, cultural, and regional identities. Assimilation merits a different kind of literary and cultural interest once immigration restrictions have been enacted; the association of American identity with consumption also changes in the wake of the 1929 market crash. Visual and dramatic texts from this period continue to interrogate the diverse subway crowd, yet they do so in a way that emphasizes the isolation of each passenger. Accounts of the subway as melting pot depend less on the blending together of different cultures than on the structural similarity of their experiences. While popular calls for intermarriage and adaptation to American norms continue, the literary and cultural responses to the subway put a greater focus on the monadic consciousness of its passengers, whether English-speaking or not.

## The International Express

In the 1920s, elements of ethnic difference entered into dialogue with—and risked being completely subsumed by—the sameness of the subway crowd. Scholars have noted a change in the art and literature of the New York City subway in the 1930s and 1940s, a turn away from the representation of the subway crowd as a collective and toward an interest in individual passengers and their mental states. I conclude this chapter with the suggestion that this change should be understood in ethnic terms. William Saroyan's little-discussed play *Subway Circus* and Walker Evans's much-admired subway photography project *Many Are Called* register a change in the understanding of American multiculturalism, one that persists in contemporary writing about the New York City subway. Photographers and playwrights may shift their focus toward the existential isolation of the prototypical passenger, but they continue to explore the subway as an ethnically diverse space, one characterized by pluralistic separation as much as by assimilation. Although *Bronx Express* marked the sense of separation between the observant Jewish world of the Bronx and the consumerist world of Manhattan, the art of the late 1930s and early 1940s moves away from the idea of ethnic subway subjectivity as liminal or suspended between worlds. In this way it brings the New York subway crowd from the era of the melting pot into the era of what Horace Kallen envisioned as an "orchestra" (124) and later theorists of multiculturalism have called a "salad bowl." Rather than emphasizing hybridity or a play between similarity and difference, these texts establish a kind of equivalence between otherwise incommensurable experiences of passengers from different backgrounds.

*Many Are Called* is the best-known work of modern art that takes the passengers of the New York City subway as its subject. In the late 1930s and early 1940s, Walker Evans surreptitiously photographed passengers in IRT trains—perhaps even the Bronx Express—using a camera hidden in his coat. The portraits are from a medium distance, framing between one and three passengers sitting on the opposite bench. The one exception to this focus on small groups is a shot of the whole subway car reacting to a blind accordion player walking down the central aisle.[20] The critical interest in these photographs has resided chiefly in their ability to register an authentic interiority: in subsequent introductions to the book, both Luc Sante and James Agee see the subjects as unposed, with their guard down (15); Susan Sontag agrees that "their expressions are private ones, not those they would offer to the camera" (37). Though Evans presents the subway crowd in one picture at the end of the series, his chief concern is the reproduction of individual passengers in all of their individuality. Michael Brooks understands this development in the visual culture of the New York subway as a shift from the external to the internal as well: "The progress from Marsh's subway images to Evans's is partly a movement from outward bustle to inward experience. The shift in emphasis is even more striking in several paintings of the forties that tend to show the crowd only by implication while dramatizing the personal or existential angst of individuals" (169). Evans takes on a deeply American project of registering differences paratactically rather than classifying them as types. Sontag suggests that this catholic embrace of subject matter puts Evans in the same category as Walt Whitman. Both engage in "the leveling of discriminations between the beautiful and the ugly, the important and the trivial"; for Evans, "each thing or person photographed becomes—a photograph; and becomes, therefore, morally equivalent to any other of his photographs (Sontag 31). *Many Are Called* emphasizes the privacy and singularity of the individual subway rider's experience, but it also exposes the seriality of that experience: this is one ride among many and one passenger among many.

Although Evans is not a photographer particularly concerned with ethnic difference, his aesthetic is based on a kind of irreducible particularity of the thing photographed. That places him in sharp distinction to caricaturists of the 1920s like Osip Dymov and Reginald Marsh, humorists who inevitably focus on a play between the particular and the stereotypical. Of course, Evans took the pictures that made up *Many Are Called* in a markedly different political climate from that of the 1920s. Marsh and Dymov were considering questions of ethnic difference in an era when US culture was deeply engaged with the question of assimilation. Ethnic quotas were set in 1921, and the immigration restrictions of the Johnson-Reed Act went into effect in 1924. By the late 1930s the issue of the melting pot had ceased to be quite so pressing. Assimilation had moved to the back of the national consciousness, supplanted by concerns about racial differences within American culture and economic disparities between rich and poor. An article in *Fortune* magazine written in celebration of the New York World's Fair in 1939 establishes just how old-fashioned the matter seemed: "It is probably some time since most [Americans] have thought seriously about the alien in our midst. The 'immigration problem' had slipped quite out of the national consciousness by 1929, when Congress drove the last long nails of the quota system into our frontiers. What once had been a flood of more than a million immigrants a year became and has remained a trickle of around 50,000" ("The Melting Pot" 74). Though it's two decades later, this article still exhibits the proliferation of metaphors that Sarah Wilson identifies in the Progressive Era discourse of assimilation (4). Migration is commonly naturalized, and here the human tide that was once a disastrous flood has been reduced to a harmless trickle. The alarmist language that marked nativist sentiment and animated the implicit violence in *Bronx Express* no longer exerts much force.

The article attempts to remedy this lack of national thought about the immigrant, mostly through a nationality-by-nationality tour of the most prominent immigrant groups in New York City. Some critics have focused on one element of the article that suggests a continued interest in ethnic assimilation. The caption above the image of a crowded subway car reads: "The New York–born sons and daughters of immigrants already outnumber their parents and intermarry three times as often. Already the faces of any Coney Island subway crowd betray the beginnings of an interracial type" ("The Melting Pot" 77). Obviously the residents of New York no longer observe the strict demarcations of ethnic difference that animated ethnic drama of the 1920s. Yet this image of the subway as a scene of interracial blending is undercut by the rest of the article, where the many smaller, black-bordered images of typical ethnic life echo the division of the article into individual sections headed "Italians," "Germans," and so on. Tracy Fitzpatrick finds New York writers and artists of the 1930s to be uneasy when they confront the increasingly ambiguous ethnic identity of subway passengers; while assimilation renders some New Yorkers more fit to be considered Americans, it transforms others into frighteningly illegible figures (106). The ideal form of ethnic difference, we might suggest, is one that is easily recognizable.

The Armenian American writer William Saroyan makes ethnic difference visible throughout his career.[21] This theme appears in Saroyan's first play, *Subway Circus,* which was written in 1935 and published in 1940. This never-produced drama consists of ten scenes that represent the fantasies of ten different passengers on a single subway car. Generally these dreams explicitly enact wish fulfillment: a cripple dreams that he is a circus acrobat; a clerk confesses his love to a co-worker. Most important for the purposes of this argument are the scenes that perform a kind of condensed racial allegory. One section is called "Africa-Harlem Express"; others depict Italian and Yiddish-speaking Jewish immigrants whose dreams take place in their native language. The monotonous roar of the subway between scenes creates a structural equivalence between what would otherwise be utterly disconnected fantasies of passengers who share the train. Saroyan's play highlights an emergent sense that the subway is both a space of isolation and one of ethnic pluralism; the scenes featuring immigrant passengers are paradoxically the most positive and the most detached from the collective experiences of the passengers.

*Subway Circus* shares a number of formal and thematic concerns with *Bronx Express:* both imagine the subway car as a dream space, use those dreams to critique the consumerist mentality of modern American culture, and borrow from popular forms of performance in order to do so.[22] Saroyan uses vaudeville structures "to persuade audiences of the fallacy of the myth of success, money-worship, and the materialistic creed of the nation" (Aguilera Linde 21), taking a similarly critical attitude toward consumerism. Yet the backdrop for Saroyan's scenes is a far different one from the culture of the 1920s. The immigrant subway passengers show neither an interest in American culture nor an expectation that they must adhere to its norms; on the contrary, it is the Americans who are shown compulsively conforming to the expectations of popular culture, particularly as presented in movies and magazines. The dreams of a Yiddish-speaking patriarch and an Italian fruit peddler offer a model for resistance, the former through his sense of connection to a racial past and the latter in his pure expression of joy through song.

While Saroyan undoubtedly essentializes these characters, he also places them in dialogue with their fellow passengers on the train by staging each of their scenes in the same way. In doing so, he suggests the ways that technology structures urban experience, rendering each dream "morally equivalent" to the next. Saroyan specifies in his production note for the play:

> A light falls upon the person whose dream is to be revealed. The subway train divides in the middle, in darkness, and the place of this person's dream is revealed. The dream unfolds while the sound of the moving subway continues.
>
> The play begins with the subway and ends with the subway. Begins and ends with the real world. The beginning and end of each dream is the subway: except for the subway and these dreamers aboard, these dreams could not be. (Saroyan 5)

All these dreams are to be staged in the same fashion, with the opening up of dream space performed onstage through a literal opening up of the subway train. The subway car thus frames and echoes the individual passenger's unconscious mind, with nonnaturalistic movement of theatrical space signaling the movement into subjective mental space. Yet this is not pure interiority, since the "sound of the moving subway continues" throughout each dream, insisting on the connection between the fantasies of all the passengers, regardless of their background.

The New York subway continues to be defined as a space that encompasses cultural differences, though we see an increasing sense of atomization in postwar representations of the subway crowd. Moving further and further from the utopian synthesis of Zangwill, imagined encounters on the subway are fewer and further between, and when contact takes place, it is understood as taboo. This is particularly true in the work of African

American writers. Think of the unnamed narrator's uncomfortable proximity to a white woman on the subway in *Invisible Man,* the aggressive flirtation that erupts into violence in *Dutchman* (written by Amiri Baraka, then known as LeRoi Jones), and the total disorientation of self in *The Owl Answers.*[23] Even when more contemporary visions of the subway shy away from dramatizing racial tensions, they imagine difference within the subway crowd as chaotic at best, criminal at worst. Paul Cadmus's *Subway Symphony* and Red Grooms's *Ruckus Manhattan* present typical subway crowds of the 1970s—the former in a large-format painting, the latter in an immersive mixed-media environment.[24] Like Reginald Marsh, both these artists work in the satiric mode. Unlike Marsh in his sketches of the subway crowd, however, these artists eschew representing a sense of shared purpose among the passengers. The tribalism of *The Warriors,* Walter Hill's cult film of 1979 based on a Sol Yurick novel, seems to be a logical extension of their comically grotesque visions. So does the image of the subway presented in the January 1992 episode of *Seinfeld* called "The Subway," with its nudists, con artists, and gamblers. As with the best episodes of that show, the joke is how well the main characters fit in with this motley crew.

Like the vision of the subway as underworld that became part of the popular image of New York City in the last third of the twentieth century, the vision of the subway crowd in this era inverts any of the optimism still associated with the discourse of the melting pot. No one melts, and the traits that distinguish passengers from one another are all negative. The anxiety about the subway crowd burst dramatically to the surface in the Bernhard Goetz shootings in 1984,[25] as well as Atlanta Braves pitcher John Rocker's ESPN interview in 2000, in which he famously derided the 7 train to Queens, which Mets fans would ride to Shea Stadium, as one where you might sit "next to some kid with purple hair next to some queer with AIDS right next to some dude who just got out of jail for the fourth time right next to some 20-year-old mom with four kids" (Pearlman). Rocker's list offers a conservative mirror image to the one presented in the works of Evans and Saroyan; instead of ethnic diversity, he imagines a diversity of deviance. Even the repetition of the word "four"—the mother with four kids, the convict who has served four terms—suggests a kind of eugenic paranoia, one that imagines the subway car as a place where these types of New Yorkers endlessly replicate.

Yet Rocker's homophobic and anti-immigrant sentiment marked the tail end of a forty-year streak of pessimism about the subway as a vehicle of multiculturalism, one that coincided with a downturn both in the city's finances and in subway safety. The image of the subway as a metaphorical melting pot persists in the twenty-first century, and the very train that he so scorned has replaced the Bronx Express as its representative. On July 26, 1999, First Lady Hillary Rodham Clinton designated the 7 train a "National Millennium Trail," calling it the "International Express." She proclaimed: "The Number Seven Train through Queens, New York, connects a series of immigrant neighborhoods and is a metaphor for the migration of all the world's people to America's shores. Pakistani, Irish, Romanian, African-American, Italian, Korean, Hispanic, Indian, Argentinean and other ethnic neighborhoods are connected and available for exploration and cultural discovery on this route from Sunnyside to Flushing" (White House Millennium Council). Here the subway takes on the discursive properties ascribed to the melting pot; it is valuable not just as a connector between different "immigrant neighborhoods" but as a stand-in for all immigration to America. This designation put the subway line in the company of such storied paths through American history as the Underground Railroad and the trail followed by the explorers Lewis and Clark. It codifies an attention to history as produced in transit rather than pinned down in fixed locations, the distinction that Paul Gilroy has memorably made between "routes" and "roots."

A number of stories in the media have since developed this understanding of the 7 train as the symbol of diversity. CNN comments on the multilingual quality of business in Queens ("Travel: The No. 7"), the *New York Times* on its cultural vibrancy (Brawarsky); somewhat grandiosely, the *Christian Science Monitor* calls it "the living lab of this experiment we call 'America'" (Sosa). Yet in all of these stories, the focus shifts from the immigrants' movements between Manhattan and Queens to their self-sufficient lives within the borough itself. We might uncharitably read the "Millennium Trails" announcement as a call for postmillennial slumming, since the availability of the neighborhoods "for exploration and cultural discovery" implies that non-ethnic Americans will be the ones doing the discovering. The *Times* article celebrating the "International Expressions" festival imagines ethnic neighborhoods as stops on "a monorail," turning the stretch of Queens into a smaller and more authentic Epcot Center. Unlike *Bronx Express*, the coverage of the 7 train appears resolutely from the perspective of the visitor: though these destinations seem worlds away, they are "less than a half-hour ride from Grand Central Terminal" (Brawarsky). It depends on the new generation of multiethnic American writers to unpack this discourse from an insider's point of view as Dymov did; perhaps Gary Shteyngart or Gish Jen will imagine a *Flushing Express* in response.

The subway car and the subway system often play conflicting roles in the cultural imaginary of New York City. While the car itself can be a site of clashes between passengers of different ethnic backgrounds, the subway system helps imaginatively put those ethnic groups in their proper places. The subway line becomes an imaginative structure for celebrating and containing pluralism. Although the (white Anglo-Saxon) people at the center now acknowledge that they may have something to learn from the (ethnic) people at the periphery, the hierarchy between center and periphery remains. In this way, the claims that Carolyn Marvin makes about nineteenth-century media hold true for twentieth-century transportation. The residents of Manhattan may venture to Queens for excellent Thai noodles or Greek pastries, but these foods are supplementary, not a central part of New York's culture.

For African American writers in modern New York, however, the subway can undo the established relation between center and periphery. As we see in the next chapter, the prose writers of the Harlem Renaissance establish an image of the subway as an uncanny repetition of the railroad, one that undoes the unidirectional flow of nineteenth-century migration narratives. Rather than equating travel north with travel toward a life of freedom, they suggest that the habitual and circular movement of the subway allows for an uncanny repetition of southern knowledge in northern space. Writers such as Rudolph Fisher and Ralph Ellison repeat the ironic lessons of their turn-of-the-century predecessors, particularly James Weldon Johnson, for whom the freedom promised by the train is illusory at best. In their narratives, southern migrants flee their pasts, which continue to confront them in the underground spaces of the northern city. Whereas pluralist ethnic writers insisted that ethnicity could be contained in discrete neighborhoods, African American writers used the uncanniness of the subway to insist that northern and southern culture remain intertwined.

# CHAPTER 5

# UNCANNY MIGRATION NARRATIVES

In the early twentieth century, Jewish New Yorkers could assimilate to the broader understanding of white American culture (as nineteenth-century German Jews did) or maintain their cultural specificity in a manner more common among the eastern European immigrants who came to the United States around the turn of the century. Some early-arriving German Jews take pains to distinguish themselves from their working-class brethren, a distinction we can see from William Dean Howells's novel *A Hazard of New Fortunes* (1890) to Alfred Uhry's play *The Last Night of Ballyhoo* (1996). In the early twentieth century, class bias within African American culture takes on a similar character, particularly in the post–World War I era popularly known as the Great Migration, when a massive population of working-class southern blacks moved to northern cities.[1] As Kevin Gaines's work shows, the reception of southern migrants by their northern brethren was not as warm as might be imagined; the influx of working-class laborers threatens the elites' sense of their own progress and identity (88–89). Consequently, "the better class" of northern African Americans asserts their claim to that title by mocking or otherwise differentiating themselves from the new arrivals. They do so in a discourse that is very often filtered through discussions of transportation technology.

For educated African Americans, public transportation presents not only the opportunity for mobility but the opportunity for harassment as well. The Harlem Renaissance gadfly George Schuyler discusses the difficulties encountered by "the better class" of African Americans in a 1930 *American Mercury* essay, "Traveling Jim Crow," in which he celebrates the American desire for travel but decries the lack of access to decent accommodations for African Americans on the road. We learn the strategies that educated black passengers use to avoid harassment while taking a trip by train: one woman dons an apron when her train crosses the Mason-Dixon line, "a badge of servility" that renders her less likely to be disturbed in the dining and sleeping cars (Schuyler 425). Schuyler presents the American landscape as a minefield of bad experiences: for instance, in some cities white taxi drivers will pick up black passengers, while in others they will not. Owning an automobile in this period is attractive to African Americans, he suggests, not merely as a badge of wealth but as a means of avoiding precisely these kinds of pitfalls.[2]

Although the racism in effect in post–*Plessy v. Ferguson* America is contemptible,[3] Schuyler finds it so for a specific reason: racial segregation of public accommodations lumps together black travelers of all classes indiscriminately, even though "a hotel or rooming-house quite satisfactory to stevedores, laborers and field hands would hardly be to the taste of a school teacher, a physician or an artist" (424). The ideology of "uplift" and the cultivation of refined taste mean nothing in such circumstances. Public transportation is a fraught topic for upper-class black writers because it's yet another space where collective judgment takes place in the bluntest of racial terms.

In a section of her autobiography *Dust Tracks on a Road*, Zora Neale Hurston illustrates this dilemma as it arises on the New York subway. A college-educated couple boards the subway, returning home to Harlem from a concert given by the soprano Marian Anderson. They are attractive and cultured, and they take great pride in the achievements of black inventors, sculptors, and singers. They are feel themselves to be exemplary in "the eyes of the entire coach" (Hurston 773) until two more black passengers board at Seventy-second Street. Hurston describes them as "scabby-looking," "dirty and smelly," the polar opposite of the first couple (773). Even their language separates them from the two refined graduates of Barnard and Yale: while the concert-goers are quoted directly and speak in uninflected English, the working-class black passengers "woof, bookoo, broadcast, and otherwise distriminate [*sic*] from one end of the coach to the other" (773). Curiously, the slangy dialect of these passengers is not conveyed directly; instead, it infects the narrative voice itself. The subject of their conversation is equally lowdown: instead of talking about cultural uplift, they trade jests about how each man beats his woman. "Barnard and Yale" are horrified. They imagine that the white passengers see not them but their "scabby-looking" brethren as typical of the race (774). As in the Jim Crow cars on the railroads, subway cars cause the black bourgeois a deep anxiety because of the "forced grouping" of all black passengers (774).

In this chapter I unpack the racial, spatial, and temporal anxieties associated with African American subway ridership. Reading the Great Migration through the lens of subway movement shows us how technology both underpins and complicates the class consciousness of black intellectuals in the period. Unpacking the subway's meaning in dialogue with alternate forms of transportation such as the railroad and the automobile offers a more historically and geographically specific understanding of how African Americans moved through the country in the early twentieth century, as well as how they understood the meaning of that movement. These forms of transportation connote differences in class, gender, region, and even history. Initially the migrants in the stories I describe are shown grappling with the unfamiliar technologized landscape by using southern folk imagery; even after they acclimate to the city, the subway and other underground sites function as uncanny spaces where southern memories and figures return. The technology of the subway holds this status in African American fiction, I argue, because its hidden tunnels offer a model for imagining personal and regional history that depends on repeated underground circulation rather than unidirectional migration or memories rooted in southern places that persist in northern locales. Like Hart Crane, African American fiction writers find in the subway a model for partial and provisional connection to the past.

The subway had a direct impact on the development of Harlem as the capital of black culture. "In a very real sense," writes Brian McCammack, "Harlem would not have existed as blacks knew it in the 1920s and '30s had subway planners not built a line up Lenox Avenue decades earlier" (976).

Critics from James Weldon Johnson onward have described the meager population of African Americans in the Tenderloin District at the turn of the century, the real estate speculation along the soon-to-be-built Lenox Avenue line, the construction delays, and the desperate landlords who finally rent to black tenants at inflated prices.[4] Perhaps the most emblematic subway ride to Harlem is the one undertaken by King Solomon Gillis, the central character in Rudolph Fisher's 1925 short story "The City of Refuge," who typifies the mix of enthusiasm, naïveté, and materialism seen in literary migrants of the era.[5] Gillis's initial emergence from the disorienting, mechanized subway space into the utopia of Harlem became a defining experience of migration to New York City, one repeated thousands more times in the years to come.

In fact, Gillis's arrival was a cliché by the time he engaged in it. Small-time crook Mouse Uggam tells his bootlegger boss that he spotted Gillis "where you find all the jay birds when they first hit Harlem—at the subway entrance. This one come up the stairs, batted his eyes once or twice, an' froze to the spot—with his mouth open" (Fisher, *City of Refuge* 38). This dismissive attitude toward novice Harlemites was not limited to small-time crooks. David Levering Lewis invokes Fisher's most famous character in his assertion that racial uplift was not able to cross class lines. "It was clear to the articulate and civic-minded of Harlem," writes Lewis, "that a metropolis of New Negroes was not to be made with the thousands of Gillises stumbling out of the 135th Street subway or swaying up Lenox Avenue atop overloaded carts and trucks" (34). Unlike the (wealthier) German and (poorer) Russian Jews who arrived in New York at different times and settled in different areas of the city, black New Yorkers of all classes lived chiefly in the same neighborhood. This led to the kinds of divisions described by Lewis, whereby the "articulate and civic-minded" Harlemites evinced a deep suspicion of the newcomers, who were mostly southern, rural, and working class. Gillis and his ilk "stumble" out of the subway instead of moving smoothly through the crowd, while their "overloaded carts and trucks" suggest the presence of cultural baggage as well as their embarrassing abundance of literal baggage. The presence of "thousands of Gillises" in the Harlem streets reshaped modern African American culture toward what Kenneth Warren calls a "telos of urbanization" (398), one that changed the terms under which African American leaders operated. Urban development, real estate, and transportation all defined the borders of the community.

The subway runs through the history of Harlem and the history of the Harlem migration narrative. Indeed, Langston Hughes collapses his subway journey with his journey to literary fame in a late essay in *Freedomways* which begins, "On a bright September morning in 1921, I came up out of the subway at 135th and Lenox into the beginnings of the Negro Renaissance" (*Essays on Art* 395). This connection between narrative and neighborhood develops in Fisher's "City of Refuge" and a later and better-known novel influenced by the story, Ralph Ellison's *Invisible Man.* Lawrence Rodgers points out the parallel between the two stories, in which both protagonists emerge into Harlem and gaze wonderingly at the black policemen (2). Similarly, both narratives imagine the subway as the belly of a whale and its passengers as Jonah. Most interesting to me is their shared understanding of the subway as a vehicle with both a diegetic function and a metaphorical one: the fulcrum between a southern past and a northern future, it also serves as a repository for southern folk knowledge and personal history that reappears in uncanny ways. Migration narratives play an important role in shaping the image of Harlem presented by the black intelligentsia. These posit Harlem as the logical end to any African American's journey, and they test the limits that race and class place upon the archetypal American narrative of self-invention.

Throughout this chapter I highlight the ways in which the subway facilitates what Leigh Anne Duck calls "temporal collisions," instances when a text violently foregrounds "the region's and the nation's multiple temporal forms" (8). This occurs both when migrants are juxtaposed with their more urbane counterparts and when their narratives call upon the tropes of earlier migration and slave narratives. The disjunctions between migrants and more cosmopolitan Harlemites can be understood not merely as a culture clash but as a clash between different understandings of historical time. And the difficulties that poor migrants face can be understood less as failures in character than as failures in temporality. Because of this radical difference between modern and premodern ways of life, southern migrants were imagined as pathologically unable to adapt to northern schedules and routines (Duck 120). Even for writers like Hurston, who did depict the southern African American experience and not just the escape from it, the South's appeal was thought to be "uncanny—a dangerous nostalgia for an experience inaccessible to modern subjects and, furthermore, inextricably linked to racist exploitation" (Duck 116). The migrants present in northern cities serve a similarly uncanny purpose. In his essay "The 'Uncanny,'" Sigmund Freud discusses the uniquely creepy feeling that comes from the recognition of a repressed experience or idea from one's past (217). Migration narratives offer assimilated African American readers the uncanny experience of recognizing repressed truths about their own experiences.

The subway serves as an important northern technology for exploring the uncanny recurrence of southern figures and beliefs. Because underground movement by subway is not bound by the direct connective logic of aboveground movement, African American writers use it to imagine a complex continuity between temporalities. The abrupt movement of the subway can be thought of as a figure for the disjunctive, repetitive, and irrational relation to tradition portrayed in these narratives. The subway entrance, in a sense, spans folk and modern time. In doing so, it gives African American writers an opportunity to reconsider and extend the metaphors of modernity that earlier writers had associated with the railroad.

## The Railroad and the Subway

The train has played a central role in African American self-definition, from antebellum spirituals to contemporary novels like Colson Whitehead's *John Henry Days* (2001).[6] So why do modern African American writers consider the subway along with, or even instead of, the train? In part they do so in order to scale down the promise of that mythological machine; a journey between areas of the city is less remarkable than one between regions of the country. Yet the subway ride is not merely a fallen imitation of the railroad journey north. Writers of these modern migration narratives locate new possibilities for representing African American culture in the passivity, spatial restriction, and repetition of subway movement, elements that reframe our understanding of migration by railroad. The subway offers a ghostly image of a Jim Crow train car while simultaneously suggesting a new model of African American mobility. For early twentieth-century writers, it is a form of transit that stages the temporal disjuncture of African American life, in part by repeating and revising ideas first presented in narratives of the railroad.

The representation of the railroad in African American culture becomes a central symbol of freedom and independence. Lawrence Levine highlights the importance of movement as a theme in African American music from the early nineteenth century onward (261). The railroad regularly appears as a vehicle of liberation in gospel, folk, and blues songs. As Mark Simpson reminds us, Americans assume a connection between motion and new forms of consciousness: travel leads to alienation from familiar truths, which in turn leads to a more refined understanding of oneself in relation to the world (9). He also notes that the mobility of slaves troubles this model; so too does the mobility of post-Reconstruction migrants. African American culture after *Plessy v. Ferguson* understood railroad movement in a more nuanced way: while it offered freedom of movement from place to place, the necessary price was restricted movement on the train itself.

Wolfgang Schivelbusch theorizes the perception of railway passengers as "panoramic," with the passing scenes experienced as a distanced blur or spectacle (52–69). Because it is rooted in spatial restriction, African Americans' movement by train cannot wholly be understood by using the same model of perception. In most cases, African American movement by train does not allow for the leisure and detachment inherent in this way of seeing. Nineteenth- and early twentieth-century African American railroad passengers tended to experience a limited perspective, whether riding in a crowded Jim Crow car, a cramped railway kitchen, or the hiding place of a stowaway or hobo. An extreme version of this limited perspective can be seen in the spatial disorientation of slaves escaping north by the Underground Railroad, since movement between "stations" had to follow an evasive, indirect path and usually took place in darkness or in hiding (Siebert 54–55, 62). In perhaps the most dramatic example, detailed in *The Narrative of Henry Box Brown* (1849), a slave ships himself to freedom by hiding in a two-by-three-foot wooden box and traveling in a mail coach (Rodgers 127).

Although African American railway passengers in the twentieth century were not as restricted in their movements as Box Brown, they too had to reshape their subjectivity into acceptable forms, like the educated woman who wears an apron to pass as a servant. Because of its restricted perspective and disorienting accommodations, African Americans in this period often find that travel by railroad is uncanny. Schuyler mentions many other passengers for whom booking passage and traveling by railroad means confronting the previously known and repressed truths about racial prejudice in America. Moving from the railroad to the underground space of the subway also emphasizes the disorientation that is constitutive of Ernst Jentsch's definition of uncanniness. For Jentsch, the uncanny is "something one does not know one's way about in" (Freud, "The 'Uncanny'" 195). Freud reframes his mentor's ideas about disorientation as repressed recognition; in discussing the word's etymology, he points out that *heimlich* means pleasantly familiar but also hidden and concealed (199). Railroad movement thus can be connected to subway movement in African American culture because both share the element of deceit and obscurity utterly absent from white passengers' understandings of the railroad.

The trope of the railroad as a site of claustrophobia continued even after slavery ended, with the narrator of James Weldon Johnson's *Autobiography of an Ex-Colored Man* stowing away in a Pullman porter's linen closet (65). Both Johnson's narrator and Box Brown suffer for their journeys, feeling the social restrictions of race and class imprint themselves on their bodies. The Ex-Colored Man, writes Johnson, is "bumped and bruised against the narrow walls" of his compartment (65), physicalizing how the narrator repeatedly chafes against the restrictiveness of possible roles for educated African Americans. Box Brown "narrowly avoided permanent injuries" (Rodgers 127) from his journey, which suggests more fatal possibilities for fugitive slaves. The railroad is not an escape from the physical constraints of the passenger's body but a stark reminder of them.

Fisher depicts the claustrophobia of subway space as a physically felt link with that of the railroad. The claustrophobia of Gillis's subway ride is clearly associated with the railroad, as we can hear in the fellow passenger's joke, "Wha' d'ye think this is, a baggage car?" (Fisher, *City of Refuge* 35). This jest about Gillis being laden with bags also evokes Jim Crow railroad cars, which often doubled as baggage cars. Gillis has traded restricted movement shared with members of his race alone for restricted movement shared equally with all city dwellers. In this way, the subway functions quite differently from the northern streetcar, a form of transportation that is repeatedly figured in terms of absolute difference from its southern counterpart. The Progressive Era journalist Ray Stannard Bakker calls "street car relationships" between black and white passengers "symbolic of new conditions" (30). According to Julia Lee, even Asian memoirists of this period understood the streetcar to be a more egalitarian space than the train (361). The streetcar's openness to the air and the absence of the severe overcrowding seen on subways made it more clearly a physical alternative to the cramped railroad as well as the explicitly segregated southern bus.[7] The subway, however, maintains the restrictions of the railroad in an urban environment. Because of their palpable similarity, the subway becomes the most prominent form of northern transit continually to evoke the southern past emotionally, even as it contradicts many tenets of Jim Crow segregation. White modernists often deploy the claustrophobic subway as a spatial metaphor for the modern subject's new insignificance in relation to the urban infrastructure. Subway migration narratives, by contrast, participate in the African American cultural tradition that portrays confinement as a necessary precondition for freedom. Thus the physical restriction inherent in subway movement offers a means for migrants to imagine their journey as it relates to a larger African American tradition.

At the turn of the century the African American migrant would have entered New York City by ferry, in the same fashion as any other new arrival. Manhattan could be reached overland only by the Brooklyn Bridge (Ballon 19). Trains moving up the eastern seaboard from Philadelphia, Baltimore, and points south stopped at Jersey City. There the entire railway crowd would debark and board ferries to Manhattan, which caused a bottleneck of tremendous proportions. Thus the railroad plays a central role in turn-of-the-century migration narratives, but it does not account for the distanced visions of New York in Paul Laurence Dunbar's *Sport of the Gods* (1902) and James Weldon Johnson's *Autobiography of an Ex-Colored Man* (1912).[8] Dunbar observes that "the provincial coming to New York for the first time" must feel "a thrill as he crosses the ferry over the river filled with plying craft and catches the first sight of the spires and buildings of New York" (49). For Johnson's Ex-Colored Man, the initial vision of New York City is a "fatally fascinating" allegory for the temptations of modern urban life. A parody of the Statue of Liberty, "she [meaning the city] sits like a great witch at the gate of the country, showing her alluring white face and hiding her crooked hands and feet under the folds of her wide garments" (89). In these accounts the narrator gives his readers a sense of the city encountered at a distance, an experience that decreases in importance once the railroad, the underground tunnel to Pennsylvania Station, and the subway join together as a technological ensemble.

Alterations in the built environment of New York City at the dawn of the Great Migration made migration qualitatively different from what it had been in the past—both more efficient and more passive. Railroad movement was streamlined in 1910 with the opening of Pennsylvania Station; trains could now tunnel beneath the Hudson River and emerge in

Manhattan.[9] This tunneling into New York had narrative consequences as well as geographic ones: Harlem began to seem less like a conscious destination and more like the inevitable end to an underground journey. In the era when the automobile promised heightened agency, the railroad and the subway conspired to take it away. The first two paragraphs of "The City of Refuge" put this distinction in sharp relief by illustrating how little Gillis has to do with his own journey north. As he stands poised on the subway steps at 135th Street and Lenox Avenue, King Solomon Gillis thinks back over how he has arrived there. He remembers "the railroad station, the long, white-walled corridor, the impassible slot machine, the terrifying subway train" (Fisher, *City of Refuge* 35). The "long, white-walled corridor" in Fisher's description is a tunnel that connects the area of Pennsylvania Station where railroad passengers exited their trains with the entrance to the subway. Although the 135th Street station in Harlem opened as part of the initial IRT line in 1904, the subway connection to Harlem inside Penn Station did not open until 1917, making it almost exactly coincident with the Great Migration (Pirmann). Gillis's journey through the railroad station to the subway, and his subway ride to Harlem, are described concretely and thoroughly; his railroad journey from Washington, DC, to New York, on the contrary, is not described at all. And the "slot machine," a defamiliarized vision of the subway turnstile, underscores Gillis's sense that luck alone has sent him north: he drops a nickel in, and the machine decides if it will allow him to keep moving.[10] The arrival of migrants in Harlem seems to have less to do with their willpower than with a series of external forces guiding them there.

The subway works against the dominant trope of the *New Negro* anthology, which associates the South with the past and the North with the present and future. For Alain Locke, who initiates this connection in his introductory essay "The New Negro," migration is a conscious journey in time as well as space. History is no longer linear. He argues that northern migrants "hurdle several generations of experience at a leap" (Locke 4). This future-oriented rhetorical strategy may have been the easiest way to emphasize the urgency and the novelty of his cultural project. The emphasis on migrants' lack of explicit agency offers an important corrective to the optimism of Locke and the boosters of the New Negro. The passivity and disorientation of migrant subway passengers affiliates them with both earlier literary migrants and present-day city dwellers.[11] In this way, subway migration becomes an important figure for effecting the partial and provisional identifications that Kenneth Warren finds to be so important in the creation of a diasporic community (393). Migrants do not separate themselves from modern urban subjects by submitting to the subway; instead, their feeling of passivity and disorientation anticipates sensations that modern commuters deal with every day. Gillis makes sense of his first subway ride as an imagined submission to a fantastic machine. He feels "as if he had been caught up in the jaws of a steam-shovel, jammed together with other helpless lumps of dirt, swept blindly along for a time, and at last abruptly dumped" (Fisher, *City of Refuge* 35). A steam shovel transporting soil to an industrialized northern space, the subway seems to be a machine of the Great Migration in miniature. This racialized imagery is turned back on itself, however, since *all* the passengers, black and white, are "helpless lumps of dirt." The subway should be understood as a machine that epitomizes New York City's constant development, both racial and spatial.[12]

The repeated movement of the subway, like the repeated movement of migrants into Harlem, is a mindless cycle; both are forces of city life that don't care who or what they're consuming. The subway mitigates the apparent linearity of railroad migration. The railroad gives the illusion of a unidirectional trip, one that migrants carry with them when they first emerge in Harlem. We see this process at work in Langston Hughes's descriptions of "Southern Harlem" as well. Though the new Harlemites may be "dressed in rhythmic words, painted in bright pictures, dancing to jazz," he still imagines them "ending up in the subway in morning rush time—*headed downtown*" (*Essays on Art* 397). Yet this element of the urban infrastructure also transports commuters between work and home. The cyclical quality of subway movement, then, works against any sense of linearity or progress in the migration narrative. As we will see in the following section, the southern past is equally cyclical: never fully abandoned upon arrival in the northern city, it returns at unexpected moments and confronts the narratives' protagonists with unexpected reminders of their history.

## Southern Time in Northern Space

The influx of migrants from the South complicated the experience of urban African American culture. These new arrivals brought southern folkways into northern cities that had defined themselves in opposition to the region:

fast where the South was slow, forward-thinking where the South was backward-looking, modern where the South was traditional. The "articulate and civic-minded" citizens of Harlem to whom David Levering Lewis refers were anxious about accommodating migrants into the collective black culture of the 1920s not only because they belonged largely to a different class but because they seemed to belong to a different time as well.[13] In this section I delineate some of the ways that modern migration narratives understood this blurring of the line between southern and northern time. Here I develop Leigh Anne Duck's argument that Harlem Renaissance writers are deeply concerned with "the paradoxical nature of modern time: though it may be understood to be uniform across space, not all subjects in all spaces are understood to participate in it uniformly" (117). Although the stewards of the Harlem Renaissance imagine time in teleological terms, the newcomers participate in modern time only insofar as they use modern transportation. The presence of migrants in Harlem Renaissance narratives, like the presence of the subway that transports them to Harlem, works against the teleology of progress but is also enabled by technological innovation.[14]

Fisher and Ellison find in the restrictive movement of the subway and the relationship between the subway and the city a means of articulating the complex and troubled relationship between tradition and modernity, a central concern of African American literature from the Harlem Renaissance to the present day. As in *Bronx Express*, African American migration narratives emphasize just how difficult the acculturation to norms of urban life was for these immigrants. "Black Southerners" may have been, in Andrew Huddle's terms, "remade in the urban crucible," but their southern identity and folk knowledge were not immediately "stripped away" (260). Instead, the play between regions, temporalities, and ways of knowing constitutes much of the conflict in migration narratives. The way their protagonists grapple with the relationship between old and new illustrates the difficulty in reconciling past and present. Fisher, for instance, shows us how the southern migrant's move to the city carries on southern realities even as it disavows them; Ellison's novel implies that the only way African Americans can deal with their personal and cultural history is through an acceptance of the past as something that rises up into the present at unexpected moments and can never be entirely hidden or rewritten.

Much of the critical discussion of migration narratives has focused on the need for spaces or figures that reinforce communal southern mores in the northern city.[15] In her influential essay "City Limits, Village Values," Toni Morrison suggests that African American characters in the city succeed or fail depending on their connection to the ancestral past they have left behind (43). More interesting to me than valuing folk knowledge over street smarts (since by the end of "The City of Refuge" the central character has both) is thinking about how the subway offers a space and a model for the subterranean linkage between regions and temporalities. We begin to see this relation to the past as soon as the migrant protagonists board the subway. Confronted with an utterly disorienting urban scene, they call upon their rural knowledge in order to make sense of it. Although the knowledge is imperfect, indeed somewhat humorously so, it helps them begin to forge connections between the lives they've left behind and the lives they're beginning.

With this focus on the subway as a vehicle of connection between southern and northern culture, I turn now to the concerns that prevail in current conversations about Rudolph Fisher's importance to the African American literary canon. Critics often discuss Fisher's stories as attempts to construct an urban black culture that partakes equally of the folk and the modern.[16] Characters who embody folk values tend to be the heroes, tempering the effect of the city through appeals to shared history or culture. For example, the grandmother in "The Promised Land" tries to stop her grandsons from fighting by throwing the Bible at them (Fisher, *City of Refuge* 82); in "Common Meter," bandleader Fess Baxter transports a dancehall crowd with an old-style southern blues number (Fisher, *City of Refuge* 182). In "The City of Refuge," however, King Solomon Gillis is not the font of ancient wisdom his name suggests. Rather than a cultural repository, Gillis is a comic type—the country fool who thinks his luck will change once he comes to the big city. And though Gillis maintain's a connection to his rural past through flashbacks as well as his friendship with fellow Waxhaw, North Carolina, native Mouse Uggam, neither can prevent him from going to jail. The character's reliance on southern imagery in northern space is important not because it comforts Gillis with familiar elements of his past, but because it shows the reader just how strange his experience feels.

Fisher, Ellison, and the migrants they portray all look at the daily life of Harlem from the perspectives of outsiders. In this way we can see how migration as a plot point enables the writer to engage in a common narrative strategy of modernism: defamiliarization. In one of the most experimental passages of "The City of Refuge," Gillis maneuvers his way through Pennsylvania Station, boards the subway, and rides it to Harlem. But rather than describing Gillis's actions, the narrative evokes the shifting noises of the city that surround him. Fisher thus illustrates the bewilderment of his migrant protagonist by presenting a decontextualized catalogue of "strange and terrible sounds":

> "New York! Penn Terminal—all change!" "Pohter, hyer, pohter, suh?" Shuffle of a thousand soles, clatter of a thousand heels, innumerable echoes. Cracking rifle-shots—no, snapping turnstiles. "Put a nickel in!" "Harlem? Sure. This side—next train." Distant thunder, nearing. The screeching onslaught of the fiery hosts of hell, headlong, breath-taking. Car doors rattling, sliding, banging open. "Say, wha' d'ye think this is, a baggage car?" Heat, oppression, suffocation—eternity—"Hundred'n turdy-fif' next!" More turnstiles. Jonah emerging from the whale. (35)

Like Charles Ives's *Central Park in the Dark* and Georges Antheil's *Ballet Mecanique,* this part of Fisher's story creates an urban symphony of disorientation.[17] Few of the sounds are described in full sentences: they are telegraphic, dependent on gerunds that suggest motion in progress. In a story marked elsewhere by an ironic distance from its protagonist, this passage collapses Gillis's and the narrator's perspective to remarkable effect. The cacophony of city life, when heard anew through a migrant's ears, can still shock even the most jaded New Yorker. Authors choose to tell the story from the perspective of arriving migrants, notes Farah Jasmine Griffin, in order to "document the impact of urban modernism, dislocation, and confusion on them" (49). They often do so using narrative techniques that render the reader equally dislocated and confused. In this way the defamiliarization of migration narratives enacts a kind of slippage between the unsophisticated new arrival and the sophisticated reader.

In his extended attention to Gillis's initial subway ride, Fisher focuses on an experience of urban modernity that white modernist writers tend to shun. According to the historian Emily Thompson, southern African Americans moving to northern cities "would have experienced an aural transformation" (132), with a wide range of noises that they would have had no experience in processing. Throughout this passage we see Gillis trying to make sense of his surroundings by using southern folk knowledge. He repeatedly attempts to understand northern space in southern terms: he compares his tiny apartment to a chicken coop and imagines the values of Harlem dwellers as similar to those of his southern black community.[18] Underground he uses religious imagery—Jonah, the "fiery hosts of hell"—to reckon with the sublimity of the unfamiliar space. Perhaps most revealingly, Gillis hears echoes of southern violence in the subway. His anxiety about fleeing his southern crimes leads him momentarily to locate himself in a remembered landscape, one where men with rifles pursue him. He mishears his surroundings, then corrects his perception: "Cracking rifle-shots—no, snapping turnstiles." As we will see again when I discuss the conclusion to "The City of Refuge," Fisher suggests that misrecognition can sometimes offer a truer sense of the subject's relationship to his or her surroundings than correct perception might. Like Hungerproud's dream of being lynched, Gillis's sense of danger on the subway is wrong on the surface, but his mishearing reveals an understanding of the parallels between spaces and situations that he could not consciously articulate. His disoriented sense perception links past and present, marking this space of transit as a true space of transition.

In the Harlem Renaissance in particular, images of southernness were used ironically as a way for characters to resist the "uplift ideology" of the era, which held that hard work at the white man's game would translate into material gain and upward mobility (Gaines 2–3). The sense of disappointment in the outcome of the Great Migration comes to the fore in Wallace Thurman's play *Harlem,* written with William Jourdan Rapp. Jasper Williams, the son who encouraged his family to move to the North, calls Harlem "the city of refuge"; his mother dismissively calls it the "City of Refuse" (Thurman 322). One conversation between the Williams patriarch and a fellow migrant compares the subway unfavorably to the experience of the South:

> JENKS: I stood all the way up in de subway. Thought I never would get home. Come up on de local. The jam and push of de express was too much fo' me.
>
> FATHER: Dat's one thing. Dey may lynch you down home, but dey shure don't squeeze you to death on no subway. (Thurman 328)

Thurman's dialogue would have been understood ironically by a Broadway audience; although the pressures of urban life are intense, they hardly compare to the threat of a possible lynching. The father's reply foregrounds the difference between southern and northern mechanisms of control over African American workers: while the former operate through threats of violence, the latter operate through the subtle domination of mechanized routine (Griffin 74). Again we see radical defamiliarization through the construction of metaphors that span regions: the apartment building as an urban chicken coop, the subway ride as a slow lynching.

Here Thurman contrasts the violence of the South with the temporal regulation of the North in much the same way as Langston Hughes's essay "The Negro Artist and the Racial Mountain," in which Hughes calls the irregular rhythms of jazz a "tom-tom of revolt against weariness in a white world, a world of subway trains, and work, work, work" (*Essays on Art* 35). Though the northern city may be associated with the present and the future, writers of the Harlem Renaissance associated their work with earlier temporalities, even the "primitive" time associated with "tom-toms," offering their readers and listeners an alternative to their Taylorist workday. Hughes undercuts a common criticism of migrants in the period. He also notes the stark division between modern and premodern (one might say primitive) ways of life discussed by Leigh Anne Duck, but he values the latter instead of the former. Hughes uses that presumed disjunction to point out that it is not the migrants but rather northern time itself that needs fixing.

Ralph Ellison focuses on the physicality of the subway in an equally estranging way, one that offers a useful corrective to readings of the subway as a vehicle of equality and freedom.[19] The narrator of *Invisible Man* conveys his urban experience with a rural image when he boards the New York subway, where "everyone seemed to stand with his head back and his eyes bulging, like chickens frozen at the sound of danger" (158). He narrates the difficulty of adjusting to a new social code and the discovery that southern knowledge can succeed in some instances and fail in others. In doing so, he turns the whole subway car into a henhouse. This ridiculous image evokes the stereotype of black poultry thieving so popular in minstrel shows, but then it is quickly transformed into something more threatening. The narrator finds himself "crushed against" a white woman, and he fears that his proximity will start a race riot, as the mere suggestion of sexual interest in the same woman would have done in his hometown. The difference between South and North is made clear when the narrator looks around and finds that "no one was paying [him] the slightest attention" (158). Though this may be true, the leap from one set of rules to another is too much for the narrator to process, and he eventually becomes so uncomfortable that he debarks before his intended stop.

In migration narratives of the period, the subway functions as an underground link between northern and southern culture. The migrant may call on southern knowledge to help orient himself in the modern city, or he may use southern "spaces, rituals, and belief systems" to maintain a sense of continuity (Griffin 52). Both of these models assume a conscious deployment of memory and history, however, whereas the authors of this period were far more interested in the unconscious mind and its mixed emotional realities. Rudolph Fisher's short stories repeatedly show the internal conflicts of migrants to Harlem who mourn their lost communities even while embracing the opportunities available in the otherwise harsh city. Similarly, we see Ellison's narrator struggle to come to terms with his own past. The New York subway system functions as an important site for reconciling these mixed emotions because it is a site of underground linkages and repetitions. In the next section we see how the subway's representation of the southern past makes an impact on the self-conception of modern migrants and modern readers. Although the uncanny recurrence of the past can be frightening, Ellison's novel in particular shows how it can lead to insight and laughter.

## The Uncanny Subway

"The City of Refuge" and *Invisible Man* reveal the problems with reading migration as a linear, progressive movement. Although Fisher's protagonist committed murder and Ellison's merely offended a white college trustee, both imagine their exodus to Harlem as a clean break from the past. This proves impossible, however, since the central characters encounter figures whom they knew in the South. Mouse Uggam is just as surprised by Gillis's appearance at the subway entrance as Gillis is by Uggam: at first neither recognizes the other. Uggam still manages to take advantage of his fellow small-town North Carolinian once he remembers their previous association. Similarly, the narrator in *Invisible Man* repeatedly encounters foods, objects, and even people from his southern past. The novel ends with his spotting Mr. Norton, the trustee, on a subway platform; the white man who indirectly caused his banishment from college is now the one who's lost. Migration does not allow for an escape from the past, we learn, because movement north *isn't* one way or restricted to migrants who want to begin their life anew.

Encounters with the past take place at unexpected moments as characters wander the streets of Harlem. "One had to be on guard," Ellison warns in his essay "An Extravagance of Laughter," "because reminders of the South could spring up from behind the most unlikely of facades" (160). Sometimes these chance meetings have a positive effect, as in Rudolph Fisher's story "The South Lingers On," when Ezekiel Taylor sings a hymn to himself and hears it taken up by a chorus that includes members of his former congregation (61). Sometimes they have negative, even fatal consequences, as they do when Helga Crane in Nella Larsen's *Quicksand* finds temporary shelter in a storefront church where "people were singing a song which she was conscious of having heard years ago—hundreds of years it seemed" (110–11).[20] The prominence of this narrative structure in the fiction of the Harlem Renaissance in particular reminds us of the complicated relationship between North and South, modernity and tradition. The strongholds of slavery- and post-slavery-era African American culture, such as religion, song, and food, are the most common reminders of the southern past, though they are not wholly positive ones. For Helga Crane, for example, the revival meeting draws her into marrying a southern preacher and abandoning her cosmopolitan life for oppressive small-town domesticity. Leigh Anne Duck refers to the "allure" of southern rural life to African American authors of this era as an "uncanny" one, since its appeal comes allied with a recognition of the repressed truths about racism and economic hardship in that region (116). Imagining that a return to the South will solve the problems of northern life is only a form of nostalgic amnesia.

A sense of the difficulty in bridging southern tradition and northern modernity recurs throughout Harlem Renaissance fiction. Larsen's *Passing* (1929) includes a brief joke that belies a deeper sadness at the inability of modern African Americans to acknowledge and learn from their past. That novel famously ends with a raucous party where Clare Kendry, who has been passing for white, falls to her death just after her racist husband discovers her secret. At a more restrained party earlier in the novel, the protagonist, Irene Redfield, shatters a teacup. She jokingly tells her white friend Hugh Wentworth that she plans on blaming him for the accident.

Then she details the teacup's history: "It was the ugliest thing that your ancestors, the charming Confederates ever owned. I've forgotten how many thousands of years ago it was that Brian's great-great-grand-uncle owned it. But it has, or had, a good old hoary history. It was brought North by way of the subway. Oh, all right! Be English if you want to and call it the underground" (221–22). The cup is the talisman of the southern slave past (perhaps stolen from the master or given to a loyal house slave); the joke, however, transforms it into a meaningless commodity. Rather than reckoning with the material history of this object, Irene seems grateful that she no longer has to deal with an ugly thing in her house.[21]

The ease of movement on the subway eviscerates the material experience of northern migration. To collapse the Underground Railroad with a quick commute uptown is to ignore the important distance traveled by Irene's husband's ancestor. Reducing a migratory journey to a quick trip on the subway, Larsen mocks the middle-class woman's avoidance of difficult racial truths. Similarly, inflating Gillis's subway ride to a slave's escape on the Underground Railroad, Fisher mocks the migrant's exaggerated sense of his own importance. The mechanization of modern life has made the journey north easier but less heroic. Gillis is a comic figure in part because he still thinks of himself in the monumental terms of the past. Both "The City of Refuge" and *Invisible Man* use the subway to complicate the relation between the past and the present. These authors reimagine the tropes of earlier migration narratives in subway space and the way those narratives use the juxtaposition of past and present movements north in order to map more clearly the melancholy and irony of the Great Migration.

One of the most important issues addressed in Alain Locke's introduction to *The New Negro* is the diversity of Harlem's population. He imagines the neighborhood as "the laboratory of a great race-welding," one where peasants and poets, West Indians and South Carolinians all work together to construct a collective culture (7). Yet Rudolph Fisher's stories insist upon the difficulty of bringing these disparate parts of the population into a whole. The inability to assimilate is true on the level of language as well as appearance. John McCluskey astutely notes "the clash of dialects" in "The City of Refuge," reading it as a sign of differing understandings of "the codes of the streets" (11). A question like "Wha' dis hyeh at, please, suh?" (Fisher, *City of Refuge* 36), which Gillis asks Uggam before they recognize each other, can no longer be understood purely as a signifier of racial difference, as it might have been in Harriet Beecher Stowe's novels or the poetry of Paul Laurence Dunbar.[22] Nor does dialect function as a measure of authenticity, as it often does for Hughes and Hurston. Instead, Gillis's dropped *r*'s and overly polite questions mark him as both nonnative and old-fashioned. Black urban speech, we find, is no monolithic norm. Uggam, his drug-dealing boss, and a West Indian shop clerk all speak distinct strains of nonstandard English (to say nothing of the white detectives and the Italian shopkeeper). Fisher's use of multiple forms of dialect articulates a central problem of the Harlem Renaissance: How can the different populations of Harlem imagine themselves as part of the same culture when they do not speak the same language or share the same history?

Both Fisher and Ellison use the migration narrative as a genre for meditating on the transitional quality of African American culture. Gillis functions as a comic type because of his associations with the past. Before he encounters Mouse Uggam, Gillis gapes at a black policeman directing traffic and a beautiful girl in green stockings. Both of these figures embody the promise of the modern city: the policeman shows that black men can hold positions of power, while the woman suggests sexual availability. Gillis's countrified appearance clashes dramatically with that of modern African Americans. His "tan-cardboard extension-case" is a comic prop; his "black, shining brow" and slow smile call to mind the visage of a blackface minstrel (Fisher, *City of Refuge* 35).[23] Fisher suggests that at this transitional moment in the life of the "New Negro," old and new forms of blackness will uncomfortably coexist in the same space and time.

The persistence of images and tropes from blackface minstrelsy persist throughout the twentieth century; these racist caricatures are based on the assumed temporal disjunction between blacks and whites, North and South, upper and lower classes. Kevin Gaines imagines the prevalence of minstrel imagery in the late nineteenth and early twentieth centuries as a response to the increasing numbers of country-born African Americans moving to northern cities: the production of grinning, watermelon-eating figures represented a kind of wishful thinking that blacks would remain in the South and in the past (72). After watching the police shoot his friend Tod Clifton, the narrator of *Invisible Man* boards the subway back to Harlem in a daze. As he waits for the train, he thinks about "those of us who shoot up from the South into the busy city like wild jacks-in-the-box broken loose from our springs" (439), suggesting a connection between migrants and the dancing

Sambo dolls that Clifton had been selling when he was killed. The uncanny, at least in Freudian terms, is the fearful recognition of a repressed belief in an externalized object. The lifelike automaton in *The Tales of Hoffman* seems uncanny because it blurs the line between subject and object, as children do when they imagine their dolls to be living beings (Freud, "The 'Uncanny'" 209). For Ellison's narrator, the Sambo dolls are uncanny because they embody both the disjunction between past and present and the gap between his own self-image and the racist caricature that the white world sees.

Indeed, the whole subway scene follows a chain of associations, connecting Clifton to southern migrants, then to a group of zoot-suit-wearing young men, all of whom the narrator imagines as existing outside of the dominant historical narrative espoused by the organization he has joined known as the Brotherhood. This is an important section of the novel, one in which the narrator begins to develop a more fluid and all-encompassing sense of African American history. He does so in part because of an increasing understanding of the multiple temporalities contained within urban black culture. Whereas the zoot-suited passengers are "transitional" (441), he imagines himself as a "throwback" (442), repeating the oratorical ideals of Frederick Douglass and Booker T. Washington long after they are relevant. The issue of "temporal collisions" (Duck 8), then, applies to the migrant's personal confrontation with modernity as well as his reconciliation with a wider sense of African American history. Although *Invisible Man* describes the sense of history present in this scene in Marxist terms as a spiral or the groove in a record, the subway scene seems to offer alternate interpretations: Clifton's life as a salesman of racist dolls is a metaphorical jump in front of a moving subway train (439), but the subway passengers are all people "outside of historical time" (440). The subway, then, is both a linear force of progress eschewed by Clifton and a circular underground temporality that resists teleology. The technological ensemble plays a similar role in this genre as it does in the modernist poetry discussed in chapter 3, short-circuiting a narrative of linear evolution in favor of juxtaposition and circularity.

The figures who appear at the beginning of "The City of Refuge" all reappear in an underground nightclub in the final section as well, suggesting a reconsideration of Gillis's first encounter with Harlem in a submerged landscape of restricted vision like that of the subway car. As the story ends, Gillis has been betrayed by Mouse Uggam and is about to be taken away by two white detectives. He spots the girl with the green stockings, now being kissed against her will by her white escort. Gillis rises from the table to help her, but the white policemen take this move as an attempt to flee. As Gillis fights the policemen, we hear his fragmented thoughts about the violence inflicted on black farmers back home: "Five of Mose Joplin's horses. Poisoning a well. A year's crops. Green stockings—white—white—" (Fisher 47). As with Gillis's mishearing of rifle shots in the subway station, he recognizes the parallels between southern and northern structures of power. Aside from the fantasy of sexual freedom evoked by the green stockings, this catalog suggests that there is no difference between north and south, that the power and authority of southern mob rule that killed horses and poisoned wells now resides in the white detectives. The lynching he escaped, Gillis thinks, may be unavoidable. The black traffic cop arrives as backup, however, and reminds Gillis that northern encounters really are different.

Gillis's encounter with the traffic cop suggests that visions of a possible racial collectivity can be intimated only in moments of submission to the larger forces of urban authority. Throughout "The City of Refuge," Gillis has affirmed the promise of Harlem by repeating to himself the refrain, "even got cullud policemans." The officer "awaits his rush," but Gillis stops in wonder, repeating that same refrain. He reacts bodily to the black policeman's presence as well: "Very slowly, King Solomon's arms relaxed; very slowly he stood erect; and the grin that came over his features had something exultant about it" (47). The repetition of "very slowly" assumes an incantatory quality similar to his marveling refrain; the slowed-down movements briefly take control of a situation characterized by speed and violence. Gillis assumes the physical posture he displayed on the subway steps, but he is now "erect," betraying a pride and power that he has not shown before, with an "exultant" minstrel grin more consciously and proudly deployed (Fisher 47). Though based in misrecognition, this encounter is truly a re-vision of Gillis's introduction to Harlem, one that he accesses through a physicalized refusal to rush toward his predetermined fate. Instead of engaging in another version of the criminal flight that brought Gillis to Harlem in the first place, he slowly relaxes, accepting his place in the underground space of the cabaret and, indeed, in Harlem. Though fleeting and deeply ironic, Gillis acclimates to the play between agency and submission that serves as a necessary part of newly self-aware migration.

The Invisible Man ends his journey with an uncanny subway encounter that emphasizes the exchange between regions and races that has been a part of his life from its beginning. He recognizes the northern college trustee Mr. Norton, who wishes to board a train for Centre Street and asks the narrator for directions (577). Norton does not recognize the young man, who cryptically alludes to their ill-fated journey together to the homestead of the incestuous Truebloods and to the Golden Day saloon. The narrator insists on the connection between their lives, one that persists even in northern space. When they had first met years earlier, Norton had said that the narrator could "tell him his fate" by thriving in his career and letting Norton know what kind of impact his donation to the college had made (44). Now the narrator claims, "I'm your destiny, I made you" (578). The subterranean connections that the subway facilitates do not merely connect migrants' old lives to their new ones; they also implicate the white power structure that made migration a possible (and even a necessary) response to the racial and economic difficulties of the South. The subway, then, helps the narrative move toward the wary reciprocity of its concluding question: "Who knows but that, on the lower frequencies, I speak for you?" (581). Leigh Anne Duck reads the narrator's first public speech as a spokesman for the Brotherhood as marking the inception of his ability to "imagine and articulate affiliations" (241). The conclusion is where this imagined community reaches across racial lines and indeed breaks down the barrier between speaker and reader.

The process of partial identification that takes place in both of these encounters—Gillis's with the policeman and the Invisible Man's with Norton—should be differentiated from the conventional understanding of the uncanny: whereas the psychoanalytic uncanny evokes a shudder of horror, this African American revision brings a ripple of laughter. Gillis grins broadly even as he is arrested, and the Invisible Man "laugh[s] hysterically" after Norton ignores his remarks and hops aboard an express train (579). In his essay "An Extravagance of Laughter," Ellison recounts an incident when he was seized with an equally paradoxical fit of laughter. It occurs while he is attending a theatrical production of Erskine Caldwell's *Tobacco Road.* The play serves as an uncanny reminder of the southern whites he had tried to avoid while attending college in Alabama (147). Although he had attempted to repress that knowledge of southern ignorance and racism, it returns in the form of a hit Broadway play. Confronted with the absurd images of southern whiteness, Ellison describes his response as one of "helpless laughter" (186), laughter that recognizes the absurdity of his own experiences of southern racism and expresses relief that someone else has also recognized and re-created them. Even though neither "The City of Refuge" nor *Invisible Man* ends on a wholly optimistic note, both of them do imagine the possibility of redressing past grievances or at least reimagining the past in a new (underground) light.

## Race and Technology

The subway plays a central role in African American migration narratives because it can echo past histories while remaining resolutely modern. The literary depiction of the subway journey to Harlem should be of broader interest to historians of technology because it helps complicate discussions in the still nascent field. As Bruce Sinclair, Rayvon Fouché, and Carolyn de la Peña have all discussed, race has become a subject of central interest to technological historians only within the past decade or so.[24] The kinds of writings I have been discussing highlight how new transportation technologies helped black intellectuals understand the conflicting temporalities at work in the modern city. Throughout the works of Fisher, Larsen, Thurman, Hughes, and Ellison, migrants experience folk and modern time in subway space. Although these authors are not inventors, and they seldom describe themselves as passengers, they nevertheless play an important part in shaping the symbolic associations between race, class, temporality, and technology. To conclude this chapter, I identify some of the questions raised by these texts and the ways in which they point to future areas of research.

First and foremost, the interest in the subway as a vehicle of poor, rural migrants tells us that we need to pay attention to intersections of race, class, and region when we talk about technology. Public transportation is often implicitly cast in both racialized and lower-class terms. Blaine Brownell, for example, observes that black car ownership signified upward mobility because it allowed the owner to escape the racism and segregation of the streetcar (35).[25] Yet even with this association reinforced by multiple histories of black automobility, there are notable and interesting exceptions. Hardly an upper-class character, King Solomon Gillis owned a car, which he sold to a bootlegger for train fare. In this period, tenant farmers commonly owned cars as well (Brownell 36). How does their use and understanding of the automobile differ from that of the black middle-class driver constructed in the pages of the travel guidebooks that Cotten Seiler describes? The stories told in and about the Harlem Renaissance tend to focus on the use of the subway by migrants just arriving. The regular commute to work, the day trip to Coney Island don't carry the same weight in the stories that black intellectuals told themselves about the culture of Harlem in this period. So we need to think about the different impacts that transportation technology has on its passengers, depending not only on their color but on their class and culture as well.

Studying the subway as a central space in histories of the Great Migration also tells us that we need to broaden our conceptions of agency. Intellectuals of the period—and even critics today—continually emphasize that migrants made a conscious choice to move to the North, that they were not mere pawns in a larger historical game (Locke 7, Levine 267). At the same time, the stories told about technology in the period, such as the advertisements in the *Chicago Defender* for the trains tagged "Bound for the Promised Land," made the migration seem all but inevitable (Bontemps and Conroy 163). The play between passivity and activity becomes one of the most important elements of subway migration narratives. Although the migrants seem to be swept north to Harlem against their will, the narratives also highlight the lack of agency felt by all passengers on the subway. They emphasize physical passivity and repetition, revealing just how similar the migrant's first subway ride is to the everyday experience of city life. In this way, subway narratives move beyond the critical position that considers "technology as material oppression," a position that Rayvon Fouché finds reductive because it "strips black people of technological agency" (640–41). Instead, they model an imaginative practice of precisely that kind of agency.

In this chapter I have suggested that attending to the smallest components of migration, such as the subway ride that functions as the last step on the journey to Harlem, may yield large dividends in terms of understanding how that migration shaped African American consciousness. Subway migration narratives thus highlight the need for a critical exploration of local movement that serves as a complement to the critical interest in interregional and international circulation. The study of public transportation is inevitably going to be one about race and class. African Americans make up a disproportionately high percentage of America's public transit riders. According to the 2008–2010 American Community Survey, self-identified white respondents constituted 76.8 percent of the total population but only 51.3 percent of public transit riders. African American respondents skewed in the other direction: although they were only 10.8 percent of the total population of respondents, they represented 24.6 percent of the public transit riders (US Census Bureau). The percentages are even higher in Atlanta, where the Metropolitan Atlanta Rapid Transit Authority (MARTA) system transports around one-third of its African American residents to work every day (Bullard, Johnson, and Torres 56). As the Great Migration reverses itself with more African Americans returning to the South, we will need more detailed and local explorations of these issues.

The subway serves a complex and often contradictory set of purposes in African American migration narratives: it is a site of communion and alienation, a space understood in folk terms, and a figure of modernist defamiliarization. The subway functions as a vehicle of partial and provisional connection between otherwise disparate regions and their concomitant ways of life. In this respect, African American writers understand the chief problem of migration quite similarly to white ethnic writers of the same period. Both take the subway to find a usable past and to keep the present from overwhelming them.

Subway migration is never singular. Fisher's and Ellison's narratives use the repetitive movement of the trains to underscore the city's perpetual oscillation between restriction and freedom. The subway suggests a more pragmatic and less utopian migration, one that acknowledges that it is following preestablished and well-trodden paths. As we'll see in the conclusion, the past becomes a source of communal feeling for contemporary writers—writers who call upon the tropes of modernist subway writing in order to understand their post-postmodern city. For Colson Whitehead, the materiality of the subway ride calls into being a momentary sense of community; for Jonathan Lethem, the traces of the past in his favorite subway station connect his autobiography to that of his Brooklyn neighborhood. As urban renewal erases much of New York's history, these post-9/11 authors use the subway system as a model for a kind of collective urban unconscious that maintains this connection between individual memories and the city of the past.

# CONCLUSION

# THE PRIVATE SUBWAY IN THE POSTMODERN CITY

Since the 1950s New York City's population has fallen and risen; its economy has gone through several cycles of boom and bust. The threat of crime, allied to the subway in the popular imagination from the 1960s onward, was counteracted through aggressive (some say too aggressive) policing in the 1980s and 1990s. Criminologist George Kelling and political scientist James Wilson's "broken windows theory," which posits that an environment of apathy toward minor crimes encourages more serious violations, had a major influence on the powers within the New York City Transit Authority and Transit Police. As Robert Huber of the Transit Authority pointed out in 1982, the subway was "under-capitalized from the beginning" (qtd. in Theroux). The nickel subway fare, the third rail of local politics until mid-century, left the system with a tight budget; as a consequence, maintenance and the purchase of new equipment were deferred as long as possible (Hood, *722 Miles* 222). That abdication of responsibility, coupled with a decreasing tax base and a loss of federal funding, led to a deterioration of the system.

The era of insolvency and disrepair that followed from the late 1960s through the 1990s seems disconnected from the "golden age" that preceded it (Hood, *722 Miles* 214). The same is true of subway stories in this period: dystopian descriptions became extremely common from the 1970s through the 1990s, setting contemporary rides in sharp contrast to the good old days of the modern subway.[1] But contemporary writing about the New York subway displays a number of features and attitudes that more closely track with modernist attitudes toward the transit system. Late twentieth- and early twenty-first-century New York writers embrace the subway in ways as varied as did those of the early twentieth century: novelists explore the psychological and historical resonances of the tunnels; poets hear echoes of their predecessors and see their ghosts underground; and playwrights, perhaps inheriting the optimism of Osip Dymov, continue to stage the subway as a melting pot. Throughout these new subway stories, the transit system gives structural coherence to an otherwise chaotic urban space. For contemporary artists and writers, the New York City subway becomes part of what Warren Susman calls the "usable past," an evocative image that is repeatedly brought into dialogue with new social and historical forces. The subway is a potent symbol for present-day city dwellers, I argue, because it offers continuity through an individual's history and serves as a shared experience among New Yorkers whose lives seem otherwise irredeemably different from one another.

As New York City moves through periods of rapid change, the subway connects its artists and writers with the past, offering a bulwark against what Max Page calls the city's "creative destruction," an "urban condition of unstoppable and inscrutable development and redevelopment, destruction and rebuilding with no apparent end" (*Creative Destruction of Manhattan* 258). This creative destruction is inseparable from the city's history over the breadth of the twentieth century and into the twenty-first: Richard Le Gallienne muses on "ever-new" New York in the pages of *Harper's Magazine* in 1911, while Robert Moses takes it as a mandate in mid-century, and Rem Koolhaas celebrates it in the 1970s. To conclude my investigation of the modernist subway culture, I examine its echoes in the postmodern and postindustrial cultural sphere, especially in the realm of the personal essay. Postmodernist writers, artists, and musicians imagine the subway as a repository for earlier personal history, a kind of underground museum of their memories.

The New York subway makes it possible for these technological tale tellers to visualize continuity even while the city changes around them: though some lines have changed names and others have disappeared, the basic structural elements of riding the subway remain the same. Like their modernist counterparts, these artists imagine the subway as a technology that mediates between individual memory and the impersonal city. Indeed, the subway can be understood as a technology that intercedes between people and the things they have built that have expanded beyond a human scale: the automobile, the elevator, and the Internet browser all serve a similar purpose. Subway stories remind us that technologies of mobility neither fully control nor are controlled by their passengers. Instead, they highlight certain ways of seeing and preclude others. And what we see with the extended modernist attention to the subway is a method of cataloguing that kind of cultural interplay. The texts discussed in the previous chapters offer provisional answers to intractable questions: What's the best way for art to engage with modern life? How do we deal with a diverse population? How do New Yorkers orient themselves within an ever-changing city?

This conclusion treats a number of different genres and media, examining the New York City subway's role as a link between private experience and collective memory in the early twenty-first century. My touchstones are essays by Colson Whitehead and Jonathan Lethem, two genre-hopping writers whose fiction and essays chronicle New Yorks both real and imagined. Their subway writings imagine the city's public spaces as an archive of myriad private moments. Whitehead's impressionistic book of essays *The Colossus of New York* (2003) follows in the tradition of the urban sketch (Lopate 31), taking on a voice that is at once autobiographical and impersonal in order to exemplify the typical New York experience.[2] Whitehead considers the transit system as the node where personal history and urban history most commonly intersect. With essays titled "The Port Authority," "Subway," and "JFK," as well as a recurrent meditation on moving from one apartment to another, a reader gets the sense that New Yorkers are perpetually in motion (Butler 73). The opposite is true for Jonathan Lethem, who begins his autobiographical essay "Speak, Hoyt-Schermerhorn" standing on a platform and thinking about the titular station's history—which even he knows is "using it wrong" (44). The essay, first published in *Harper's* magazine in 2004 and expanded in Lethem's 2006 essay collection *The Disappointment Artist,* shows just how thoroughly one subway station can be implicated in a person's understanding of himself. Like Lethem's novel *The*

*Fortress of Solitude* (2003), "Speak" interrogates his relation to the gentrifying Brooklyn neighborhood where he grew up in the 1970s; he places this personal experience in dialogue with the development of the subway system and the traces of its history that remain visible.

In his discussion of the "postmodern sublime," Joseph Tabbi suggests that an autobiographical turn such as the one that we see in contemporary subway writing may be a way of grounding a narrative that deals with a period of history marked by instability and technological innovation (3). At the same time, Whitehead and Lethem carry on a tradition begun by postwar essayists such as Alfred Kazin, E. B. White, and Joseph Mitchell. (Indeed, Lethem refers to Kazin's memoir *A Walker in the City*, finding in it a clue to one of the mysteries of the Hoyt-Schermerhorn station.) All of these men wrote regularly for the *New Yorker*, and all participate in what Bryan Waterman calls a "nostalgic strain" (233) of postwar New York writing in order to preserve a history that seemed to be passing them by. Yet what I'd foreground is not their sense of loss but the sense that the subway itself retains traces of their memories. As Kazin begins *A Walker in the City*, he considers how the subway structures his return home to Brownsville and, indeed, his memories of Brooklyn in general: "There was always a stirring of my heart at Hoyt, where the grimy station platform was suddenly enlivened by Abraham and Straus's windows of ladies' wear. Atlantic Avenue was vaguely exciting, a crossroads, the Long Island railroad; I never saw a soul get in or out at Bergen Street; the Grand Army Plaza, with its great empty caverns smoky with dust and chewing-gum wrappers, meant Prospect Park and the stone path beside a meadow where as a child I ran off from my father one summer twilight" (9). The 3 train thus shapes Kazin's consciousness and indeed structures urban memory on a larger scale by dividing the journey into stops. Some of these stops, such as Grand Army Plaza and Atlantic Avenue, correspond to the places in Brooklyn located aboveground; others, such as Hoyt, include a piece of the building that extends from the stop into the neighborhood; the Bergen Street station, however, seems disconnected from the city above, both for Kazin and for anyone else with whom he has shared the train. These ellipses in Kazin's understanding are not a cause for alarm; instead, they merely reflect his own interpretation of the subway map, not as a regulated representation of a system in which all stations are equal but as a map of his memories. As a former Brooklynite who lived two blocks from that mysterious Bergen

Street stop, I have a map of the borough that is understandably quite different from Kazin's. In the next section I unpack the autobiographical function of subway stories, suggesting how the modernist texts I have discussed throughout this book anticipate contemporary concerns with narrating personal experiences in an era of rapid technological change.

## Constructing Autobiographies

As we saw in chapter 1, the early newspaper accounts of the subway helped model a new kind of movement through the city. The stories discussed there suggest the benefits and drawbacks that passengers might encounter when they abandon a visually focused form of orientation in favor of a more unconscious mental map. Instead of the bird's-eye view of the city that makes the observer feel godlike and disembodied, the view from within the subway car depends on visual and aural cues mixed with a general physical sense of how far one has traveled along a particular line. For contemporary authors, the everyday knowledge that comes from subway travel serves a secondary purpose: tracing their memories through a city that may otherwise have changed beyond recognition. The persistence of the subway in a city that has continued to remake itself and deny its past serves as a tangible, embodied connection to that past. Placing themselves in the same position, riding the same train over the same route, they can relive the same memory.

In Whitehead's book and Lethem's essay we see the impact of postmodern thinking about pluralism and the impossibility of a totalizing view from above: the subway, like the city, is experienced only from an embodied perspective. Any desire to represent the abstract perspective, the map, has fallen by the wayside. The narrator of *The Colossus of New York*, for example, claims: "My first city memory is of looking out a subway window as the train erupted from the tunnel on the way to 125th Street and palsied up onto the elevated tracks. It's the early seventies, so everything is filthy. Which means everything is still filthy, because that is my city and I'm sticking to it" (Whitehead 4–5). In the face of his insistence that "my city" is different from yours and that it is rooted in a particular period of time, the subway can no longer serve as a model for unifying New York City as a spatial whole. Instead, it unifies individual experiences across time.

The essays that I discuss in this chapter, then, return to the issue raised in chapter 1—how the mental map of the subway relates to that of the city above—from an autobiographical perspective. How might the subway, and other technologies like it, help present-day city dwellers imaginatively relate to their pasts when much of the evidence of those pasts is erased? Early twentieth-century subway riders had to learn to live like moles, keeping track of their location in space without any external visual cues. We might imagine contemporary New Yorkers as moles in historical terms, locating themselves in *time* with few external visual cues to remind them of their past. Lethem values the Hoyt-Schermerhorn stop because it is a "functional ruin" ("Speak" 46), still used by riders on a daily basis but nevertheless displaying legible signs of a New York culture that has passed. The station is also one of the few places that have stayed basically the same since Lethem first began visiting it as a child; though crime has decreased and shoppers shop at different stores, the police substation and the mezzanine-level shop windows remain.

Although I have only briefly alluded to other cities' subway lines throughout this book, I should point out that European authors are equally interested in moving away from a regimented understanding of the subway map as a regulated, top-down representation of city space. Instead they tend to imagine their cities' subway maps much like Kazin does, as evocative condensations of an individual's movements through the city, with overdetermined areas and absences depending on personal experience. The first chapter of Marc Augé's book *In the Metro* (originally published in French in 1986) thinks through the moment when a Paris Métro passenger's "inner geology" intersects with the "subterranean geography of the capital city" (4). Augé's natural metaphor, whereby consciousness is a rock formation with "sedimentary layers" of memories (4), brings the passenger's mind into dialogue with the subway tunnel without evoking the infernal or repressed associations of the underworld. The London Underground brings about similar meditations in the writing of Virginia Woolf.[3] In *Jacob's Room* (1922), she considers the analogical relationship between Tube stops and the neighborhoods into which they open. Woolf observes that most stops are to most people "eternally white letters upon a blue ground. Only at one point . . . does the name mean shops where you buy things, and houses in one of which, down to the right, where the pollard trees grow out of the paving stones, there is a square curtained window, and a bedroom" (Woolf 67). Each passenger's knowledge (or lack thereof) associated with each proper name can be understood as a reflection of his everyday life, especially his sense of home. As the imagined passenger moves from the abstraction of station names to the particularity of a neighborhood, the prose too becomes more detailed and located in space. These meditations on the deeply subjective understanding of the city open up the possibility for a comparatist treatment of transportation technology, one that is unfortunately beyond the scope of this book.

Longtime New Yorkers like Whitehead and Lethem may recognize their history in subway stations, but more recent arrivals write their way into them. When she moved to New York City in 2003, the Pakistani American artist Asma Ahmed Shikoh began a series of paintings titled *Home,* in which she inscribed her immigrant identity onto prototypical icons of the city such as the Statue of Liberty and Forty-second Street. Her painting *Van Wyck Blvd; Home Series* (2005) (fig. 4) re-creates the entire New York City subway map with one major difference: all the station names and instructions appear in Urdu. Shikoh inscribes her language of origin onto the Metrocard in another painting, elevating and defamiliarizing a token of subway travel so common that it tends to escape most New Yorkers' notice (much like the Greek key coffee cup that is now a design icon). The use of Urdu has a dual effect: it makes the icons unfamiliar to New Yorkers who do not speak the language, and it creates a shared space for fellow immigrants who do. Yet Shikoh sees the act of painting these images as a deeply individualistic one that helps her to "build a personal territory within the city" and assert her "presence" and "identity" on a map that is generally understood to be impersonal (Shikoh).

As Tracy Fitzpatrick has shown, visual artists have found the subway map to be a useful icon for staging the interaction between the officially sanctioned use of subway space and the lived realities of individual passengers (138–42). Several contemporary works reconstruct the subway map in a form that abandons its directive purpose. Al Hansen's *Manhattan Venus* and *Brooklyn Venus* (1994) cut voluptuous female figures out of the maps, celebrating the tactile pleasures to be found in the disconnected space. Nina Katchadourian's *Hand-Held Subway* (1996) excises the colored lines that mark subway routes, paring the map down to pure motion; she then photographs this tangled mass of paper in the palm of someone's hand. The sense of touch as a means of engagement with representational space comes into play in Shikoh's work as well. She describes "painting the subway map and translating minute, tiresome details" as paradoxically "therapeutic for an estranged person who is trying to identify with a new city"

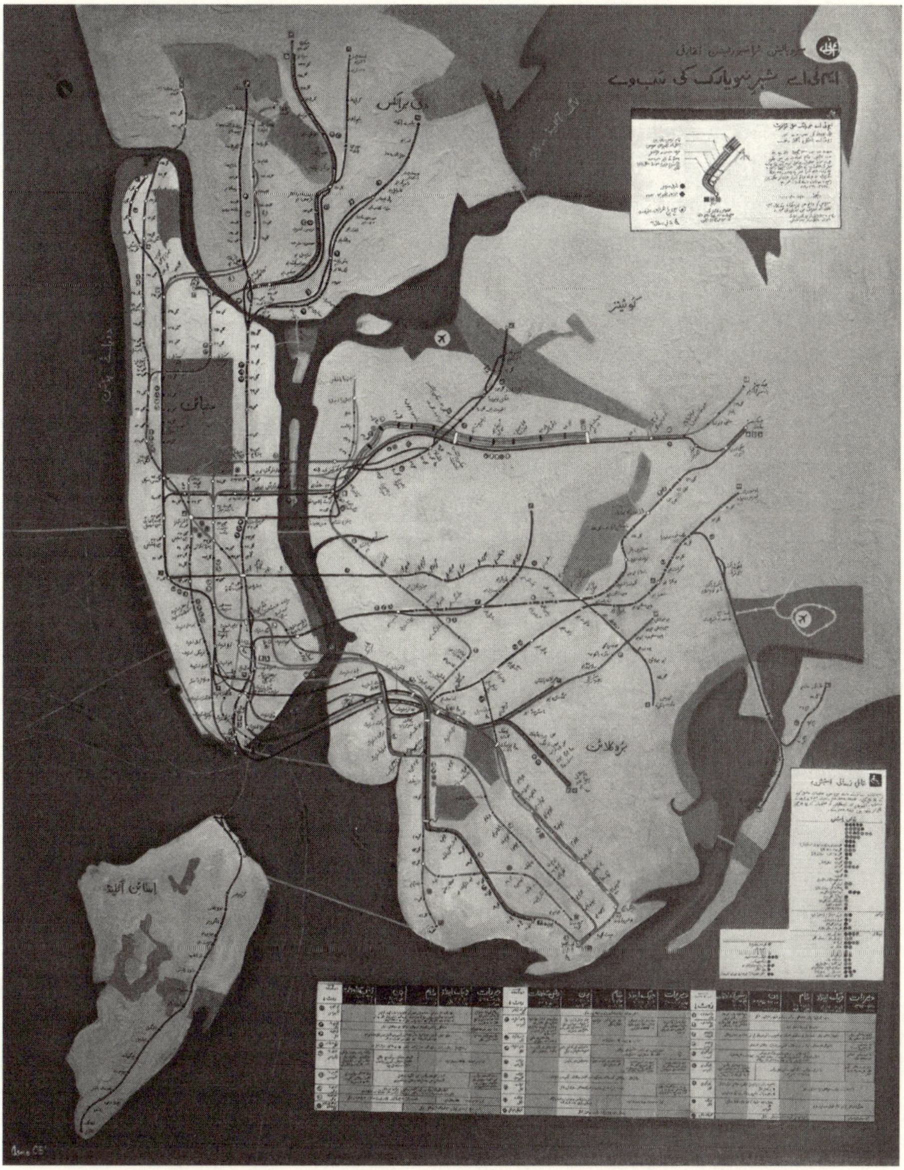

Figure 4. Asma Ahmed Shikoh, *Van Wyck Blvd; Home Series,* 2005. © Asma Ahmed Shikoh.

(Shikoh). Her attentive engagement with the specificity of the subway map helps Shikoh feel more at home in the city, since it has led to an intimate knowledge of the system's layout, schedule, and rules.

In an era defined by technologies of abstraction and disembodiment, the subway becomes an important technological trope for city writers arguing in favor of the knowledge gained only in the lived reality of urban space. The particularity of Shikoh's and Whitehead's narratives underscore the present-day emphasis on multiple and subjective urban histories. One might assume that the subjective quality of subway experience would serve to divide them. Whitehead makes no claims to inclusivity. He concludes his opening chapter, "City Limits," with the claim that his book "contains your neighborhoods. Or doesn't. We overlap. Or don't" (*Colossus* 11). Some urban stories simply do not intersect with one another. Yet Augé points out the "paradox" that this too can be a point of connection between people: "Isn't the first virtue of personal recollections, inspired by a somewhat dreamy consultation of the subway map, that of having us sense something like a feeling of fraternity?" (10). Subway stories spin away from grand narratives of urban prosperity or decline, instead focusing on local experience as the only truth worth sharing.

A number of recent subway texts are multiply authored accounts, emphasizing the contemporary feeling that the train can be understood only from a variety of perspectives. *Subway Stories* (1997), a film collection directed by Jonathan Demme, Abel Ferrara, and eight others, includes romances, cautionary tales, and character sketches among its ten short films. *The Subway Chronicles* (2006), an essay collection edited by Jacquelin Cangro, adopts a similar tack: Lethem's and Whitehead's meditative takes on the subway brush up against descriptions of egg salad sandwiches and homeless men leering at centerfolds. The very structure of these texts suggests the multiplicity of the subway crowd and the privacy of the subway experience in a way that echoes William Saroyan's *Subway Circus,* which I discussed in chapter 4. The subway ride in the late twentieth and twenty-first centuries maintains the aesthetics of the discrete and anecdotal subway ride well established by the 1940s.

In Colson Whitehead's New York, everyone has his own private version of the city. This concern with the categorical experience of life in New York can perhaps best be seen in the most-quoted passage from the book: "No matter how long you have been here, you are a New Yorker the first time you say, That used to be Munsey's, or That used to be the Tic Toc Lounge. That before the internet café plugged in, you got your shoes resoled in the mom-and-pop operation that used to be there. You are a New Yorker when what was there before is more real and solid than what is here now" (*Colossus* 3–4). Authenticity for Whitehead has less to do with arriving before a particular time than with feeling the passage of time since you've been there. No New Yorker will have the same definition of what "was there before" that is "more real and solid," since those specific details are inflected by when you arrived, where you lived, and what you paid attention to. Instead, New Yorkers are defined by their shared sense of nostalgia, truly a structure of feeling in the sense that Raymond Williams used it. I turn now to the prevalence of nostalgia in contemporary subway writing, particularly nostalgia for the less reliable, less comfortable, and more dangerous subways of the past.

## Mythicizing Urban History

Hart Crane's poetry may seem arcane to present-day readers, but his poetic impulse throughout *The Bridge* is one practiced by myriad present-day New Yorkers. When Crane sought details about New York for his epic poem, he looked for ones that would convert "[his] own image of the city into legend" (Lethem, "Speak" 53). The name of a onetime cabdriver graces Crane's Native American warrior in the section on Pocahontas; he chooses a subway stop (Gravesend) that fits thematically within his descent to the underworld. Both of these choices recast typical New York encounters in ways that amplify their excitement and implicitly put the protagonist in a more heroic light. In his essay on a subway stop with a less evocative name, Jonathan Lethem acknowledges his love for culture that does the same kind of work, helping him cope with riding the subway as a child by elevating its everyday risks to operatic heights. Both Crane and Lethem tell stories about technology that help them construct a more stable and authoritative relationship to their pasts.

At first the Hoyt-Schermerhorn stop is interesting to Lethem merely because it is his stop. "When you're a child," he says, "everything local is famous. On that principle, Hoyt-Schermerhorn was the most famous subway station in the world" ("Speak" 45). But Lethem comes to understand that his subway station is in fact famous, because it served as the filming location for many of the emblematic subway movies of the 1970s. As a younger man, Lethem sees a film crew shooting a scene for *The Warriors*

(1979), an adaptation of Sol Yurick's novel about New York City street gangs. The film has become a cult classic, celebrated by rappers and transformed into a video game in 2005. Why would a low-budget exploitation film in which young men flee outlandish pursuers (some on roller skates, others dressed as demonic baseball players) become a touchstone for New Yorkers of Lethem's generation? He claims that it did so because it transformed the real fears associated with the subway into a fantastic form. The gritty but glamorous gang, narrowly escaping danger and returning to their home on Coney Island, allows viewers who experienced 1970s New York City to "preen in [their] old fears" ("Speak" 53). Even shameful experiences that Lethem describes, such as his ostensibly playful stalking of a girlfriend from the subway station to her doorstep, enact a desire to identify with the criminal underclass rather than with bourgeois bohemians like his parents. We can understand the chief concern of autobiographical subway writing, then, as finding a mode of narration that articulates a personal understanding of urban space while avoiding the solipsistic perspective that sees public space only in terms of private experiences.

Though their essays display the sophisticated, anecdotal ease of middlebrow urban sketches, I'd suggest there's another form of city writing that might help us better understand Lethem's and Whitehead's vision of the subway: graffiti writing. Both authors grew up in New York in the late 1970s and early 1980s, the boom years for graffiti.[4] Lethem's interest in graffiti is well documented: he wrote the introduction to a collection of graffiti photographs, and he follows the lives of two teenage graffiti writers in *The Fortress of Solitude.* Colson Whitehead has expressed more interest in B movies, but he acknowledges an affinity for the graffiti artist and painter Jean-Michel Basquiat in an interview with Kevin Young (Whitehead, "A Short Distance to the Blues" 34). More than a strictly autobiographical connection, though, graffiti offers us a local context for thinking about how an individual's identity might circulate through the postindustrial city.

The subway is inescapably tied to graffiti culture in this era, with artists' short pseudonyms (known as "tags") festooning the inside of cars and murals covering the outside. Graffiti polarized the cultural landscape in the 1970s and 1980s: Claes Oldenburg and Norman Mailer embraced it, while Alfred Kazin and Paul Theroux decried it. Whether they read it as artistic or narcissistic, all of the critics agreed that graffiti is a gesture of personal expression.[5] The graffiti writer's "tag" becomes his or her personal identity within the graffiti-writing community. That "tag" is often written in a near-illegible script called "wild style." For Susan Stewart, the fact that the signature can't be read by outsiders makes it all the more individualistic: "The graffiti writer's goal is a stylization inseparable from the body, a stylization that, in its impenetrable 'wildness,' could surpass even linguistic reference and serve purely as the concrete evidence of an individual existence and the reclamation of the environment through the label of the personal" (212). When graffiti writers tag a subway car, they reclaim an impersonal urban space by literally making their mark on it. Lethem and Whitehead forgo an objective urban history in favor of one based in the personal, the gestural, and the embodied. Like the rhetoric of walking for de Certeau and the style of the graffiti writer for Stewart, the anecdote and the small-scale personal experience are imagined as traces of urban life as it is lived.

Graffiti writing evokes nostalgia in part because it signifies an era when young, disenfranchised residents of the city could harness elements of the urban infrastructure to their own ends. Whereas Mervyn Kurlansky, John Naar, and Norman Mailer saw graffiti as a minority group's protest against the white, Taylorist city, I am more interested in how graffiti writers took advantage of modernity in order to facilitate their work: timing it according to train schedules, for example, or interchanging the cap from one can to another to alter the spray of paint.[6] The subway system itself becomes a technology of publication, "a communication network on which the names and messages of graffiti writers circulate throughout the city" (Cooper and Chalfant 23). Their names travel through neighborhoods that they would normally not enter, rendering the impersonal, postindustrial city knowable in a way that it wasn't before. As New York becomes slicker and more consumer oriented, I suspect that this personal mark on the city will only gain cachet.

References to practices of riding and tagging the subway in the 1970s and 1980s serve as badges of authenticity in the hip hop world, rhetorical opportunities for artists simultaneously to evoke a shared history and highlight their knowledge and firsthand experience. Tupac Shakur's "Old School" (1995) lists important rappers, DJs, fashion trends of the 1980s; these are interspersed with accounts of youthful indiscretions, including one described in language that is strikingly immediate: "Forget the TV, about to hit the streets and do graffiti / Be careful don't let the transit cops see me" (qtd. in Forman 1). While Shakur may use lyrics such as these to make his lyrical persona seem tougher, the song as a whole is a giddy homage to shared culture. The Beastie Boys do much to aestheticize the period in "Stop That Train," a portion of the twelve-minute "B-Boy Bouillabaisse," the collection of fragmentary songs that concludes *Paul's Boutique* (1989). The song describes a "D train ride to Coney Island vacation" in which the fellow passengers include drug users and prostitutes as well as well-dressed businessmen. This is a diverse crowd, a modern-day version of the "Subway Crush" sketched by Reginald Marsh (see chapter four). Even at 4 a.m., people read newspapers in English (the *New York Post*) and Spanish (*El Diario*), "Sweating like sardines in a flophouse fraternity" (Beastie Boys). Here the lyrics suggest just how crowded the subway was through a portmanteau metaphor: "sweating like pigs" and "packed like sardines" are compressed into "sweating like sardines." As in modernist writing, the evocation of animals in these lyrics operates on two levels, making concrete the dehumanizing component of subway riding while at the same time betraying a certain pride and sense of membership in the tough "fraternity" that can withstand such conditions.

Colum McCann's novel *Let the Great World Spin* (2009) subtly critiques the nostalgia for 1970s New York City even while acknowledging the role it plays in bringing people together. Fernando, a thirteen-year-old street photographer, searches out the graffiti masterpieces most difficult for other photographers to reach. His pursuit is paralleled with protagonist John Corrigan's mission among the prostitutes in the South Bronx, though Fernando's story ends with him selling a photograph of Philippe Petit's tightrope walk between the Twin Towers, and Corrigan's with a deadly car crash. Artistic immersion in this culture seems to have more direct rewards than immediate involvement in the everyday life of its inhabitants.

Tags also appear in Michael Elmgreen and Ingar Dragset's installation *End Station* (2005), a meticulously re-created platform for the nonexistent "13th Street" station. There, the tags coexist with a single trash can full of historically overdetermined refuse: newspapers alluding to the Reagan presidency and the AIDS crisis, a Converse tennis shoe, drink cans for the prototypically 1980s diet soda Tab, and a bag from a 1987 Museum of Modern Art exhibition (Fitzpatrick 148; Allen, "Elmgreen"). The graffiti function in the same way as the Guerrilla Girls poster on the subway station wall, reminding viewers of the possible responses to mindless consumerism and political silence in that era. The tags can also be understood in relation to the hypodermic needles, condoms, and cigarette butts in the trash, since all are traces of the physical presence of other passengers—passengers who have been engaging in illicit activities.

As in McCann's novel, the focus on the marginal lives of drug users, prostitutes, and graffiti artists lends an air of bohemian authenticity to the outsider who observes this strain of city life. Yet by presenting an odor-free, abandoned subway station in an art gallery, this re-created history is divorced of context. It exists more as a streamlined, idealized memory of that period in history, one that overlays the messier, more complex version. Elmgreen and Dragset describe their installation as a display of memory's "erroneous machinery" (Allen, "Elmgreen"), connecting the workings of the New Yorker's mind with the nonexistent platform and the train that never comes. "End Station" should not be understood as parodic, however; it reminds viewers that the underground associations made in subway space may not be based in reality. For contemporary writers, subway histories are subjective, multiple, and emotionally true even when factually questionable. This is the case with the nostalgia that arises in even the most pessimistic missives. Alfred Kazin's 1973 essay "Please, How Do I Get Out of Here?" acknowledges that his memory of the Great Depression–era subway may be distorted by allowing, "No doubt I am fondly misremembering my earlier years on the subway." Indeed, Kazin was misremembering key details about subway lines, and several letters to the editor correct his facts ("Letters: Subway Transitives").

We need to understand technological nostalgia not in terms of its accuracy but in terms of the emotions and identifications animating it. Expressing admiration for *The Warriors*, for example, is a means of imaginatively connecting oneself with the New York City that preceded the urban renewal of the Giuliani administration. This desire has only grown as time has passed. When the movie was screened at Coney Island and Tompkins Square park, thousands of New Yorkers showed up to watch, including many who were born after the film's premiere. For young people who move to New York City today, nostalgia for the city in the 1970s articulates a set of bohemian desires that have been repeated for more than a century: the desire to live cheaply within an artistically fertile and diverse community. Woody Allen's 2011 film *Midnight in Paris* makes the same point about another city, suggesting that his central character's desire to live among Lost Generation artists and writers has less to do with the time period or the Parisian setting than with the companionship that these people provide. So rather than dismissing this desire for authenticity as impossible or childish, we might understand nostalgia for an earlier moment in New York's history as a mode of collective identity making. Those who long for the past are expressing very particular ideas not only about the present-day city they wish to inhabit but also about what group they imagine themselves belonging to within that city.

Coupled with these desires is a sense of belatedness, a sense of having missed the most exciting period of New York's history. Melissa Bradshaw points out in her history of Greenwich Village bohemianism that "mourning this lost authenticity" becomes a central "part of being a bohemian" (158). Even the models for bohemian life inevitably borrow from lost ways of life imagined to be more authentic: the chronicle of East Villagers' artistic struggles in *Rent* borrows its plot structure from a Puccini opera set in 1830, and the very term "bohemian" ascribes to those Parisian artists the lifestyle that they imagined Romany (or Gypsies) to lead. Andreas Huyssen's writing on urban remembrance suggests that "city culture" is particularly prone to cycles of dismissal and nostalgia in which "the resisted new is bound to become the basis for another glorified past some time in the future" (*Present Pasts* 87). When critics study nostalgia, then, they need to ask what is being glorified about the past and why it holds such an appeal for a particular group in the present day. What needs is the imagined past fulfilling that the present cannot?

## Creating Communities

As I discuss in chapters 4 and 5, American Yiddish plays and African American migration narratives both depict subway riding habits as clues about group membership. In both cases onlookers read the protagonists as primitive figures who don't belong in the midst of Manhattan's bustling commercial energy. To ride the subway inappropriately is to give oneself away as a tourist, a new arrival, non-urban. These stories may mock vulnerable populations for their incomplete acclimation, but they also show the acclimation process in exacting detail. Rudolph Fisher may describe King Solomon Gillis's face by using minstrel-show terminology, but he also describes Gillis's journey through Penn Station's depths with cognitive precision. Osip Dymov shows exactly how much information about American advertisements Hungerproud has soaked up while sleeping on the subway. In these modernist subway stories, we see how New Yorkers are made.

Colson Whitehead and Jonathan Lethem are equally interested in how the subway habit shapes its passengers. In his review of *The Colossus of New York*, Phillip Lopate calls the city mindset in the book "a sort of group psychology, fabricated under stress" (32). The trials of the subway passenger are reimagined as a source of cohesive identity. Routines of subway riding, particularly in the post-9/11 era, offer New Yorkers a sense of collective pride and self-definition.[7] This is far from a novel idea: in the midst of his bleak 1982 essay "Subway Odyssey," Paul Theroux offers two anthropological assessments of the ways that the subway reinforces group coherence even in that grim age. First, he mentions a linguistic quirk that I still observed in the early 2000s: "Most New Yorkers refer to the subway by the now-obsolete forms: IND, IRT, BMT. No one intentionally tries to confuse the stranger; it is just that, where the subway is concerned, precise directions are very hard to convey." Referring to the subways by their older system names is not merely an individual habit; signs on the walls in MTA tunnels continue to do the same thing. But in the case of passengers, it is difficult not to read some intentional mystification into their choice of words.

Along with in-group knowledge about the city's past, one characteristic that has been ascribed to city dwellers since the days of Georg Simmel is a blasé attitude. In a humorous essay published in the *New Yorker* in 1995, Calvin Trillin shares the struggles of Greenwich Village residents who can no longer complain about their newly renovated subway station. "Expressions of enthusiasm" more emphatic than "it could be worse" mark the speakers as naïve rubes from "Iowa or Idaho or one of them" (Trillin 102). Beneath his jocular tone, Trillin gets at an important shared belief that defines New York subway culture: to be urban is indeed to be blasé. New Yorkers in the 1990s were beginning to process the changing landscape of the subway system, which included newly air-conditioned cars stripped of graffiti. If complaining about the subway had helped strangers bond while waiting for a train, what might they do now? One way that New Yorkers define themselves in Trillin's essay is in opposition to tourists; instead of becoming a New Yorker once something that you knew has disappeared, you are a New Yorker when the subway no longer impresses you.

Concerns about regional and national identity fall by the wayside in Lethem's and Whitehead's work, perhaps because both writers were born in New York City. Assumptions about the pluralism of the subway crowd seem to be second nature to writers in the new millennium.[8] As a self-contained system that enables myriad different pathways through it, the New York City subway models the kind of community desired by these contemporary writers, one that Tamar Katz describes as "simultaneously coherent and argumentatively, profusely multiple" (814). Cohesive multiplicity animates the narrative choices made by both authors: they wish to describe a shared history without suggesting that it is the only history. A focus on subway planners and builders might imply a master narrative, but a focus on subway riders fragments in a thousand different directions. The subway system, then, is the structure that brings together both their points of view.

Whitehead and Lethem oscillate between embodied, partial perspectives on the subway and more omniscient, retrospective narratives. In this way, both authors imagine the subway, and the subway station in particular, as the prototypical intersection of urban planned space and intimate personal experience. Whitehead's authorial voice in *The Colossus of New York* moves between first-, second-, and third-person narration, implicating the narrator in the action and then extricating him from it. Whitehead has been criticized for the de-historicized quality of his book, particularly as a response to September 11 (Li 88, Lopate 33). He eschews all but the broadest outlines when giving the history of particular neighborhoods, focusing instead on prototypical New York experiences like moving from one apartment to another, walking down Broadway, taking a cab home after drinking too much. To my mind, the lack of detail gives the book a map-like quality, dealing in the structures of New York life rather than their particular iterations.

For Whitehead, the subway is a space of isolated collectivity. In his essay titled "Subway," the first-person voice occurs only in the plural: "We are stuck in the tunnel on account of a police action at the station ahead of us" (*Colossus* 55). He describes subway habits in anthropological terms—"There's a culture for platforms and a culture for between stations" (50)—and imagines the roar in a tunnel as a sound that can awaken primal instincts. Much of the essay is concerned with the difficulty of subway riding even for the most experienced passengers; every trip presents an opportunity for an awkward encounter, a missed connection, or a stained pair of pants.[9] Yet as Katz points out, "the physical movement of the train imposes unity on the subway's occupants, and this unity staves off an imaginary loss" (824). Although their individual attitudes divide them, they nonetheless do "a little dance" together "without rehearsal" (*Colossus* 57). "Subway" presents the practice of urban civility as a never-ending negotiation between the individual's need to get somewhere quickly and his need to be part of a community along the way.

Jonathan Lethem puts a double emphasis on the local near the end of his essay when he begins to page through newspaper clippings mentioning the Hoyt-Schermerhorn station. Most of these stories deal with moments of terror—shootings, passengers trapped beneath trains, and the like. Yet instead of being overwhelmed by the violence and danger of city life, Lethem instead considers the everyday life of the passengers involved in these incidents. The history that he worries about losing is not the history recorded in newspapers but the memories of people involved in it. The "lapping of human moments" ("Speak" 55) that he imagines as the life force of the station is not as dramatic as a train crash, but it is just as insistent and constitutive in constructing the history of the station. Unlike the poets of the subway sublime in the early twentieth century, Lethem characterizes this sublime experience as one defined by the crowd rather than the space that it moves through. The tide of passengers breaks for a moment on the platform and then moves on, spreading throughout the city. Even a local history of a subway station cannot be localized.

Lethem mentions the dangers of subway riding in the 1970s, but his image of the New York subway is quite different from the dystopian subway of *The Warriors* and Joseph Sargent's film *The Taking of Pelham One Two Three*, or even the utopian subway of graffiti and street artists like Keith Haring. Some contemporary novels try to bridge the divide between the pessimism of the recent past and the optimism that preceded it. Yet rather than understanding these grim novels as depictions of the failure of urban infrastructure, I argue that they are more concerned with interpersonal connection and local history. Colum McCann's *This Side of Brightness* (1998) and John Wray's *Lowboy* (2009) call upon images of the subway as ominous underworld while simultaneously imagining it as a possible site of authentic interpersonal contact. Both novels parallel their protagonists' convoluted thinking with their physical movement through the subway system. Lowboy, a paranoid schizophrenic teenager, escapes from a mental institution and leads missing persons detective Ali Lateef on a wild goose chase through the streets and tunnels of the city; Treefrog, the homeless protagonist of *This Side of Brightness*, lives in the tunnels. More important, the subway serves as the only way for these mentally unstable characters to relate to the city and to the people in it. The subway enables Treefrog, then known as Clarence Nathan Walker, to bond with his grandfather, a sandhog in the multiethnic group of laborers who helped clear the underwater tunnels between Brooklyn and Manhattan. One day the two of them walk the tunnels together, trying to find the site of a tunnel blowout. When they return to the station, Walker is unable to help his grandfather get back up onto the platform, and the man is killed. This is the moment of Walker's psychic break; his guilt leads him to molest his daughter and lose his family. Lowboy similarly finds himself to be most at ease in the subway, although it too is the place where he has been most antisocial, pushing his girlfriend Emily onto the tracks. Although Lowboy and Treefrog have deeply troubled connections with their family and friends, these novels ensure that readers can imagine the world from their perspective.

Even when Lowboy is at his most messianic, insisting that he can prevent the world from ending by climate change, his actions are understood in deeply interpersonal and embodied terms: to lower the earth's temperature, he must lower his own temperature by having sex with a girl. That he wants to lose his virginity in the City Hall station—the beautifully decorated, long-deserted station at the end of the 6 line—shows the intimate connection between global, urban, and personal history. McCann too looks to the past as a source of consolation and opportunity for reimagining the future: although racism warps his grandparents' experience aboveground, the tunnel where Treefrog's grandfather worked provides the most curiously utopian image of a true melting pot in the novel. McCann and Wray fuse the optimistic social engagement of Progressive Era subway writing with the dark fascination that characterizes urban writing in the era of white flight. In doing so, they suggest how knowledge of our infrastructure's history grounds particular and collective memories.

## Imagining Annihilation

Writing about technology in the modern United States has always been ambivalent. For every transportation technology, stories proliferate that imagine its catastrophic failure. Wolfgang Schivelbusch notes that even the most celebratory paeans to the railroad still grappled with "the ever-present fear of a potential disaster" (130). To futurism founder F. T. Marinetti and science fiction writer J. G. Ballard alike, the thrill of a speeding automobile always contains within it the imagined possibility of a crash.[10] The subway system's immensity, discussed again and again in the magazine poetry of the 1910s, necessarily suggests by contrast the smallness of human life and the failure of the poet's imagination in the face of such an indescribable spectacle. In this literary engagement with the subway as a sublime space, we can see the beginnings of the discourse imagining the risks of everyday city life in the wake of 9/11.[11] "All dwellers in cities must live with the stubborn fact of annihilation," wrote E. B. White, haunted by World War II (54). Both modern magazine poetry and postmodern subway writing aim for a middlebrow audience, evoking pathos by juxtaposing the fragile human body with the technological landscape.

The experiences of September 11 have made a tremendous impact both on the collective identity of New Yorkers and on the artistic reimagining of subway space.[12] Devin Zuber discusses the ways that subway stations became canvases for public mourning and political critique in the early 2000s. Flyers depicting the missing, flowers, and other mementoes were posted throughout the subway system (Zuber 280). Because these memorials were decentralized, traces lasted far longer there than in the more centralized memorials aboveground. As these makeshift memorials disappeared, street art critiquing the war on Iraq arose in its place. Zuber discusses two subway artists whose work responded to the Iraq war: Paul Chan, who created downloadable posters with photos of Iraqi citizens to be posted in the subway, and Copper Greene, an anonymous artist whose resituation of the hooded Abu Ghraib prisoner in an iPod advertisement is perhaps the most iconic critique of the period (281–83).[13] The subway plays the part of a transitory public square with the voices of dissent replaced by anonymous posted images.

For Colson Whitehead, *The Colossus of New York* began as a "side project" but became a place for processing his own grief and reimagining his relation to a changed city (Selzer 400). The first chapter of *Colossus* appeared in a slightly different form two months after the Twin Towers fell, in the November 11 issue of the *New York Times Magazine.* That version, as critics have noted, addresses the events of September 11 more directly than does the revised chapter. Whitehead writes, "The twin towers still stand because we saw them, moved in and out of their long shadows, were lucky enough to know them for a time" (Whitehead, "The Way We Live Now"). In the book, "The twin towers" is replaced by "our old buildings," generalizing the problem of loss to include even those New Yorkers who have arrived since the fall of 2001. The near-wordless paranoia about the new dangers of the city creep into the "Subway" chapter, where one character's "heart speeds up before his mind can process the fear" that results from being stuck between subway stations (*Colossus* 56). "It could be apocalypse above for all you know," the narrator wryly claims, "and who wouldn't think disaster, stuck in the tunnel like that" (56). Although 9/11 functions as a particularly traumatic realization of their fantasies, Max Page's book *The City's End* shows that artists, writers, and filmmakers have imagined the destruction of New York City for more than a century. Page understands Whitehead's attitude as a kind of hometown pride that acknowledges implicit danger: "Owning New York means surrendering to its rapid change, and the threats it constantly survives" (*City's End* 229).

The subway has long served as an imaginary source of and respite from those apocalyptic visions. Being stuck in a tunnel makes Whitehead's passenger "think disaster," but it is "apocalypse above" and not disaster within the subway that comes to mind. This reflects a feeling that can be seen in *The Subway* (1929), an Elmer Rice play in which an outer-borough secretary named Sophie Smith has an affair with the upper-class artist Eugene Landray. He imagines New York City being destroyed. The city's "steel towers" topple, and humanity flees underground to hide in the subway tunnels. He envisions "the city razed flat . . . a mountain of rubble and twisted steel . . . and humanity penned . . . penned in the subway . . . every orifice choked with rubble . . . great pipes bursting . . . gas-mains . . . sewers . . . and mankind perishing . . . drowned . . . suffocated . . . buried alive in the grave of concrete and steel it has built for itself" (Rice, *Subway* 96). This passage gives us a sense of how ominous, even dangerous is the interdependency among elements of the urban infrastructure: when the tunnels collapse, mankind is not only buried in rubble but also drowned in the water and sewage of burst pipes and suffocated by gas from ruptured mains. Yet the subway maintains life as well. The artist concludes his story with scientists "from the new civilization on the Congo" digging through the rubble of a destroyed New York and finding "the body of a young girl . . . preserved miraculously . . . inexplicably . . . through all those centuries . . . a young girl asleep . . . warm . . . radiant . . . in that chamber of death" (98). Even when New York seems poised to change irrevocably, the subway maintains a connection to the lived reality of its listener. Sophie recognizes herself in the young girl of Eugene's story and swoons.

Eugene Landray's dramatic monologue serves two purposes in *The Subway:* it transforms New York City into a quasi-mythological realm, and it seduces Sophie. The subway writing that I have discussed serves a similar purpose, rendering the daily grind of a subway ride into a timeless truth about city life and welcoming the audience into the realm of cosmopolitan readers who can see it as such. Whitehead ironically calls the totality of cultural production glamorizing New York City "the brochure" (*Colossus* 3). But how does a focus on the subway help these essayists convert their readers and make them fall in love with the city advertised in that fabled brochure? First, it's important to remember that both texts began their lives as magazine essays. Although neither appeared in the *New Yorker,* both began their lives in magazines that imagine a similar level of worldliness in their readership. They also assume a familiarity with New York City geography and culture: *Harper's* has offices in New York City, and the *Times Magazine*—particularly in the wake of 9/11—is invested in presenting life in Manhattan as both unique and uniquely American. In this way we can understand both of these essays as utilizing the tropes of cosmopolitan provincialism that Thomas Grant sees as the defining quality of writing published in the *New Yorker* (32). New York City is imagined as a self-contained world, one that might interest readers in the rest of the country but certainly interests its own residents.

*The Colossus of New York* and "Speak, Hoyt Schermerhorn" assume that their readers are fellow New Yorkers, or if not, then that they are sophisticated enough to be both familiar with and interested in the workings of the New York City subway. It might be useful, then, to understand these essays as participating in what Trysh Travis calls a "high middlebrow culture" (254). Like the *New Yorker* essayists to whom they are indebted, Whitehead and Lethem engage in a sophisticated and specific form of popular writing, one that appeals to educated reader on an affective level. Their essays create an imagined community of New Yorkers, one that might include readers who have only visited the city and others who have never been there. Travis emphasizes that the bonds created by the *New Yorker* should be understood as valid, not merely the byproduct of a desire to sell more magazines. The felt response to New York writing in the twenty-first century is similarly valid in that it expresses (along with the desire for cultural capital) a desire for the kind of lived community felt in subway space. I conclude my meditation on contemporary subway writing by considering the critical possibilities that arise in contemplating subway space from a historical perspective as well as a personal one.

## Riding the Local

Throughout this conclusion a keynote of nostalgia for an earlier era in New York's history sounds again and again. This nostalgia has less to do with a desire to return to the past, I argue, than with a desire for a particular kind of urban space that is lacking in the present day. When writers and artists suggest that the New York subway is a palimpsest on which the history of the recent past can be read, they are protesting the lack of this legible history on the city streets.[14] And when they celebrate the particulars of New York subway nomenclature or behavior, they are arguing in favor of a tactile, local form of transportation and against a dematerialized, globalized movement. Fredric Jameson does not specifically refer to the subway when he says that postmodern literature's focus on technology is "itself a figure for something else," the unimaginable network of global capitalism (*Postmodernism* 35); contemporary personal narratives find in the subway an infrastructural figure of resistance to the multinational reach of global capital in the postmodern city. They do so not because the subway is an intrinsically superior technology or one that harkens back to a golden age before global capitalism. Instead, what these authors recognize in the subway is its ability to create an environment where people relate to one another in an anonymous but intimate way. Indeed, the subway serves as a kind of neutral territory where people with otherwise hugely different lives might come into contact with one another. Although it precedes the interstate highway system and the Internet, modern writing about the subway anticipates the decentralized layout and the impersonal modes of sociability that the later networks enable. Subway stories remind us that it is not utopian to imagine technologies bringing about new kinds of interpersonal relations, but also that narratives shape the understanding of those new relations.

Spaces of public transit have long been symbolic sites of social conflict in US history; think of *Plessy v. Ferguson*, the Zoot Suit Riots, or the Montgomery bus boycotts. But these conflicts occurred in part because of the ways they brought Americans of different political persuasions together in a public, mechanized space. Many typical New York subway stories are possible only because of the kinds of journeys that the infrastructural framework makes possible. If the commute from the Lower East Side to the Bronx didn't pass through Times Square, Osip Dymov might not have understood the Jewish New Yorker's commute in such commercial terms; without the Hoyt-Schermerhorn stop's ghost platform, it would not have been such a popular location for movie shoots. Cities may no longer serve as the manufacturing centers of the United States, but they have become increasingly important as tourist destinations. Their infrastructure, particularly public transit, offers an alternative way of living to the decentralized car culture to which most of those visitors are accustomed.

Studying the literary representations of technology gives us a clearer sense of transportation technology's diverse ridership and the competing meanings it can hold for different populations. Like Jacob Lawrence's paintings depicting railroad migration, Rudolph Fisher's short stories valorize the experience of migrants encountering new technology at a pivotal time. While African Americans from the South may not have felt their subway rides to be symbolic of an entry into modernity, the black bourgeoisie who had already settled in the North did, in part because their comfort with the technology set them apart from their less acclimated brothers and sisters. King Solomon Gillis's subway ride certainly reads differently in the middlebrow, nationally distributed *Atlantic Monthly* than it does in the *New Negro* anthology. The users of a given technology are seldom a monolithic group; when they are portrayed as such, scholars of technology need to ask who might be interested in doing so. In order to understand its purpose in culture, we need to look at stories told about technology from a rhetorical perspective, asking who's doing the talking, how that person is establishing credibility or manipulating emotions, and what kinds of audiences are being addressed or imagined.

This genealogy of subway stories reminds us that transportation technologies are not only literal but also literary: they transport us, but they also shape and direct our understanding of the space surrounding us. In literary-critical terms, a metaphor has two parts, the tenor and the vehicle. Whereas the tenor is the thing being described in a metaphor, the vehicle is the concrete object that takes on symbolic descriptive power: love is a rose, for example, or the United States is a symphony. In both of those metaphors, certain nuances of the former concept come into clearer focus when put into dialogue with the latter. To call the nation a symphony, for example, highlights how individual cultures combine in an aesthetically pleasing way to produce a whole that's greater than the sum of its parts. The New York subway helps scholars and city dwellers understand the metaphorics of technology because it becomes the vehicle in so many different kinds of metaphors. At the beginning of his essay titled "Spatial Stories," Michel de Certeau calls upon technology as a metaphorical vehicle: "In modern Athens, the vehicles of mass transportation are called *metaphorai.* To go to work or come home, one takes a 'metaphor'—a bus or a train. Stories could also take this noble name: every day, they traverse and organize places; they select and link them together; they make sentences and itineraries out of them. They are spatial trajectories" (115). Subway stories, then, are doubly metaphorical. They serve as vehicles for the dreams and anxieties of modern and contemporary urban life, and they "traverse and organize" space in a way that helps their tellers and their audience make sense of it. As I have shown throughout this book, the metaphorical exploration of technology can have a deep psychic impact on Americans: it can narrate our isolation, or it can enable us to imagine that we are part of a larger whole. Subway stories show us how to remain in close and even uncomfortable quarters with all kinds of people in order to reach our destination.

# Notes

## Introduction

1. By calling the texts in this book "modernist," I mean to point out a number of their commonalities beyond that of publication date. In contemporary critical parlance, "modernism" can designate both a literary period—usually "about 1890 to 1945" (Mao and Walkowitz 738)—and a range of formal devices employed by writers in that period. For recent contestation of the periodization of modernism, see Friedman, "Definitional Excursions" and "Periodizing Modernism."
2. Financed by millionaire Augustus Belmont, the Interborough Rapid Transit Company's subway line ran from City Hall up the east side of Manhattan to Grand Central Terminal, connected to Times Square, and then ran up the west side of Central Park. At 103rd Street, the subway branched off into two lines that extended into the Bronx (Interborough Rapid Transit and Cudahy 24–25). Clifton Hood's *722 Miles* is widely regarded as the definitive academic history of the New York subway's construction and expansion. For a more popular account, see Cudahy, *Under the Sidewalks*.
3. Indeed, Randy Kennedy ("A Day in the Subway") emphasizes the many ways in which the infrastructure has stayed the same over time: "The levers [the dispatcher] moves look like the ones her predecessors moved when the subway started. The

trains she dispatches still run on the same kind of wheels (steel), sit atop rails of the same gauge (4 feet, 8.5 inches) and draw the same blue-sparking direct current (625 volts) from the ominous third rail."

4. Sidonie Smith also discusses the interplay between different types of movement and different forms of writing when she says, "If the mode of moving a body through space affects the traveler who moves through spaces as that body, then the mode of motion informs the meaning that the traveler sends back home in narration" (xii).
5. Jonathan Crary is another critic who sees modernist aesthetics intertwined with modernization: "Any effective account of modern culture must confront the ways in which modernism, rather than being a reaction against or transcendence of processes of scientific and economic rationalization, is inseparable from them" (85).
6. As Mark Bahnisch notes, "In one sense, the minute division of labour characteristic of Taylorism, and the alienated work which is its consequence, have become a floating signifier written into central narratives and myths of the 20th century" (54). For Fordist efficiency in modern narratives, see Banta, *Taylored Lives.* For Taylorism in modernist poetry, see Tichi 257–67.
7. See Seiler 25–29 for a discussion of how scientific management works against earlier conceptions of individualism in this period.
8. For an analysis of the subway in relation to New York's reputation as an "unfinished city," see Bender 23, 40. For the subway as an instance of the urban underworld, see Pike, *Metropolis on the Styx* and "Urban Nightmares."
9. I discuss the critical history of the subway as underworld in chapter 1.
10. For a thorough guide to the history of this critical tradition, see de la Peña, "Slow and Low Progress."
11. In his important 1963 essay "The Modern City as a Field of Historical Study," Oscar Handlin considers "the appearance of the common carrier" to be a "critical breakthrough" in the size and complexity of the modern city (12).
12. For further discussion of these early forms of urban transit, see Cheape; Cudahy, *Cash, Tokens, and Transfers;* Fischler.
13. See Stilgoe 8 and Douglas 4.
14. Wolfgang Schivelbusch discusses the ways in which train travel altered the modern sense of time (see 33–44). Many critics also discuss the importance of time as a regulating force in the modern city. See Handlin 14 and Kern 15.
15. The city began dismantling elevated lines in 1939. See Stalter, "Farewell to the El," for a description of the social and cultural response to the razing of the final holdout, the Third Avenue El, in 1955.
16. Recent critical attention to the elevated train has emphasized its panoramic quality and the distanced relationship to the city sights (particularly the lives of the poor) that resulted. See Brooks 36–46; Haenni 36–48; Tichi 247–48. In the few instances when the El is represented from the perspective of a Bowery apartment, it is generally an oppressive urban force. See Kirby 165.
17. See Augé 70; Gitelman and Pingree xv; and Marvin 4.
18. See Seiler 25–30 and Lears.

19. For a discussion of nineteenth-century codes of politeness, see Kasson, *Rudeness and Civility*, especially chap. 4, "Venturing Forth: Bodily Management in Public." For a description of the crowded buses and horsecars of mid-nineteenth-century New York City, see Brooks 8–10.
20. See Hood, "Changing Perceptions."
21. For discussions of panoramic visuality as it affected modern subjectivity, see Friedberg 20–29 and Kirby 7.
22. For further discussions of the railroad as a vehicle of cinematic visuality, see Kirby.
23. See Stalter, "The Subway Crush."
24. See Kuklick, "Myth and Symbol in American Studies," for the classic critique of this critical approach.
25. See Bramen 159–60 and Zurier 86–103 for a history of this tradition, generally said to have begun with the character sketches in the London *Spectator.* Zurier finds it particularly useful to distinguish the European tradition of the flâneur as discussed by Baudelaire and Benjamin from the "host of mobile urban observers" (91) seen in American culture by the turn of the twentieth century. I attempt to do the same, since the perspective of the subway writer often moves between a detached flânerie and a more invested style.
26. See Mumford, *Technics and Civilization* 333; Meikle 19–38; and Dinerstein 12.
27. In using the word "liminal," I call upon its meaning in Victor Turner's anthropological study of liminal states of being during rites of passage, as referred to in *The Ritual Process: Structure and Anti-structure.* Performance studies, with its focus on the interaction between individuals and their environment, has certainly influenced my thinking about the function of subway space. Since the subway commute tends to be an everyday occurrence rather than a structured ritual, I will not pursue further connections between Turner's thinking and my topic.

## 1. Forming the Subway Habit

1. Tracy Fitzpatrick follows the claims made by the *World* in dating this phrase to an editorial from April 8, 1893. While the editorial may have given the first detailed explanation of this desire, the phrase certainly appeared in print prior to that date.
2. W. Joseph Campbell sets Ochs's paradigm of straight news, established as the norm by 1897, against two other models: the "journalism of action" seen in William Randolph Hearst's *New York Journal* and the literary-minded feature story popular in Lincoln Steffens's *New York Commercial Advertiser* (70–71). The *Times*'s famous slogan "All the News That's Fit to Print" explicitly positions the paper's objectivity against the exploitative and sentimental positions taken by its competitors. This makes the paper's subway speculations all the more surprising.
3. Here I follow John Urry's call for practitioners of mobility studies to explore how people, goods, and ideas cut across borders (3).
4. This possibly apocryphal quote appears in a number of variants throughout histories of the New York subway. I take this version from Edward Hymoff's 1961 *Popular*

*Mechanics* article "Underground City" (264), one of the many mid-century magazine articles exploring the subterranean infrastructure of New York City.

5. These lyrics are taken from the original cast album of *On the Town* (Bernstein, Comden, and Green). The Broadway show debuted in 1944, with the film version following in 1949.
6. For a critical history of the use of these two terms, see Thacker, *Moving through Modernity.*
7. Perhaps the most influential book on this subject has been Rosalind Williams's *Notes on the Underground,* which considers the resonance of nineteenth-century excavation and underground construction projects on the literature and culture of the era. Preceding Williams by a few years, Wendy Lesser's *Life below the Ground* surveys a broader range of literary representations of underground space over a longer period, focusing less on technological innovations. David Pike considers the relationship between the mythological underworld and the material and metaphorical underground in two books, *Subterranean Cities* and *Metropolis on the Styx.* He makes a wide-ranging historical argument about the relationship between the different spaces in the "vertical city" (*Subterranean Cities* 5).
8. Though I allude to some possible explanations, it is beyond the scope of this book to consider thoroughly the historical and cultural differences that led New York writers to a different conception of subway space from those of their French and British counterparts.
9. For an analysis of the "underground films" of the 1970s and 1980s, see Pike, "Urban Nightmares."
10. For further discussion of the tension between horizontal and vertical models of New York life, see Taylor 51–67.
11. This trope continues in the late twentieth century and into the twenty-first. Jennifer Toth's (now somewhat discredited) journalistic account of the "mole people" who live in the tunnels beneath New York, published in 1993, carries the idea of the subway mole to its extreme. Even the long-delayed construction of the Second Avenue subway line, now under way, uses a machine nicknamed "the Mole" to bore new tunnels without disturbing the city above (Sargent, "The Line").
12. Some subway lines are elevated, chiefly on the northern fringes of Manhattan and in the outer boroughs. Many authors are drawn to these moments of emergence from the underground tunnels, using them to mark a shift in perspective or a realization of some sort on the part of their protagonists.
13. In this example we see how the *New York Times,* like the population of New York, moved north. Its original building stood at 113 Nassau Street in lower Manhattan. The *Times* then moved to 41 Park Row, a building that faced City Hall, in 1858. For further history of 41 Park Row, see Dunlap.
14. For the foundation of the literary understanding of modernity as an era of ephemerality, see Baudelaire and Berman. For the foundation of contemporary models of modernity based in the assumption that the modern city provides shocks to the individual consciousness, see Simmel. For a discussion of modernity as the era of speed, see Duffy.
15. For a history of modern velocity, see Schnapp and Duffy.

16. In *The Culture of Time and Space, 1880–1918,* Stephen Kern lays the groundwork for thinking about technology in this way. See especially 109–80 and 211–58.
17. I borrow the distinction between a system and a regime from Colin Divall's essay "Mobilizing the History of Technology," where he "encourages thinking in terms of a transport *system* (single mode) or *regime* (multimode)" (951).
18. Lankevich notes that Brooklyn was the third-largest city in the United States by population from 1860 to 1890. As consolidation took place in 1898, and population was measured every ten years, it had become part of Greater New York by the time populations were counted again.
19. See Brooks 70 for the debate on "subway air."
20. As Jameson points out in his talk on cognitive mapping, the converse is true as well: "Urban alienation is directly proportional to the mental unmapability of local cityscapes" ("Cognitive Mapping" 283). Later in this chapter I consider how the subway functions as a whole system and as a constitutive part, since it is both what Lynch calls an "environmental image" and a vehicle for constructing such an image of the wider city.
21. See Melman for an analysis of this book and the many cultural imitators and parodies it spawned.
22. My interpretation of elevated visuality is thus quite different from Amy Kaplan's influential take on William Dean Howells's New York novel *A Hazard of New Fortunes.* She argues that "the moving lens of the L masters the city's rapid pace by framing the spectacle of working-class life in a series of domestic still lives" (50). Most critical attention to the elevated train has followed Kaplan's argument.
23. See Ziegler for a reading of subway space similarly inspired by de Certeau.
24. Mark Simpson discusses this ideology in his introduction to *Trafficking Subjects: The Politics of Mobility in Nineteenth-Century America.*

## 2. How the Subway Became Sublime

1. Although the genealogy of the term "technological sublime" has been rehearsed elsewhere, I will do so here as well. First alluded to in Perry Miller's *Life of the Mind* and developed in Leo Marx's *Machine in the Garden,* the concept, particularly in nineteenth-century American culture, is most fully developed in David Kasson's *Civilizing the Machine* and David Nye's *American Technological Sublime.*
2. Chester Firkins was born in Minneapolis in 1882. He attended the University of Minneapolis as an undergraduate. He then moved to New York and worked as a journalist while widely publishing his verse in magazines including *The Independent, Puck,* and *The Smart Set.* His only book of verse appeared in 1916, a year after his early death; its sections include "Poems of City Life" on New York themes and "Poems of the Northwest," which deal with his home state. The juxtaposition of these two sections suggests that the "cityscape poetry" of the early twentieth century may owe as much to the "local color" magazine fiction of the late nineteenth century as it does to the poetry of Walt Whitman and Charles Baudelaire. Brief biographies of the brothers may be found in Schilplin 169–72.

3. The earliest poem discussed in this chapter, "On a Subway Express," was published in 1908. Anthologies of urban verse, particularly New York–centered verse, appeared in the late 1910s and early 1920s.
4. Many of the sources that I discuss and questions that I respond to in this chapter came from thinking through Newcomb's essay " 'The Housetop Sea': Cityscape Verse and the Rise of Modern American Poetry." Newcomb develops his argument about this period in American verse in his book *How Did Poetry Survive?,* which unfortunately was released too recently for me to respond to in this study.
5. Nye shows how one's perspective on the sublime depends on economics as well: "The older forms of the technological sublime embodied the values of production, and literally embodied the gaze of the businessman as he surveyed a city from the top of a skyscraper or appreciated steel mills from the window of a passing train" (*American Technological Sublime* 294). Nye sets this type of relationship to the technologically sublime sight outside the window in opposition to the consumerist spectacle of Las Vegas, where the mirrored and lavishly lit sights "destroy normal spatial relations" (295).
6. One other common category of American railroad poetry describes the passengers riding on the railroad. I address Henry David Thoreau's "What's the Railroad to Me?" as a precursor to the genteel critiques of city poetry. I do not discuss folksongs and work songs of the nineteenth-century railroad in this chapter simply because they were outside the purview of these genteel writers, though I do bring them up in chapter 5 in relation to the migration narratives of Harlem Renaissance writers. For a compilation of railroad poetry that spans high and low sources over the past two centuries, see Hedin.
7. Morley had similar credentials to the critics of subway verse. Along with his reputation as a poet, he was known as a novelist, a newspaper columnist, and later as an "an arbiter of middlebrow taste" for serving as a member of the selection committee for the Book of the Month Club (Rogers-Carpenter 709).
8. A professor of Romance languages at the University of Minnesota, Phelps wrote extensively on Italian language and literature. It is no surprise, then, that her depiction of the subway system would make reference to the *Inferno:* "Dante pilgrimaging where / Lucifer was hurled / Journeyed not thus debonair / Through the underworld" (23). Here it should be noted that the comparison to the underworld is not an exact parallel, since the subway ride underground is far more "debonair" than that of the passenger's predecessors.
9. According to nycsubway.org, "Broadway at this point is in a deep valley and the transit designers had a choice of a viaduct or deep tunnel with steep grades at either end. They chose a viaduct to allow the subway to remain relatively level" ("Station: 125th Street").
10. For the Transcendentalists and the Romantics, the sublime was far more commonly experienced in nature. Indeed, we might equally understand these different ways of experiencing sublimity as Protestant (an unmediated one-on-one experience) and Catholic (mediated and collective) versions of the sublime. Thanks to Ben Johnson for this suggestion.

11. For a discussion of Whitman's interest in the urban crowd, see Brand 156–85.
12. The juxtaposition of "the children" with "the factory," along with Patton's interest in feminine labor, suggest that this figure may be female. The central thesis of the poem—that individual city dwellers find peace in subway space—does not depend on the gender of the speaker. The author's name appears below the poem as "M. F. Patton."
13. By mid-century, Garrett Ziegler suggests, people's fear of the subway system has been sublimated: "As their wonder decreased, so too did their fear" (292).

## 3. Minding the Gaps in Modernist Poetry

1. Using Alice Notley's *Descent of Alette* as her central text, Julia Bloch argues that the subway can be understood as a figure of complex poetic lineage in the work of later poets as well.
2. See especially Balestra and Versluys.
3. An approximation of the poem's layout in its original version follows (Pound, "In a Station of the Metro"):

   IN A STATION OF THE METRO
   The apparition    of these faces    in the crowd:
   Petals    on a wet, black    bough.

4. In this way Reed puts a new spin on an old critical trope: that *The Bridge* fails to achieve its own poetic ideals, whether intentionally or not. See Riddel, Schultz, and especially Dickie.
5. Crane regularly mocked subway ads. Sam Loveman, a friend of Crane's, said that "riding on the subway was just one *holocaust of laughter* because he saw double meanings in all the ads, and usually obscene meanings. He claimed that most of them had some sexual or phallic undercurrent of meaning. I doubted that, although very frequently he was right or seemed to be right" (Unterecker 181).
6. The humanization of subway advertisements recurs throughout American modernism, both high and low. In the next chapter I discuss a Yiddish play whose hero dreams that he encounters the trademarked characters in the ads that surround him on the Bronx Express. Similarly, Busby Berkeley's "I Only Have Eyes for You" sequence in the movie *Dames* shows a man riding the subway with his sweetheart; when she falls asleep on his shoulder, he looks at the ads featuring female figures, imagining each face turning into the face of his beloved. See Dinerstein 212–15. This repeated motif suggests the prevalence of "car cards" as a part of city life and a deep compulsion to humanize them.
7. For British poetry that deals with the London subway as a site of visual encounters, see Thacker, *Moving through Modernity* and "Uncompleted Life."
8. See Huyssen, "Mass Culture as Woman," for the classic formulation of this argument.
9. The Baroness Elsa von Freytag-Loringhoven undertakes a similar poetic project in her poems "Subjoyride" and "Sense into Nonsense 2: Subjoyride," where she mixes and matches advertising slogans (99–103).
10. Indeed, the kind of self-definition and resistance to interpretation evoke Charles Baudelaire's and Walt Whitman's poems to passers-by.

11. For a reading of this poem as a failed attempt at romantic contact, see Nickowitz 105–7.
12. The first extended attention to Crane's queer poetics came in Thomas E. Yingling's *Hart Crane and the Homosexual Text.* Yingling reveals how *The Bridge* accounts for the movements of desire in the relationship between body and machine (225–26). For more recent readings of Crane's queer poetics, see Dean; Reed, *Hart Crane* 39–70; Snediker 43–78.
13. See Rice, *The Subway* 31, where groping passengers are transformed into animals, and Chase 4, calling New York subway cars worse than Chicago stockyards.
14. Michael Trask calls this new form of temporality "episodic time" and connects it to the anonymous and replaceable laborer in Crane's poetry (138).
15. Parker was an upper-class woman posing as working class to write her account. Some of the most striking details of her first weeks working at a chocolate factory have to do with the conscious and unconscious ways she had to alter herself physically to become accustomed to that routine. Thanks to Pamela Caughie for introducing me to this and the Bryn Mawr summer school source as well.
16. See especially Trask 108–41.
17. See Hood, *722 Miles* 135–61, for a discussion of New York City subway expansion under the Dual Contracts.
18. According to Crane, this section of the poem takes its place-names from a "boozy truckdriver" he spoke with "in a lowdown dive" who "lived out there" and "died at Floral Park, Flatbush" (Crane 539–40). Like the cab driver who claimed that "Maquokeeta" was his "Indian name" (Crane 512)—providing the name for the warrior in "The Dance"—this truck driver invests Crane's poem with a sense of authenticity. Although the monologue is spoken in subway space, it also evokes the hoboes of "The River," suggesting the transient quality of working-class life across the country.
19. Many people have made this argument, but the most thorough is Lensing.
20. Brian Reed describes this critical tradition, noting that the lines have "long been understood as a reference to tearoom trade, that is, sex in public restrooms" (*Hart Crane* 165).
21. This suggests another connection between Crane's and Poe's poetic strategies: "Poe had, to an exceptional degree, the feeling for the incantatory element in poetry. . . . It has the effect of an incantation which, because of its very crudity, stirs the feelings at a deep and almost primitive level" (Eliot 31).
22. Brian Reed discusses the previous critical understanding of Crane as a literary disciple of Walt Whitman, a view first presented by Yvor Winters in 1947 and revised by Harold Bloom, who sees in their relationship a central example of his concept of the "anxiety of influence" (Reed, *Hart Crane* 19–21).
23. For an important dissenting opinion, see "From Poe to Valéry" a 1948 essay in *To Criticize the Critic and Other Writings* in which T. S. Eliot disavows Poe for his immaturity and inconsistency before he finally acknowledges Poe's importance to poetry (27).
24. Cecelia Tichi calls the poem "a good example of the design formed largely of components manufactured, so to speak, in the word factories of the advertising agencies" (280).

25. See Armstrong 90–95 for a discussion of physical fragmentation in Poe and its wider literary import.
26. See Reed, *Hart Crane* 169–246, and Khalip.

## 4. Underground Assimilation in Ethnic Drama

1. I should acknowledge Tracy Fitzpatrick's excellent reading of this cartoon, though I disagree with her assertion that the African American figures are "the most highly exaggerated" in it (104); when an eastern European woman wears a headscarf and an Italian-looking man sports not only a mustache but also an organ grinder's hat, we are in the realm of caricature and not flesh and blood.
2. For a history of the melting pot as a metaphor, especially pre-Zangwill, see Sollors, *Beyond Ethnicity* 66–101. These calls to abandon ethnic difference continue throughout the twentieth century, from Theodore Roosevelt's suspicion of "hyphenate" Americans to the Ford Motor Company's Americanization pageants to the culture wars of the 1980s and 1990s.
3. Appropriately enough for a play about interborough movement, it was not until 1968 that *Bronx Express* played on the Lower East Side, the presumptive home of Yiddish theater. The Folksbiene theater reimagined the play that year, with new advertising characters such as Miss Clairol and the Marlboro Man (see Shepard). The English version was revived with new songs at the New York International Fringe Festival in 2005, directed by Miriam Weiner.
4. The English translation used in the 1922 production at the Astor Theater is in the Billy Rose Theatre Collection at the New York Performing Arts Library. Later drafts of this adaptation, which was changed substantially in the course of production, can be found in the Charles Coburn papers at the Hargrett Rare Book and Manuscript Library, University of Georgia Libraries.
5. Since the subway functioned both as a vehicle of agency for women and as a site for reinscribing them into socially determined roles, it may be understood within the wider critical discussion of women and mobility in the nineteenth and twentieth centuries. Nancy Bentley discusses "the sensations of risk in modern mobility" throughout the work of Edith Wharton (246). For an extensive discussion of women's narratives of mobility, see Smith, *Moving Lives.* For a discussion of the ways that early automobile discourse constructs the car as both fashionable and domesticated, see Seiler 50–60.
6. Although space prevents me from describing the connections between Dymov's work and that of American expressionist dramas by Eugene O'Neill, Elmer Rice, and others, they are certainly worth pursuing. Indeed, *Bronx Express* demands a reconceptualization of the canon of American expressionist drama, since its December 1919 Yiddish-language debut precedes that of O'Neill's play *The Emperor Jones,* which opened at the Provincetown Playhouse in November 1920.
7. For a history of the movement focused on its contribution to stagecraft and acting style, see Wainscott 91–140.

8. In her history of New York subway art, Tracy Fitzpatrick notes that the diversity of subway reading material becomes a shorthand way of understanding the diversity of the riders (105).
9. See Robert Park's study *The Immigrant Press and Its Control* (1922) for a description of the role that immigrant newspapers play in the process of Americanization. Park mentions *Bronx Express* by name in this book. He notes that "the Jews have a group of contemporaneous playwrights whose plays deal with American life" and singles out Dymov (whose name he spells "Ossip Dimoff") as a writer who "has only recently come from Russia" and put on a play "at the Madison Square Garden Theater in the winter of 1920, called 'The Bronx Express,' which is a very clever satire on Americanization" (129–30).
10. The New York City subway that takes passengers to the Bronx is "non-Aryan" by metonymy, since most of its passengers at that time would have been Jewish. I discuss the intraurban migration to Brooklyn and the Bronx later in this chapter.
11. If, as Presner suggests, "the 'arcade' counts as the best material witness to nineteenth-century Paris" and the railroad system "the best material witness to German/Jewish modernity," then the subway system counts as an equally vital "material witness" to New York Jewish modernity (2).
12. For further discussion of the Jewish intraurban movement to Brooklyn and the Bronx, see chapter 2 of Deborah Dash Moore's *At Home in America,* especially 19–36.
13. For a discussion of the ways that the railroad has affected modern conceptions of time, see Kern 12, Schivelbusch 33–44, and Presner 59–62.
14. Thanks to Alison Shonkwiler for helping me formulate the ideas in this paragraph.
15. In *Ethnic Modernism,* Werner Sollors remarks on the prominence of streetcars in modern American ethnic literature. See 35–37.
16. See Harshav and Harshav 37 for the works of A. Leyeles, the Introspectivist poet who wrote in Yiddish journals such as *Po'eyze* and *In Zikh.* His 1926 poetic sequence titled "New York" included three poems set in the subway. In the first, he calls the crowd "A living tangle"; in the second, the underground system of tracks is a "nightmare tunnel-land"; in the third, a white woman and an African American man standing close together in the car evoke not a vision of racial harmony but one of lynching (Harshav and Harshav 99, 101, 103).
17. See Sollors, *Beyond Ethnicity.*
18. Hasia Diner's *In the Almost Promised Land* discusses the coverage of lynchings in the South in the wake of the Leo Frank case (94–99).
19. Walter Benn Michaels notably (and controversially) associates nativism in politics with modernism in literature in *Our America.*
20. Judith Keller reads this photograph as "perhaps the most poignant and meaningful of the series" (152), using it as a starting point for considering the relationship between blindness and camera-aided vision in twentieth-century art.
21. For a discussion of Saroyan's interest in multiculturalism, see Calonne.
22. This appropriation of popular performance styles has been noted by critics. One of

the few analyses of *Subway Circus* describes its form as typical of Saroyan's dramas overall, which borrow a "jumbled mix of signs taken from vaudeville, circus, and melodrama" (Aguilera Linde 18).

23. I historicize the African American response to the subway in chapter 5, situating the literature within the Great Migration and the need to render coherent the disparate experiences of the rural South and the urban North.
24. These works of art are both discussed in Brooks 207–10.
25. See Brooks 198–205.

## 5. Uncanny Migration Narratives

1. For a recent history of the Great Migration, see Wilkerson. For earlier accounts of the Great Migration's impact on Harlem, see Johnson, *Black Manhattan* and "Harlem: The Culture Capital."
2. For further discussion of the African American driver, see Franz 131–53 and Seiler 105–28.
3. After the Civil War, African Americans were technically free to ride in any railroad car for which they had paid the appropriate fare, though many passengers had to sue to do so. See Ayers 93–100. This hard-won freedom was cut short with the transportation segregation of late nineteenth-century Jim Crow laws, which divided passengers by race in addition to the class of ticket they bought. Homer Plessy tested this law in 1892. A light-skinned African American who could pass as a white man, he boarded a whites-only car on a Louisiana train and eventually told the conductor that he was a Negro. For a thorough and lucid account of the *Plessy v. Ferguson* Supreme Court case, see Sundquist 233–49. This strategic challenge led to the codification of "separate but equal accommodations" as a principle of racial segregation in American life, even through the years where the train was a symbol of freedom.
4. See Johnson, "Harlem: The Culture Capital" (303–4) and *Black Manhattan;* Osofsky 17–35; Brooks 185; Rhodes-Pitts 15–17.
5. Extremely well received in its day, the story was originally published in the *Atlantic Monthly* and reprinted in *The New Negro* (1925). Its title became a synonym for Harlem in writing of the period (Jongh 17), and was used as a chapter title in David Levering Lewis's groundbreaking cultural history *When Harlem Was in Vogue* (25).
6. See Lee for a discussion of "the turn-of-the-century's persistent association between the railroad and racial conflict" (346). She usefully reminds us that the railroad was not only a utopian but also "an estranging experience" (347). For a historical survey of the train's importance in African American culture in the nineteenth century, see Zabel. For a selection of African American railroad poetry, see Hedin. For discussion of the train in blues songs, see Carby 13–14. For attention to the story of John Henry and the importance of the train to African American music and dance, see Dinerstein.
7. See Ellison, "An Extravagance of Laughter" 152–57, for a discussion of the difference between northern and southern bus rides.

8. *Sport of the Gods* is often described as the first migration novel (Rodgers 3).
9. For more information on the construction of Pennsylvania Station and its tunnels under the Hudson River, see Jonnes. The destruction of McKim, Mead & White's original railroad station in the early 1960s is one of New York's great architectural traumas (Diehl). For a history of Penn Station's initial construction, as well as its reconstruction beneath Madison Square Garden in the early 1960s, see Ballon and Taylor.
10. Gillis already shows himself to be a more skillful subway rider than Perryn Joel, a white journalist who poses as an African American in the story "The Man Who Passed." Sent away from Harlem by a girl who discovers his secret and fears for his safety, Joel "fumble[s] in his pocket for a nickel" as the train approaches at the story's conclusion (Fisher, *City of Refuge* 259).
11. Mark Simpson discusses an earlier displacement in narratives of the Underground Railroad, where the agency of white abolitionists is emphasized at the expense of the escaped slaves (65).
12. See Page, *Creative Destruction of Manhattan.*
13. See Carby 168–88 and Duck.
14. Thanks to Liz Reich for the phrasing of this last point.
15. See Rodgers 29–30, 168–69; Griffin 5, 110–23.
16. See Balshaw 32–36, 43; Bone, *Down Home* 156; Lenz 326–27. For a discussion of this process in the work of contemporary African American women novelists, see Dubey.
17. See Thompson 133–44 for a discussion of these modern composers who appropriated and replicated city noise. *The Autobiography of William Carlos Williams* contains a related anecdote. "As we came from Antheil's 'Ballet Mecanique,'" Williams wrote, "a woman of our party, herself a musician, made this remark: 'The subway seems sweet after that'" (qtd. in Thompson 143).
18. The dismissive metaphor of the apartment building as a henhouse—implying that the tenants are treated like and have as much space as the chickens back home—also appears in another Fisher story, "The Promised Land" (*City of Refuge* 83).
19. For the policing of African American migrants' manners in public transportation, see McCammack 979–80. Ann Petry's novel *The Street* (1946) articulates a black woman's negative response to subway space (57).
20. For a discussion of this scene as a site of temporal disjuncture, see Duck 122–23.
21. Larsen's novel deals with many of the modes of urban circulation I discuss in this chapter, including migration, racial passing, and the passer's compulsive return to Harlem. But since they are upper-middle-class conspicuous consumers, Irene Redfield and her husband, Brian, own a car and do not take the subway.
22. These earlier readings of dialect are discussed in Wideman.
23. Bone notes that the characterizations of "Harlem School" writers often "run dangerously close to the stereotype" (*The Negro Novel* 66).
24. For de la Peña's discussion, see "The History of Technology, the Resistance of Archives, and the Whiteness of Race."

25. Kathleen Franz makes a similar point, associating car ownership with uplift ideology (133).

## Conclusion

1. See Pike, "Urban Nightmares and Future Visions."
2. For a history of the urban sketch, and a lucid distinction of the "mobile urban observer" from the flâneur, see Zurier 92–96.
3. Both David Ashford and David Welsh have discussed Woolf's depiction of the subway in the larger context of British modernism and modernity.
4. The first academic history of graffiti writers and their culture is Craig Castleman's *Getting Up: Subway Graffiti in New York.* Martha Cooper and Henry Chalfant's *Subway Art* and Kurlansky, Naar, and Mailer's *Faith of Graffiti* both feature extensive photographic documentation of the subculture. Tracy Fitzpatrick analyzes the history and artistic style of graffiti and graffiti-inspired art by Keith Haring and Jean-Michel Basquiat (171–90).
5. This critical commonplace persisted in later writing about graffiti; see Barnett 27 and Ong 402.
6. Susan Stewart points out several ways that hip hop culture of this period borrows aesthetic elements of the artisanal and the mechanical (208, 215)
7. Cornelia Cody offers another take on the purpose of what she calls "The New York City Personal Experience Narrative."
8. See my discussion of the 7 train at the end of chapter 4.
9. Although Whitehead's characters worry about being stuck in the "underworld," these concerns are shown to be just one more form of improper subway riding. His next chapter, "Rain," suggests an emergence into city space that is just as difficult to navigate (*Colossus* 57–61).
10. See Schnapp, Duffy 199–261, and Brottman.
11. Recent literary and cultural criticism has almost compulsively addressed the issue of how to theorize New York City's literal and literary spaces in the wake of the World Trade Center's destruction on September 11, 2001. For just a few examples, see Keniston and Quinn, Tallack 174–81. I do not wish to underemphasize the destructive impact of the day, but I follow Colson Whitehead's lead in this chapter by treating it as one particularly destructive incident in New York City's history of creative destruction.
12. Nor is the threat of terrorist attacks on public transportation confined to New York City: since I began this project, Madrid commuter trains and the London Underground have both been bombed.
13. For further discussion of the "Abu Ghraib man" and his reproduction, see Mitchell, *Cloning Terror.*
14. In "Farewell to the El," Stalter discusses the nostalgia for the Third Avenue elevated train as an earlier mode of protesting the direction being taken in urban development in mid-1950s New York City.

# Works Cited


Agee, James. "Introduction." *Many Are Called.* By Walker Evans. 1966. New Haven: Yale University Press, 2004.

Aguilera Linde, Mauricio D. "Saroyan and the Dream of Success: The American Vaudeville as a Political Weapon." *American Drama* 11.1 (2002): 18–31.

Ahearn, Barry. *William Carlos Williams and Alterity: The Early Poetry.* Cambridge: Cambridge University Press, 1994.

Allen, Greg. "Elmgreen + Dragset + Me: The Not-Fit-to-Print Interview." Greg.org. May 5, 2005.

Allen, Woody, dir. *Midnight in Paris.* Sony Pictures Classics, 2011.

Anderson, Benedict R. *Imagined Communities: Reflections on the Origin and Spread of Nationalism.* 1983. Rev. ed. New York: Verso, 2006.

Armstrong, Tim. *Modernism, Technology, and the Body: A Cultural Study.* Cambridge: Cambridge University Press, 1998.

Ashford, David. "Blueprints for Babylon: Modernist Mapping of the London Underground 1913–1939." *Modernism/modernity* 17.4 (2010): 735–64.

Atkinson, A. S. "New Senses Developed by Subway Travel." *New York Times* December 30, 1906.

Augé, Marc. *In the Metro.* Trans. Tom Conley. Minneapolis: University of Minnesota Press, 2002.

Ayers, Edward L. *Southern Crossing: A History of the American South, 1877–1906.* Oxford: Oxford University Press, 1995.

Bahnisch, Mark. "Embodied Work, Divided Labour: Subjectivity and the Scientific Management of the Body in Frederick W. Taylor's 1907 'Lecture on Management.'" *Body & Society* 6.1 (2000): 51–68.

Baker, Ray Stannard. *Following the Color Line: An Account of Negro Citizenship in the American Democracy.* New York: Doubleday, Page, 1908.

Balestra, Gianfranca. "Poetry of the Subway." *Rivista di Studi Anglo-Americani* 6.8 (1990): 89–100.

Ballon, Hilary, with a photographic essay by Norman McGrath and a contribution by Marilyn Jordan Taylor. *New York's Pennsylvania Stations.* New York: Norton, 2002.

Balshaw, Maria. *Looking for Harlem: Urban Aesthetics in African American Literature.* London: Pluto Press, 2000.

Banta, Martha. *Taylored Lives: Narrative Productions in the Age of Taylor, Veblen, and Ford.* Chicago: University of Chicago Press, 1993.

———. "The Three New Yorks: Topographical Narratives and Cultural Texts." *American Literary History* 7.1 (1995): 28–54.

Barnett, Claudia. "The Death of Graffiti: Postmodernism and the New York City Subway." *Studies in Popular Culture* 16.2 (1994): 25–38.

Baudelaire, Charles. *The Painter of Modern Life and Other Essays.* Trans. and ed. Jonathan Mayne. London: Phaidon, 1964.

"Beach Pneumatic Transit." NYC Subway. www.nycsubway.org/wiki/Beach_Pneumatic_Transit.

The Beastie Boys. *Paul's Boutique 20th Anniversary Remastered Edition.* Audio recording. Capitol, 2009.

Bender, Thomas. *The Unfinished City: New York and the Metropolitan Idea.* 2002. New York: New York University Press, 2007.

Benjamin, Walter. *Illuminations.* Ed. Hannah Arendt. New York: Schocken, 1968.

Bentley, Nancy. *Frantic Panoramas: American Literature and Mass Culture, 1870–1920.* Philadelphia: University of Pennsylvania Press, 2009.

Berger, Meyer. "Big City Shows to Its Visitors Things Its Own People Neglect to Enjoy." *New York Times* December 7, 1947.

Berlant, Lauren. "Intuitionists: History and the Affective Event." *American Literary History* 20.4 (2008): 845–60.

Berman, Marshall. *All That Is Solid Melts into Air: The Experience of Modernity.* New York: Simon & Schuster, 1982.

Bernstein, Charles. "Blood on the Cutting Room Floor." *Content's Dream: Essays, 1975–1984.* 1986. Evanston: Northwestern University Press, 2001. 351–62.

Bernstein, Leonard, Betty Comden, and Adolph Green. *On the Town.* 1960. Audio recording. Sony, 1998.

Blake, William. *Selected Poetry.* Ed. Michael Mason. Oxford: Oxford University Press, 2008.

Bloch, Julia. "Alice Notley's Descent: Modernist Genealogies and Gendered Literary Inheritance." *Journal of Modern Literature* 35.3 (2012): 1–24.

Bobrick, Benson. *Labyrinths of Iron: A History of the World's Subways*. New York: Newsweek Books, 1981.

Bodenheim, Maxwell. *Introducing Irony: A Book of Poetic Short Stories and Poems*. New York: Boni & Liveright, 1922.

Bone, Robert A. *Down Home: A History of Afro-American Short Fiction from Its Beginning to the End of the Harlem Renaissance*. New York: G. P. Putnam's Sons, 1975.

———. *The Negro Novel in America*. New Haven: Yale University Press, 1965.

Bontemps, Arna Wendell, and Jack Conroy. *Anyplace but Here*. 1945. Columbia: University of Missouri Press, 1997.

Bradshaw, Melissa. "Performing Greenwich Village Bohemianism." *The Cambridge Companion to the Literature of New York*. Ed. Cyrus R. K. Patell and Bryan Waterman. Cambridge: Cambridge University Press, 2010. 146–59.

Bramen, Carrie Tirado. *The Uses of Variety: Modern Americanism and the Quest for National Distinctiveness*. Cambridge: Harvard University Press, 2000.

Brand, Dana. *The Spectator and the City in Nineteenth-Century American Literature*. Cambridge: Cambridge University Press, 1991.

Brawarsky, Sandee. "On the 7 Train, Living the Multicultural Ideal." *New York Times* September 22, 2000.

*Bronx Express* Clippings Folder. 1919. Billy Rose Theatre Division, Special Collections, New York Public Library for the Performing Arts.

Brooks, Michael W. *Subway City: Riding the Trains, Reading New York*. New Brunswick: Rutgers University Press, 1997.

Brottman, Mikita, ed. *Car Crash Culture*. New York: Palgrave Macmillan, 2002.

Broun, Heywood. "Drama." *New York World* April 27, 1922.

Brownell, Blaine A. "A Symbol of Modernity: Attitudes toward the Automobile in Southern Cities in the 1920s." *American Quarterly* 24.1 (1972): 20–44.

Buck-Morss, Susan. *The Dialectics of Seeing: Walter Benjamin and the Arcades Project*. Cambridge: MIT Press, 1991.

Bullard, Robert, Glenn S. Johnson, and Angel O. Torres, eds. *Sprawl City: Race, Politics, and Planning in Atlanta*. Washington, DC: Island Press, 2000.

Burroughs, John. "City Life versus Literature." *Literature in the Making, by Some of Its Makers*. New York: Harper & Brothers, 1917. 213–26.

Butler, Robert. "The Postmodern City in Colson Whitehead's *The Colossus of New York* and Jeffrey Renard Allen's *Rails under My Back*." *CLA Journal* 48.1 (2004): 71–87.

Calonne, David Stephen. "William Saroyan and Multiculturalism." *Journal of the Society for Armenian Studies* 6 (1992): 107–17.

Campbell, W. Joseph. *The Year That Defined American Journalism: 1897 and the Clash of Paradigms*. New York: Routledge, 2006.

Cangro, Jacquelin, ed. *The Subway Chronicles: Scenes from Life in New York*. New York: Plume, 2006.

Carby, Hazel V. *Cultures in Babylon: Black Britain and African America.* New York: Verso, 1999.

Castells, Manuel. *The Rise of the Network Society.* 2nd ed. Malden, MA: Wiley-Blackwell, 2009.

Castleman, Craig. *Getting Up: Subway Graffiti in New York.* Cambridge: MIT Press, 1982.

Chase, Stuart. *Men and Machines.* New York: Macmillan, 1929.

Cheape, Charles W. *Moving the Masses: Urban Public Transit in New York, Boston, and Philadelphia, 1880–1912.* Cambridge: Harvard University Press, 1980.

Clarke, Joseph Ignatius Constantine, and Elbert Hubbard. *Manhattan, an Ode and Henry Hudson, an Essay.* East Aurora, NY: The Roycrofters, 1910.

Cody, Cornelia. "'Only in New York': The New York City Personal Experience Narrative." *Journal of Folklore Research* 42.2 (2005): 217–44.

Cohen, Richard. "Poetry Underground." *New Yorker* December 28, 1992: 57–58.

Cooper, Martha, and Henry Chalfant. *Subway Art.* New York: Macmillan, 1988.

Crane, Hart. *Complete Poems and Selected Letters.* Ed. Langdon Hammer. New York: Library of America, 2006.

Crary, Jonathan. *Techniques of the Observer: On Vision and Modernity in the Nineteenth Century.* 1990. Cambridge: MIT Press, 1992.

Cudahy, Brian J. *Cash, Tokens, and Transfers: A History of Urban Mass Transit in North America.* New York: Fordham University Press, 1990.

———. *Under the Sidewalks of New York: The Story of the Greatest Subway System in the World.* New York: Fordham University Press, 1995.

Dalí, Salvador. *The Secret Life of Salvador Dalí.* Trans. Haakon M. Chevalier. 1942. New York: Dover, 1993.

Davis, Elmer Holmes. *History of the New York Times, 1851–1921.* New York: The New York Times, 1921.

Dean, Tim. "Hart Crane's Poetics of Privacy." *American Literary History* 8.1 (1996): 83–109.

de Certeau, Michel. *The Practice of Everyday Life.* Trans. Steven Rendall. 1984. Berkeley: University of California Press, 1988.

de la Peña, Carolyn. "The History of Technology, the Resistance of Archives, and the Whiteness of Race." *Technology and Culture* 51.4 (2010): 919–37.

———. "'Slow and Low Progress,' or Why American Studies Should Do Technology." *American Quarterly* 58.3 (2006): 915–41.

Derrick, Peter. *Tunneling to the Future: The Story of the Great Subway Expansion That Saved New York.* New York: NYU Press, 2001.

Dickie, Margaret. *On the Modernist Long Poem.* Iowa City: University of Iowa Press, 1986.

Dickinson, Emily. *The Complete Poems of Emily Dickinson.* 1960. Ed. Thomas H. Johnson. New York: Back Bay Books, 1976.

Diehl, Lorraine B. *The Late, Great Pennsylvania Station.* New York: Four Walls Eight Windows, 1996.

Diner, Hasia R. *In the Almost Promised Land: American Jews and Blacks, 1915–1935.* Baltimore: Johns Hopkins University Press, 1995.

Dinerstein, Joel. *Swinging the Machine: Modernity, Technology, and African American Culture between the World Wars.* Amherst: University of Massachusetts Press, 2003.

Divall, Colin. "Mobilizing the History of Technology." *Technology and Culture* 51.4 (2010): 938–60.

Dixon, Royal. *The Human Side of Animals.* New York: Frederick A. Stokes, 1918.

Douglas, Ann. *Terrible Honesty: Mongrel Manhattan in the 1920s.* New York: Farrar, Straus & Giroux, 1995.

"Drama and Music." *The Nation* September 9, 1909: 240.

Dubey, Madhu. "Narration and Migration: Jazz and Vernacular Theories of Black Women's Fiction." *American Literary History* 10.2 (1998): 291–316.

Duck, Leigh Anne. *The Nation's Region: Southern Modernism, Segregation, and U.S. Nationalism.* 2006. Athens: University of Georgia Press, 2009.

Duffy, Enda. *The Speed Handbook: Velocity, Pleasure, Modernism.* Durham: Duke University Press, 2009.

Dunbar, Paul Laurence. *The Sport of the Gods.* 1902. New York: Signet Classics, 2011.

Dunlap, David W. "150th Annivesary: 1851–2001; Six Buildings That Share One Story." *New York Times* November 14, 2001.

Dymov, Osip. "*Bronx Express* (*Bronks Ekspres*): A Dream in Three Acts with a Prologue and Epilogue." 1919–1926. *God, Man, and Devil: Yiddish Plays in Translation.* Trans. and ed. Nahma Sandrow. Syracuse: Syracuse University Press, 1999. 266–305.

Dymow, Ossip [Osip Dymov]. *The Bronx Express: A Local Comedy.* 1922. Adapted by Owen Davis Sr. Billy Rose Theatre Division, New York Public Library for the Performing Arts.

"Editorial: City Poets." *The Independent* August 15, 1912: 395–96.

"Efficiency Show a General Uplift: Improved Methods in Everything, from Kitchens to Subways, Are Now on View." *New-York Tribune* April 5, 1914.

Eliot, T. S. *To Criticize the Critic and Other Writings.* New York: Farrar, Straus & Giroux, 1965.

Ellison, Ralph. "An Extravagance of Laughter." *Going to the Territory.* New York: Vintage, 1986. 145–97.

———. *Invisible Man.* 1952. New York: Vintage, 1995.

Elmer, Jonathan. *Reading at the Social Limit: Affect, Mass Culture, and Edgar Allan Poe.* Stanford: Stanford University Press, 1995.

Emerson, Ralph Waldo. *The Collected Works of Ralph Waldo Emerson. Volume 1: Nature, Addresses, and Lectures.* Ed. Robert E. Spiller. Cambridge: Belknap Press of Harvard University Press, 1971.

Evans, Walker. *Many Are Called.* 1966. New Haven: Yale University Press, 2004.

Feinman, Mark S., Peggy Darlington, David Pirmann, and Ed Sachs. "BMT Culver Line." NYC Subway. www.nycsubway.org/wiki/BMT_Culver_Line.

Firkins, Chester. "On a Subway Express." *Atlantic Monthly* February 1908: 181.

Fischler, Stan. *Moving Millions: An Inside Look at Mass Transit.* New York: Harper & Row, 1979.

Fisher, Clive. *Hart Crane.* New Haven: Yale University Press, 2002.

Fisher, Rudolph. *The City of Refuge: The Collected Stories of Rudolph Fisher.* Ed. John McCluskey Jr. Columbia: University of Missouri Press, 2008.

Fitzpatrick, Tracy. *Art and the Subway: New York Underground.* New Brunswick: Rutgers University Press, 2009.

Flynn, Joyce. "Melting Plots: Patterns of Racial and Ethnic Amalgamation in the American Drama before Eugene O'Neill." *American Quarterly* 38.3 (1986): 417–38.

Forman, Murray. "Introduction." *That's the Joint! The Hip-Hop Studies Reader.* Ed. Murray Forman and Mark Anthony Neal. New York: Routledge, 2004. 1–9.

Fotsch, Paul Mason. *Watching the Traffic Go By: Transportation and Isolation in Urban America.* Austin: University of Texas Press, 2007.

Fouché, Rayvon. "Say It Loud, I'm Black and I'm Proud: African Americans, American Artifactual Culture, and Black Vernacular Technological Creativity." *American Quarterly* 58.3 (2006): 639–61.

Frank, Waldo. "An Introduction to Hart Crane." *Critical Essays on Hart Crane.* Ed. David Clark. Boston: G. K. Hall, 1982. 124–33.

Franz, Kathleen. "'The Open Road': Automobility and Racial Uplift in the Interwar Years." *Technology and the African-American Experience: Needs and Opportunities for Study.* Ed. Bruce Sinclair. Cambridge: MIT Press, 2004. 131–53.

Freedman, Jonathan. *Klezmer America: Jewishness, Ethnicity, Modernity.* New York: Columbia University Press, 2008.

Freud, Sigmund. *Beyond the Pleasure Principle: The Standard Edition.* 1961. Trans. James Strachey. New York: Norton, 1990.

———. "The 'Uncanny.'" *Writings on Art and Literature.* Stanford: Stanford University Press, 1997. 193–233.

Freytag-Loringhoven, Elsa von. *Body Sweats: The Uncensored Writings of Elsa von Freytag-Loringhoven.* Ed. Irene Gammel and Suzanne Zelazo. Cambridge: MIT Press, 2011.

Friedberg, Anne. *Window Shopping: Cinema and the Postmodern.* Berkeley: University of California Press, 1993.

Friedman, Susan Stanford. "Definitional Excursions: The Meanings of Modern/Modernity/Modernism." *Modernism/modernity* 8.3 (2001): 493–513.

———. "Periodizing Modernism: Postcolonial Modernities and the Space/Time Borders of Modernist Studies." *Modernism/modernity* 13.3 (2006): 425–43.

Gaines, Kevin K. *Uplifting the Race: Black Leadership, Politics, and Culture in the Twentieth Century.* Chapel Hill: University of North Carolina Press, 1996.

Garrett, Leah V. *Journeys beyond the Pale: Yiddish Travel Writing in the Modern World.* Madison: University of Wisconsin Press, 2003.

Giles, Paul. *Hart Crane: The Contexts of "The Bridge."* 1986. Cambridge: Cambridge University Press, 2009.

Gilroy, Paul. *The Black Atlantic: Modernity and Double Consciousness.* Cambridge: Harvard University Press, 1993.

Gitelman, Lisa. *Always Already New: Media, History, and the Data of Culture.* Cambridge: MIT Press, 2006.

Gitelman, Lisa, and Geoffrey B. Pingree. "Introduction: What's New about New Media?" *New Media, 1740–1915.* Cambridge: MIT Press, 2004. xi–xxii.

Graham, Stephen, and Simon Marvin. *Splintering Urbanism: Networked Infrastructures, Technological Mobilities and the Urban Condition.* London: Routledge, 2001.

Grant, Thomas. "Mythologizing Manhattan: The *New Yorker*'s New York." *American Studies* 28.1 (1987): 31–46.

Gregory, Horace. "Afterword." *In the American Grain.* 1925. New York: New Directions, 2009. 235–46.

Grey, John S. "Characters in the Cars." *Fame: A Journal for Advertisers* December 1917: 256–257.

———. "My Traveling Companions." *Fame: A Journal for Advertisers* August 1917: 167.

Griffin, Farah Jasmine. *"Who Set You Flowin'?" The African-American Migration Narrative.* 1995. New York: Oxford University Press, 1996.

"The Growth of Underground New York." *New-York Tribune* February 28, 1904.

Grynbaum, Michael M. "Cellphone Service Coming to the Subway." City Room Blog. *New York Times* September 22, 2011. http://cityroom.blogs.nytimes.com.

———. "Literary Quotations on Subway Trains Come to an End." *New York Times* December 21, 2010.

Haenni, Sabine. *The Immigrant Scene: Ethnic Amusements in New York, 1880–1920.* Minneapolis: University of Minnesota Press, 2008.

Handlin, Oscar. "The Modern City as a Field of Historical Study." 1963. *The Historian and the City.* Cambridge: MIT Press, 1966. 1–27.

"Harlem in Twenty? No Subway Express Station above Ninety-sixth-st." *New-York Tribune* October 2, 1904.

Harshav, Benjamin, and Barbara Harshav. *American Yiddish Poetry: A Bilingual Anthology.* Berkeley: University of California Press, 1986.

Harvey, David. *The Condition of Postmodernity: An Enquiry into the Origins of Cultural Change.* Malden, MA: Wiley-Blackwell, 1990.

Hedin, Robert, ed. *The Great Machines: Poems and Songs of the American Railroad.* Iowa City: University of Iowa Press, 1996.

Heinze, Andrew R. *Adapting to Abundance: Jewish Immigrants, Mass Consumption, and the Search for American Identity.* New York: Columbia University Press, 1990.

Higham, John. *Strangers in the Land: Patterns of American Nativism, 1860–1925.* New Brunswick: Rutgers University Press, 2002.

Hill, Walter, dir. *The Warriors.* Paramount, 1979.

Hollis, Karyn. "Liberating Voices: Autobiographical Writing at the Bryn Mawr Summer School for Women Workers, 1921–1938." *Rhetorical Bodies.* Ed. Jack Selzer and Sharon Crowley. Madison: University of Wisconsin Press, 1999. 98–119.

Hood, Clifton. "Changing Perceptions of Public Space on the New York Rapid Transit System." *Journal of Urban History* 22.3 (March 1996): 308–31.

———. *722 Miles: The Building of the Subways and How They Transformed New York.* Baltimore: Johns Hopkins University Press, 1993.

"How We'll Travel in the Subway." *New York Sun* September 27, 1903.

Howells, William Dean. *A Hazard of New Fortunes.* 1890. New York: Modern Library, 2002.

Huddle, Mark Andrew. "Harlem, the 'New Negro,' and the South: History and the Politics of Place." *Safundi: The Journal of South African and American Studies* 9.3 (2008): 257–70.

Hughes, Langston. *The Collected Poems of Langston Hughes.* Ed. Arnold Rampersad. New York: Knopf, 1994.

———. *Essays on Art, Race, Politics, and World Affairs. The Collected Works of Langston Hughes,* vol. 9. Ed. Christopher C. De Santis. Columbia: University of Missouri Press, 2002.

Hurst, Fannie. "'Chocolate Fudge' in the Magazines." *Literature in the Making, by Some of Its Makers.* New York: Harper & Brothers, 1917. 241–50.

Hurston, Zora Neale. "My People, My People!" *Zora Neale Hurston: Folklore, Memoirs, and Other Writings: Mules and Men, Tell My Horse, Dust Tracks on a Road, Selected Articles.* Ed. Cheryl A. Wall. New York: Library of America, 1995. 773–81.

Huyssen, Andreas. "Mass Culture as Woman: Modernism's Other." *After the Great Divide: Modernism, Mass Culture, Postmodernism.* Bloomington: Indiana University Press, 1986. 44–62.

———. *Present Pasts: Urban Palimpsests and the Politics of Memory.* Stanford: Stanford University Press, 2003.

Hymoff, Edward. "Underground City." *Popular Mechanics* April 1961: 100–105, 264–68, 270.

Ingram, John H. *Edgar Allan Poe: His Life, Letters and Opinions.* 1880. New York: AMS Press, 1971.

Interborough Rapid Transit and Brian Cudahy. *The New York Subway: Its Construction and Equipment.* 1904. New York: Fordham University Press, 2004.

*Interior N.Y. Subway, 14th St. to 42nd St.* American Mutoscope and Biograph Company, 1905. American Memory from the Library of Congress. http://memory.loc.gov/ammem/index.html.

"It Won't Be Very Soon." *New York Herald Tribune* November 19, 1938. "Third Avenue Elevated Train" Folder. Special Collections, Museum of the City of New York.

Jacobson, Matthew Frye. *Whiteness of a Different Color: European Immigrants and the Alchemy of Race.* Cambridge: Harvard University Press, 1998.

James, William. *Talks to Teachers on Psychology: And to Students on Some of Life's Ideals.* New York: H. Holt, 1899.

Jameson, Fredric. "Cognitive Mapping." 1988. *The Jameson Reader.* Ed. Michael Hardt and Kathi Weeks. Malden, MA: Blackwell, 2000. 277–87.

———. *Postmodernism, or, The Cultural Logic of Late Capitalism.* Durham: Duke University Press, 1991.

Johnson, James Weldon. *The Autobiography of an Ex-Coloured Man.* 1912. New York: Alfred A. Knopf, 1976.

———. *Black Manhattan.* 1930. New York: Da Capo, 1991.

———. "Harlem: The Culture Capital." 1925. *The New Negro : Voices of the Harlem Renaissance.* Ed. Alain Locke. New York: Touchstone, 1997. 301–11.

Johnston, John. "The Intuitionist and Pattern Recognition: A Response to Lauren Berlant." *American Literary History* 20.4 (2008): 861–69.

Jones, LeRoi [Amiri Baraka]. *Dutchman and The Slave: Two Plays.* New York: Morrow Quill, 1964.

Jongh, James de. *Vicious Modernism: Black Harlem and the Literary Imagination.* 1990. Cambridge: Cambridge University Press, 2009.

Jonnes, Jill. *Conquering Gotham: A Gilded Age Epic: The Construction of Penn Station and Its Tunnels.* New York: Viking, 2007.

Kallen, Horace Meyer. *Culture and Democracy in the United States.* 1924. New York: Arno Press and The New York Times, 1970.

Kaplan, Amy. *The Social Construction of American Realism.* 1988. Chicago: University of Chicago Press, 1992.

Kasson, John F. *Civilizing the Machine: Technology and Republican Values in America, 1776–1900.* 1976. New York: Macmillan, 1999.

———. *Rudeness and Civility: Manners in Nineteenth-Century Urban America.* New York: Hill & Wang, 1990.

Katz, Tamar. "City Memory, City History: Urban Nostalgia, *The Colossus of New York,* and Late-Twentieth-Century Historical Fiction." *Contemporary Literature* 51.4 (2010): 810–51.

Kazin, Alfred. "Please, How Do I Get Out of Here?" *New York Times* March 25, 1973.

———. *A Walker in the City.* New York: Harcourt, Brace, 1951.

Keller, Judith. "Walker Evans and *Many Are Called:* Shooting Blind." *History of Photography* 17.2 (1993): 152–65.

Kelling, George L., and James Q. Wilson. "Broken Windows: The Police and Neighborhood Safety." *Atlantic Monthly* March 1982: 29–38.

Keniston, Ann, and Jeanne Follansbee Quinn, eds. *Literature after 9/11.* New York: Routledge, 2008.

Kennedy, Adrienne. "The Owl Answers." *The Adrienne Kennedy Reader.* Minneapolis: University of Minnesota Press, 2001. 29–42.

Kennedy, Randy. "A Day in the Subway, as It Rolls Up a Century." *New York Times* October 27, 2004.

Kern, Stephen. *The Culture of Time and Space, 1880–1918.* Cambridge: Harvard University Press, 1983.

Khalip, Jacques. "Cruising among Ghosts: Hart Crane's Friends." *Arizona Quarterly: A Journal of American Literature, Culture, and Theory* 64.2 (2008): 65–93.

Kilmer, Joyce. "The Great Nickel Adventure." *The Circus and Other Essays.* New York: Laurence J. Gomme, 1916. 38–44.

———. "Subway." *The Independent* September 1, 1910: 467.

Kinnahan, Linda Arbaugh. *Poetics of the Feminine: Authority and Literary Tradition in William Carlos Williams, Mina Loy, Denise Levertov, and Kathleen Fraser.* Cambridge: Cambridge University Press, 1994.

Kirby, Lynne. *Parallel Tracks: The Railroad and Silent Cinema.* Durham: Duke University Press, 1997.

Kraus, Joe. "How *The Melting Pot* Stirred America: The Reception of Zangwill's Play and Theater's Role in the American Assimilation Experience." *MELUS: Multi-Ethnic Literatures of the United States* 24.3 (1999): 3–19.

Kuklick, Bruce. "Myth and Symbol in American Studies." *American Quarterly* 24.4 (1972): 435–50.

Kurlansky, Mervyn, Jon Naar, and Norman Mailer. *The Faith of Graffiti.* New York: Praeger, 1974.

Laidlaw, René. "Open Letters: On Gutter Verse: From an Unsympathetic Country Gentleman to His Town Cousin, Who Writes for Magazines." *The Century Illustrated Monthly Magazine* 84.4 (1912): 634–35.

Lankevich, George. *American Metropolis: A History of New York City.* New York: New York University Press, 1998.

Larsen, Nella. *Quicksand* and *Passing.* Ed. Deborah E. McDowell. New Brunswick: Rutgers University Press, 1986.

Latour, Bruno. *Reassembling the Social: An Introduction to Actor-Network-Theory.* Oxford: Oxford University Press, 2005.

Lears, T. J. Jackson. *No Place of Grace: Antimodernism and the Transformation of American Culture, 1880–1920.* 1981. Chicago: University of Chicago Press, 1994.

Lee, Julia H. "Estrangement on a Train: Race and Narratives of American Identity." *ELH* 75.2 (2008): 345–65.

Lefebvre, Henri. *The Production of Space.* Boston: Blackwell, 1991.

Le Gallienne, Richard. "The Philosopher Walks Up-Town." *Harper's Magazine* July 1911: 228–38.

Lensing, George S. "Hart Crane's Tunnel from *The Waste Land.*" *Ariel: A Review of International English Literature* 6.3 (1975): 20–35.

Lenz, Günter H. "Symbolic Space, Communal Rituals, and the Surreality of the Urban Ghetto: Harlem in Black Literature from the 1920s to the 1960s." *Callaloo* 35 (1988): 309–45.

Lesser, Wendy. *The Life below the Ground: A Study of the Subterranean in Literature and History.* Boston: Faber & Faber, 1987.

Lethem, Jonathan. *The Fortress of Solitude: A Novel.* 2003. New York: Vintage, 2004.

———. "Speak, Hoyt-Schermerhorn." *The Disappointment Artist: Essays.* 2005. New York: Vintage, 2006. 43–58.

"Letters: Subway Transitives." *New York Times* April 15, 1973.

Levine, Lawrence W. *Black Culture and Black Consciousness: Afro-American Folk Thought from Slavery to Freedom.* 1977. Oxford: Oxford University Press, 2007.

Lewis, David Levering. *When Harlem Was in Vogue.* 1981. New York: Penguin Books, 1997.
Li, Stephanie. "'Sometimes Things Disappear': Absence and Mutability in Colson Whitehead's *The Colossus of New York.*" *Literature after 9/11.* Ed. Ann Keniston and Jeanne Follansbee Quinn. New York: Routledge, 2008. 82–98.
Linde, Charlotte, and William Labov. "Spatial Networks as a Site for the Study of Language and Thought." *Language* 51.4 (1975): 924–39.
Locke, Alain. "The New Negro." *The New Negro: Voices of the Harlem Renaissance.* 1925. New York: Touchstone, 1997. 3–16.
Lopate, Phillip. "New York State of Mind." *Nation* December 1, 2003: 31–34.
Lowell, James Russell. *The Early Poems of James Russell Lowell.* Ed. Nathan Haskell Dole. New York: T. Y. Crowell, 1893.
Lynch, Kevin. *The Image of the City.* Cambridge: MIT Press, 1960.
Mao, Douglas, and Rebecca L. Walkowitz. "The New Modernist Studies." *PMLA* 123.3 (2008): 737–48.
Marcosson, Isaac F. "The World's Greatest Traffic Problem." *Munsey's Magazine* June 1913: 327–38.
Marsh, Reginald. "Subway Sunbeams: The Melting Pot." *New York Daily News* June 26, 1923.
Marvin, Carolyn. *When Old Technologies Were New: Thinking about Electric Communication in the Late Nineteenth Century.* New York: Oxford University Press, 1988.
Marx, Leo. *The Machine in the Garden: Technology and the Pastoral Ideal in America.* 1964. New York: Oxford University Press, 2000.
McCabe, Joseph. "In Search of the American Soul." *The Bookman* 45 (May 1917): 231–37.
McCammack, Brian. "'My God, They Must Have Riots on Those Things All the Time': African American Geographies and Bodies on Northern Urban Public Transportation, 1915–1940." *Journal of Social History* 43.4 (2010): 973–88.
McCann, Colum. *Let the Great World Spin: A Novel.* New York: Random House, 2009.
———. *This Side of Brightness: A Novel.* 1998. New York: Macmillan, 2003.
McCluskey, John. "Introduction." *The City of Refuge: The Collected Stories of Rudolph Fisher.* Columbia: University of Missouri Press, 2008. 1–31.
McCutcheon, George Barr. "Magazines Cheapen Fiction." *Literature in the Making by Some of Its Makers.* New York: Harper & Brothers, 1917. 157–66.
McKay, Claude. *Harlem Shadows: The Poems of Claude McKay.* New York: Harcourt, Brace, 1922.
Meikle, Jeffrey L. *Twentieth Century Limited: Industrial Design in America, 1925–1939.* 2nd ed. Philadelphia: Temple University Press, 2001.
Melman, Billie. *Women and the Popular Imagination in the Twenties: Flappers and Nymphs.* London: Macmillan, 1988.
"The Melting Pot." *Fortune* July 1939: 73–77.
Merwin, Ted. *In Their Own Image: New York Jews in Jazz Age Popular Culture.* New Brunswick: Rutgers University Press, 2006.

Michaels, Walter Benn. *Our America: Nativism, Modernism, and Pluralism.* Durham: Duke University Press, 1995.

Miller, Perry. *The Life of the Mind in America: From the Revolution to the Civil War.* New York: Harcourt, Brace & World, 1965.

Mills, Charles Wright. *White Collar.* 1951. New York: Oxford University Press, 2002.

Mitchell, Ruth Comfort. *The Night Court, and Other Verse.* New York: The Century Co., 1916.

Mitchell, W. J. T. *Cloning Terror: The War of Images, 9/11 to the Present.* Chicago: University of Chicago Press, 2010.

Moore, Deborah Dash. *At Home in America: Second-Generation New York Jews.* New York: Columbia University Press, 1981.

Morley, Christopher. "On First Looking into a Subway Excavation." *The Century Illustrated Monthly Magazine* 93 (1917): 796.

Morrison, Toni. "City Limits, Village Values: Concepts of the Neighborhood in Black Fiction." *Literature and the American Urban Experience: Essays on the City and Literature.* Ed. Michael C. Jaye and Ann Chalmers Watts. Manchester: Manchester University Press, 1981. 35–43.

"MTA—Arts for Transit | History." www.mta.info/mta/aft/about/history.html.

Mumford, Lewis. *The Culture of Cities.* 1938. New York: Harcourt Brace Jovanovich, 1970.

———. *Technics and Civilization.* 1934. Chicago: University of Chicago Press, 2010.

Nadell, Martha J. "Poetry in Motion." *Polygraph: An International Journal of Culture and Politics* 8–9 (1996): 39–48.

Namako, Tom. "Subway Hell This Weekend with a Slew of Service Changes: Subway Lines Set for Weak-end." *New York Post* April 1, 2011. www.nypost.com.

Newcomb, John Timberman. "'The Housetop Sea': Cityscape Verse and the Rise of Modern American Poetry." *American Literature: A Journal of Literary History, Criticism, and Bibliography* 76.2 (2004): 275–306.

———. *How Did Poetry Survive? The Making of Modern American Verse.* Champaign: University of Illinois Press, 2012.

———. *Would Poetry Disappear? American Verse and the Crisis of Modernity.* Columbus: Ohio State University Press, 2004.

"New York's Growth Will Soon Require a 'Fourth Dimension.'" *New York Times Sunday Magazine.* December 23, 1906. 3.

Nickowitz, Peter. *Rhetoric and Sexuality: The Poetry of Hart Crane, Elizabeth Bishop, and James Merrill.* New York: Palgrave Macmillan, 2006.

Nye, David E. *American Technological Sublime.* Cambridge: MIT Press, 1994.

———. *Narratives and Spaces: Technology and the Construction of American Culture.* New York: Columbia University Press, 1997.

O'Neill, Eugene. "The Emperor Jones." *Eugene O'Neill: Complete Plays, 1913–1920.* New York: Library of America, 1988. 1029–61.

Ong, Walter J. "Subway Graffiti and the Design of the Self." *The State of the Language.* Ed. Christopher Ricks. Berkeley: University of California Press, 1990. 400–407.

Osofsky, Gilbert. *Harlem, the Making of a Ghetto: Negro New York, 1890–1930*. 1966. Chicago: Ivan R. Dee, 1996.

Page, Max. *The City's End: Two Centuries of Fantasies, Fears, and Premonitions of New York's Destruction*. New Haven: Yale University Press, 2008.

———. *The Creative Destruction of Manhattan, 1900–1940*. 1999. Chicago: University of Chicago Press, 2001.

Park, Robert Ezra. "The City: Suggestions for the Investigation of Human Behavior in the Urban Environment." *The City*. By Robert E. Park, Ernest W. Burgess, and Roderick D. McKenzie. 1925. Chicago: University of Chicago Press, 1984. 1–47.

———. *The Immigrant Press and Its Control*. New York: Harper & Brothers, 1922.

Parker, Cornelia Stratton. *Working with the Working Woman*. New York: Harper & Brothers, 1922.

Patton, Margaret French. "On the Subway Train." *Harper's Weekly* January 25, 1913: 21.

Paul, Sherman. *Hart's "Bridge."* Champaign: University of Illinois Press, 1973.

Peacock, Molly. "Subway Vespers." *Cornucopia: New and Selected Poems, 1975–2002*. New York: Norton, 2002. 224.

Pearlman, Jeff. "At Full Blast: Shooting Outrageously from the Lip, Braves Closer John Rocker Bangs Away at His Favorite Targets." *Sports Illustrated* December 22, 1999. http://sportsillustrated.cnn.com/features/cover/news/1999/12/22/rocker/.

Petry, Ann. *The Street: A Novel*. 1946. Boston: Mariner Books, 1998.

Phelps, Ruth Shepard. "The Subway." *The Bellman Book of Verse, 1906–1919*. Ed. William Crowell Edgar. Minneapolis: Bellman Co., 1919. 23.

Pike, David L. *Metropolis on the Styx: The Underworlds of Modern Urban Culture, 1800–2001*. Ithaca: Cornell University Press, 2007.

———. *Subterranean Cities: The World beneath Paris and London, 1800–1945*. Ithaca: Cornell University Press, 2005.

———. "Urban Nightmares and Future Visions: Life beneath New York." *Wide Angle: A Film Quarterly of Theory, Criticism, and Practice* 20.4 (1998): 9–50.

Pirmann, David. "IRT West Side Line." NYC Subway. www.nycsubway.org/wiki/IRT_West_Side_Line.

Poe, Edgar Allan. *The Fall of the House of Usher and Other Writings: Poems, Tales, Essays, and Reviews*. Ed. David Galloway. London: Penguin Classics, 1986.

"Poetry in Motion®—Poetry Society of America." www.poetrysociety.org/psa/poetry/poetry_in_motion/.

"The Point of View: The Muse in Town." *Scribner's Magazine* September 1914: 407–9.

Pound, Ezra. *Early Writings*. Ed. Ira B. Nadel. New York: Penguin, 2005.

———. "In a Station of the Metro." *Poetry: A Magazine of Verse* 2.1 (1913): 12.

"Practical Subway Working." *New York Times* July 17, 1904.

Presner, Todd Samuel. *Mobile Modernity: Germans, Jews, Trains*. New York: Columbia University Press, 2007.

Reed, Brian. "Hand in Hand: Jasper Johns and Hart Crane." *Modernism/modernity* 17.1 (2010): 21–45.

———. *Hart Crane: After His Lights*. Tuscaloosa: University of Alabama Press, 2006.

Rhodes-Pitts, Sharifa. *Harlem Is Nowhere: A Journey to the Mecca of Black America.* New York: Little, Brown, 2011.

Rice, Elmer. "A New York Childhood: Joy-Riding in the Subway." *New Yorker* December 29, 1928: 21–23.

———. *The Subway: A Play in Nine Scenes.* New York: Samuel French, 1929.

Riddel, Joseph. "Hart Crane's Poetics of Failure." *ELH* 33.4 (1966): 473–96.

Rodgers, Lawrence Richard. *Canaan Bound: The African-American Great Migration Novel.* Champaign: University of Illinois Press, 1997.

Rogers-Carpenter, Katherine. "Re-envisioning 1930s Working Women: The Case of Kitty Foyle." *Women's Studies: An Inter-disciplinary Journal* 37.6 (2008): 707–30.

Rukeyser, Muriel. "Study in a Late Subway." *The Collected Poems of Muriel Rukeyser.* Ed. Janet E. Kaufman and Anne F. Herzog with Jan Heller Levi. Pittsburgh: University of Pittsburgh Press, 2005. 53.

"Runaway Hid in Subway: Boy Spent Three Days Riding Wherever B.M.T. Trains Took Him." *New York Times* January 19, 1927.

Sack, Kevin. "The State of the State, Proudly Restated; Cuomo Writes the Book on New York's Strengths, and (Surprise!) Finds Much to Like." *New York Times* April 9, 1994.

Saler, Michael T. *The Avant-Garde in Interwar England: Medieval Modernism and the London Underground.* New York: Oxford University Press, 1999.

Sandrow, Nahma. "Introduction to *Bronx Express (Bronks Ekspres): A Dream in Three Acts with a Prologue and Epilogue.*" *God, Man, and Devil: Yiddish Plays in Translation.* Trans. and ed. Nahma Sandrow. Syracuse: Syracuse University Press, 1999. 261–66.

Sargent, Greg. "The Line That Time Forgot—Second Avenue Subway." *New York Magazine* April 5, 2004: 22–26.

Sargent, Joseph, dir. *The Taking of Pelham One Two Three.* United Artists, 1974.

Saroyan, William. *Subway Circus.* New York: Samuel French, 1940.

Saxe, John Godfrey. *Poems.* 1851. Boston: Ticknor & Fields, 1855.

Schilplin, Maude C. *Minnesota Verse: An Anthology.* St. Cloud: Times Publishing, 1934.

Schivelbusch, Wolfgang. *The Railway Journey: The Industrialization of Time and Space in the 19th Century.* Berkeley: University of California Press, 1986.

Schnapp, Jeffrey T. "Crash (Speed as Engine of Individuation)." *Modernism/modernity* 6.1 (1999): 1–49.

Schocket, Eric. *Vanishing Moments: Class and American Literature.* Ann Arbor: University of Michigan Press, 2006.

Schultz, Susan M. "The Success of Failure: Hart Crane's Revisions of Whitman and Eliot in *The Bridge.*" *South Atlantic Review* 54.1 (1989): 55–70.

Schuyler, George S. "Traveling Jim Crow." *American Mercury* August 1930: 423–32.

Sconce, Jeffrey. *Haunted Media: Electronic Presence from Telegraphy to Television.* Durham: Duke University Press, 2000.

Seiler, Cotten. *Republic of Drivers: A Cultural History of Automobility in America.* Chicago: University of Chicago Press, 2008.

Seltzer, Mark. *Bodies and Machines.* New York: Routledge, 1992.

Selzer, Linda. "New Eclecticism: An Interview with Colson Whitehead." *Callaloo* 31.2 (2008): 393–401.

Sheller, Mimi. "Automotive Emotions: Feeling the Car." *Theory, Culture & Society* 21.4–5 (2004): 221–42.

Shepard, Richard F. "Theater: 'Bronx Express'; Folksbiene Yiddish Troupe Opens New Season with an Updated Comedy." *New York Times* November 17, 1968.

Shikoh, Asma Ahmed. *Van Wyck Blvd; Home Series.* 2005. Art in Embassies Program, US Department of State.

Shonts, Theodore. Letter to Frank Hedley. 1912. August Belmont Papers, ca. 1880–1938, Bulk (1904–1925). Box 4. Manuscripts and Archives Division, The New York Public Library, Astor, Lenox, and Tilden Foundations.

Shumsky, Neil Larry. "Zangwill's *The Melting Pot:* Ethnic Tensions on Stage." *American Quarterly* 27.1 (1975): 29–41.

Siebert, Wilbur H. *The Underground Railroad from Slavery to Freedom.* New York: Macmillan, 1898.

Simmel, Georg. "The Metropolis and Mental Life." *The Sociology of Georg Simmel.* Trans. and ed. Kurt H. Wolff. 1950. Glencoe: Free Press, 1964. 409–24.

Simpson, Mark. *Trafficking Subjects: The Politics of Mobility in Nineteenth-Century America.* Minneapolis: University of Minnesota Press, 2005.

Sinclair, Bruce, ed. *Technology and the African-American Experience: Needs and Opportunities for Study.* Cambridge: MIT Press, 2004.

Smith, Sidonie. *Moving Lives: Twentieth-Century Women's Travel Writing.* Minneapolis: University of Minnesota Press, 2001.

Smith, Wendy. *Real Life Drama: The Group Theatre and America, 1931–1940.* 1990. New York: Grove Press, 1992.

Snediker, Michael D. *Queer Optimism: Lyric Personhood and Other Felicitous Persuasions.* Minneapolis: University of Minnesota Press, 2009.

Sollors, Werner. *Beyond Ethnicity: Consent and Descent in American Culture.* New York: Oxford University Press, 1986.

———. *Ethnic Modernism.* Cambridge: Harvard University Press, 2008.

Sontag, Susan. *On Photography.* 1977. New York: Picador, 2001.

Sosa, Alfredo. "A Train Ride into America's Melting Pot." *Christian Science Monitor* June 15, 2006.

"Station: 125th Street (IRT West Side Line)." NYC Subway. www.nycsubway.org/wiki/Station:_125th_Street_(IRT_West_Side_Line).

Stalter, Sunny. "Farewell to the El: Nostalgic Urban Visuality on the Third Avenue Elevated Train." *American Quarterly* 58.3 (2006): 869–90.

———. "The Subway Crush: Making Contact in New York City Subway Songs, 1904–1915." *Journal of American Culture* 34.4 (2011): 321–31.

Stewart, Susan. *Crimes of Writing: Problems in the Containment of Representation.* New York: Oxford University Press, 1991.

Stilgoe, John R. *Metropolitan Corridor: Railroads and the American Scene.* 1983. New Haven: Yale University Press, 1985.

Stone, Jonathan. "Song of the Subway." *Harper's Weekly* December 30, 1911: 22.
Stover, John F. *American Railroads.* 1961. Chicago: University of Chicago Press, 1997.
"The Subway." *Seinfeld.* Dir. Tom Cherones. NBC, January 8, 1992.
"The Subway Habit." *New York Times* October 4, 1903.
"The Subway Signs." *New York Times* February 18, 1905.
"Subway Store" advertisement. *New York Times* March 23, 1905.
*Subway Stories.* Dir. Bob Balaban, Patricia Benoit, Julie Dash, Jonathan Demme, Ted Demme, Abel Ferrara, Alison Maclean, Craig McKay, Lucas Platt, and Seth Rosenfeld. HBO Home Video, 1997.
"Subway's Dark Secret Up at Columbus Circle: Tis There They Kill Unhappy Wives at 1 A.M." *New York Times* November 29, 1904.
Sundquist, Eric J. *To Wake the Nations: Race in the Making of American Literature.* Cambridge: Belknap Press of Harvard University Press, 1993.
Susman, Warren I. "History and the American Intellectual: Uses of a Usable Past." *American Quarterly* 16.2 Part 2: Supplement (1964): 243–63.
Tabbi, Joseph. *Postmodern Sublime: Technology and American Writing from Mailer to Cyberpunk.* 1995. Ithaca: Cornell University Press, 1996.
Tallack, Douglas. *New York Sights: Visualizing Old and New New York.* Oxford: Berg, 2005.
Tapper, Gordon A. *The Machine That Sings: Modernism, Hart Crane, and the Culture of the Body.* New York: Routledge, 2006.
Tashjian, Dickran. *Skyscraper Primitives: Dada and the American Avant-Garde, 1910–1925.* Middletown: Wesleyan University Press, 1975.
Tate, Allen. "Subway." *The Swimmers, and Other Selected Poems.* New York: Scribner, 1970. 105.
Taussig, Michael. *The Nervous System.* New York: Routledge, 1992.
Taylor, William R. *In Pursuit of Gotham: Culture and Commerce in New York.* New York: Oxford University Press, 1992.
Thacker, Andrew. *Moving through Modernity: Space and Geography in Modernism.* Manchester: Manchester University Press, 2003.
———. "Uncompleted Life: The Modernist Underground." *The Railway and Modernity: Time, Space and the Machine Ensemble.* Ed. Matthew Beaumont and Michael Freeman. Oxford: Peter Lang, 2007. 101–24.
Theroux, Paul. "Subway Odyssey." *New York Times* January 31, 1982.
Thompson, Emily. *The Soundscape of Modernity: Architectural Acoustics and the Culture of Listening in America, 1900–1933.* 2002. Cambridge: MIT Press, 2004.
Thoreau, Henry David. "What's the Railroad to Me?" *The Great Machines: Poems and Songs of the American Railroad.* Ed. Robert Hedin. Iowa City: University of Iowa Press, 1996. 6.
"Those Who Read in the Subway." *New York Times Sunday Magazine* June 30, 1929: 17.
Thurman, Wallace. *The Collected Writings of Wallace Thurman: A Harlem Renaissance Reader.* Ed. Amritjit Singh and Daniel M. Scott III. New Brunswick: Rutgers University Press, 2003.
Tichi, Cecelia. *Shifting Gears: Technology, Literature, Culture in Modernist America.* Chapel Hill: University of North Carolina Press, 1987.

Tifft, Susan E., and Alex S. Jones. *The Trust: The Private and Powerful Family behind the* New York Times. 1999. New York: Back Bay Books, 2000.

"To Harlem in Fifteen Minutes." *New York Evening World* April 5, 1893.

Toth, Jennifer. *The Mole People: Life in the Tunnels beneath New York City.* Chicago: Chicago Review Press, 1993.

Trask, Michael. *Cruising Modernism: Class and Sexuality in American Literature and Social Thought.* Ithaca: Cornell University Press, 2003.

"Travel: The No. 7 Bringing the World Home to Queens." CNN. February 23, 2000. http://archives.cnn.com/2000/TRAVEL/NEWS/02/23/nyc.train/index.html.

Travis, Trysh. "What We Talk About When We Talk About the *New Yorker.*" *Book History* 3 (2000): 253–85.

Trillin, Calvin. "Shouts and Murmurs: What's the Good Word?" *New Yorker* May 15, 1995: 102.

"A Trip on a Handcar through the Rapid Transit Subway." *New-York Tribune Illustrated Supplement* January 24, 1904.

Tuan, Yi-Fu. *Space and Place: The Perspective of Experience.* 1977. Minneapolis: University of Minnesota Press, 2001.

Turner, Victor. *The Ritual Process: Structure and Anti-structure.* 1969. New York: Aldine de Gruyter, 1995.

Uhry, Alfred. *The Last Night of Ballyhoo.* New York: Dramatists Play Service, 1997.

"Underground New York." *Life* November 7, 1949: 80–90.

Unterecker, John. *Voyager: A Life of Hart Crane.* 1969. New York: Liveright, 1987.

Urry, John. *Sociology beyond Societies: Mobilities for the Twenty-first Century.* London: Routledge, 2000.

US Census Bureau. *Means of Transportation to Work by Selected Characteristics.* 2008–2010 American Community Survey 3-Year Estimates, Table S0802. http://factfinder2.census.gov/.

Versluys, Kristiaan. "Voyages into the Dark: The Subway Motif in Pound, Eliot, Tate, and Crane." *Thought: A Review of Culture and Idea* 62.246 (1987): 329–38.

Wainscott, Ronald Harold. *The Emergence of the Modern American Theater, 1914–1929.* New Haven: Yale University Press, 1997.

Warren, Kenneth W. "Appeals for (Mis)recognition: Theorizing the Diaspora." *Cultures of United States Imperialism.* Ed. Amy Kaplan and Donald E. Pease. Durham: Duke University Press, 1993. 392–406.

Waterman, Bryan. "Epilogue: Nostalgia and Counter-nostalgia in New York City Writing." *The Cambridge Companion to the Literature of New York.* Ed. Cyrus R. K. Patell and Bryan Waterman. Cambridge: Cambridge University Press, 2010. 232–40.

Weiskel, Thomas. *The Romantic Sublime: Studies in the Structure and Psychology of Transcendence.* 1976. Baltimore: Johns Hopkins University Press, 1986.

Welsh, David. *Underground Writing: The London Tube from George Gissing to Virginia Woolf.* Liverpool: Liverpool University Press, 2010.

Whissel, Kristen. *Picturing American Modernity: Traffic, Technology, and the Silent Cinema.* Durham: Duke University Press, 2008.

White, E. B. *Here Is New York.* 1949. New York: Little Bookroom, 1999.
Whitehead, Colson. *The Colossus of New York: A City in Thirteen Parts.* Doubleday, 2003.
———. *John Henry Days: A Novel.* New York: Doubleday, 2001.
———. "A Short Distance to the Blues: A Conversation with Kevin Young." *Poets & Writers Magazine* 31.1 (2003): 30–37.
———. "The Way We Live Now: 11-11-01." *New York Times* November 11, 2001.
White House Millennium Council. "Millennium Trails Announcement." July 26, 1999. http://clinton4.nara.gov/Initiatives/Millennium/trails_doc.html.
Whitman, Walt. *Whitman: Poetry and Prose.* Ed. Justin Kaplan. New York: Library of America, 1996.
Wideman, John Edgar. "Frame and Dialect: The Evolution of the Black Voice in Fiction." *American Poetry Review* 5 (1976): 33–37.
Wilkerson, Isabel. *The Warmth of Other Suns: The Epic Story of America's Great Migration.* New York: Random House, 2010.
Williams, Raymond. *Marxism and Literature.* Oxford: Oxford University Press, 1977.
Williams, Rosalind. *Notes on the Underground: An Essay on Technology, Society, and the Imagination.* 1990. Cambridge: MIT Press, 2008.
Williams, William Carlos. *The Collected Poems of William Carlos Williams:* Vol. 1, *1909–1939.* Ed. A. Walton Litz and Christopher MacGowan. New York: New Directions, 1986.
———. *Imaginations: Kora in Hell / Spring and All / The Descent of Winter / The Great American Novel / A Novelette & Other Prose.* Ed. Webster Schott. New York: New Directions, 1970.
———. *In the American Grain.* 1925. New York: New Directions, 2009.
Wilson, Rob. *American Sublime: The Genealogy of a Poetic Genre.* Madison: University of Wisconsin Press, 1991.
Wilson, Sarah. *Melting-Pot Modernism.* Ithaca: Cornell University Press, 2010.
Woolf, Virginia. *Jacob's Room.* 1922. New York: Harcourt, Brace, 1950.
"Would You Live as a Mole? Well, Wait for the Subway." *New York Times* May 8, 1904.
Wray, John. *Lowboy: A Novel.* New York: Farrar, Straus & Giroux, 2009.
Yaeger, Patricia. "Introduction: Dreaming of Infrastructure." *PMLA* 122.1 (2007): 9–26.
Ybarra, T. R. "In the Subways of Four Great World Cities: Crowds, Speed, and Noise Set the New York Tubes Apart from Europe's." *New York Times Magazine* November 30, 1930: 11, 18.
Yingling, Thomas E. *Hart Crane and the Homosexual Text: New Thresholds, New Anatomies.* Chicago: University of Chicago Press, 1990.
Zabel, Darcy A. *The (Underground) Railroad in African American Literature.* New York: Peter Lang, 2004.
Zangwill, Israel. *The Melting-Pot: Drama in Four Acts.* 1909. New York: Macmillan, 1920.
Ziegler, Garrett. "Subjects and Subways: The Politics of the Third Rail." *Space and Culture: International Journal of Social Spaces* 7.3 (2004): 283–301.

Zuber, Devin. "Flanerie at Ground Zero: Aesthetic Countermemories in Lower Manhattan." *American Quarterly* 58.2 (2006): 269–99.

Zukofsky, Louis. "Mantis." *Complete Short Poetry.* Baltimore: Johns Hopkins University Press, 1997. 65–66.

Zurier, Rebecca. *Picturing the City: Urban Vision and the Ashcan School.* Berkeley: University of California Press, 2006.

Zylbercweig, Zalman. "Dymov, Osip." *Leksikon fun Yidishn Teater* [Lexicon of Yiddish Theater]. Vol. 1. New York: Elisheva Publishers, 1931. 557–62.

# Index

acculturation. *See* assimilation
Agee, James, on *Many Are Called*, 133
Ahearn, Barry, on "Rapid Transit," 89
airplane: in "Cape Hatteras," 85, 99; in "Modern Poetry," 79, 103
Aleichem, Sholem: in *Bronx Express*, 131; *Railroad Stories*, 120
Althusser, Louis, ideology defined by, 50
American Community Survey, on public transportation usage, 165
American studies: focus on literature in, 14–15; Myth and Symbol School of, 2; technological sublime as concept in, 20, 53, 195n1
Arts for Transit: and original subway builders, 7–8, as public art program, 74
assimilation, 112, 114; in *Abie's Irish Rose* (play), 131; ambivalence about, 117; consumption as sign of, 118, 123–32; in *The Jazz Singer* (film), 131
Atkinson, A. S., on subway riders as moles 38–40
Augé, Marc, on private responses to subway, 171, 174
automobile, the: African American ownership of, 21, 141, 163–64; bodily experience of, 4–5; crash of, 184–85; as individualist form of mobility, 12, 33, 74, 89, 149; public transportation as alternative to, 189

Baker, Ray Stannard, on "street car relationships," 147
Balestra, Gianfranca, on "The Tunnel," 82
Banta, Martha, infrastructure described by, 28
Baraka, Amiri [LeRoi Jones], *Dutchman*, 137
Baudelaire, Charles, as representative of modernity, 68

Beach, Alfred, pneumatic transit of, 27
Beastie Boys, nostalgia for subway in "Stop That Train," 178
Belmont, August, Jr.: employee's interest in efficiency, 43; relationship with *New York Times*, 26
Bender, Thomas, on urban development of New York City, 37
Benjamin, Walter: on cinematic techniques, 93; on tactile perception, 39
Berger, Meyer, on New Yorkers' dislike of outdoors, 35
Berlant, Lauren, on technology and contemporary history, 15
Bernstein, Charles, on poetic collage, 87
*Beyond the Pleasure Principle* (Freud), 102–3
bird's-eye view. *See* overhead view of the city
Blake, William, cited in "The Tunnel," 104
BMT. *See* Brooklyn Rapid Transit Company
Bobrick, Benson, on railroad as underworld, 28
Bodenheim, Maxwell: as modernist subway poet, 20, 84, 88; "Summer Evening: New York Subway-Station," 90–91
Bramen, Carrie Tirado. *See* intra-urban walking tour.
*The Bridge* (Crane), 84, 86, 100, 110, 175; first publication of, 81. *See also* Crane, Hart *for individual poems*
broken windows theory, 166
Bronx, growth of the, 121
*Bronx Express* (Dymov), 21, 112–19, 121–32, 135, 138–39, 154; production history of, 112, 127–29, 199n3
Bronx Express train, 119–20
Brooklyn Rapid Transit Company, 36, 96
Brooks, Michael: on cultural history of the subway, 6–7; on race and gender on the subway, 115; on the subway as underworld, 8–9; on visual culture of the subway, 133
Brower, Abraham, and urban mass transit, 10
Brown, Henry Box, slave narrative of, 146–47
BRT. *See* Brooklyn Rapid Transit Company
Bryant, William Cullen, as poet of sublime, 58–59. *See also* Fireside Poets
Buck-Morss, Susan, on advertisements, 125
Burroughs, John: city opposed to literature in, 54–55, 70; Whitman in, 58
bus, the: crowds on, 13; early forms of, 10–11; southern experience of, 147, 188

car, the. *See* automobile, the
Catholicism, 66, 75, 78, 197n10
Chase, Stuart, on subway riders as animals, 31
circulation: individual's role in, 62, 71–73; migration compared to, 142, 150. *See also* migration; traffic
City Hall station, in Wray's *Lowboy*, 184
city literature: critics of, 54–55, 58–59, 61, 68–70; in relation to literary past, 59, 99–106, 142; sublime in, 60
Clarke, Joseph, "Manhattan, an Ode," 63
class distinctions: among African American New Yorkers, 140–42, 151, 189; among Jewish New Yorkers, 140; on public transportation, 163
claustrophobia, 147–48
Clinton, Hillary Rodham, and the 7 train, 138
cognitive mapping, 19, 39–40, 44, 49–50, 81–82, 98
*The Colossus of New York* (Whitehead), 168, 170, 181–82, 185–87
Coney Island, 176, 178–79
consolidation of five boroughs, 36
consumption, criticism of, 135
Crane, Hart, 20, 79, 81, 100–101, 142, 175; *The Bridge*, "Atlantis," 82, 85, 106–9; *The Bridge*, "Ave Maria," 95; *The Bridge*, "Cape Hatteras," 85, 99, 104; *The Bridge*, "Cutty Sark," 85; *The Bridge*, "Indiana," 95; *The Bridge*, "Proem: To Brooklyn Bridge," 85; *The*

*Bridge*, "Quaker Hill," 96; *The Bridge*, "The Tunnel," 3, 79–88, 92–100, 102–9; "For the Marriage of Faustus and Helen," 91–92; "General Aims and Theories," 88, 91; "Modern Poetry," 79, 103. *See also* queer theory
creative destruction, 61, 167
culture of consent, 128. *See also* Sollors, Werner
cummings, e. e., as "impressionist," 88
Cuomo, Mario, on negative impressions of New York , 22

Dalí, Salvador, on New York City as living being, 63
Davis, Elmer, on *New York Sun*, 24
Davis, Owen, adaptation of *Bronx Express* by, 117
de Certeau, Michel: on overhead view of the city, 45, 108; on space and place, 28; on story as form of transportation, 31, 190; on "tour" vs. "map," 19, 46
de la Peña, Carolyn: on bodies and technology, 4, on race and technology, 163
Derrick, Peter: on impact of Dual Contracts, 37; on "subway suburbs," 21
dialect, 142, 158–59
Dickinson, Emily: "'Hope' is the Thing with Feathers," 76; "I like to See it lap the Miles," 56
Dinerstein, Joel, on machine aesthetics, 17
disaster, imagined in art and literature, 184–87
Divall, Colin, on historiography of public transportation, 23
Dixon, Royal, on mole as engineer, 31
drama: expressionist, 116–17, 125, 199n6; interiority in, 116, 135–36; mix of styles in, 116–18, 131; nineteenth-century American, 118; Yiddish, 112, 117, 180. *See also* ethnic drama; melodrama
Dual Contracts, for subway expansion, 21, 36–37, 110
Duck, Leigh Anne: on competing notions of time, 144, 151; on *Invisible Man*, 162; on nostalgia for South, 157
Duffy, Enda, critiques of Kevin Lynch, 39–40
Dunbar, Paul Laurence: dialect in poetry of, 159; *Sport of the Gods*, 148
Dymov, Osip, 3, 116–17. See also *Bronx Express*

efficiency, 6, 25, 31, 42–43, 55, 93, 192n6
elevated train, the, 5, 192n15; visuality of, 11, 13, 192n16, 203n14
Eliot, T. S.: Hart Crane's imitation of, 88, 96, 104; as editor of *The Criterion*, 81; "The Waste Land," 99, 105
Ellison, Ralph, 28, 139, 151–52, 165; "An Extravagance of Laughter," 157, 162–63. See also *Invisible Man*
Elmgreen, Michael, and Ingar Dragset, 178–79
Emerson, Ralph Waldo, on panoramic perception, 34
*End Station* (Elmgreen and Dragset), 178–79
essayists, postwar, 169
ethnic drama, 116, 118
ethnic identity: and food, 129–30; generational, 131; visibility of, 135
Evans, Walker, *Many Are Called*, 118, 132–34

*Fame* (trade magazine), 125
ferry, the, 148
Fireside Poets: compared to city poets, 57–60; compared to Edgar Allan Poe, 101; railroad in the writings of, 67
Firkins, Chester: biography of, 53, 195n2; "On a Subway Express," 53, 59–60, 62–64, 66; as poet of public transit, 20, 78, 106
Fisher, Rudolph, 21, 139, 151–52, 156, 165, 189; "The City of Refuge," 143–44, 147, 152–54, 156, 158–63, 201n5; "Common Meter," 152; "The Promised Land," 152; "The South Lingers On," 157
Fitzpatrick, Tracy: on cultural history

Fitzpatrick, Tracy (*continued*)
of the subway, 6; on race and gender on the subway, 115; on subway maps, 36, 172; on "Subway Sunbeams: The Melting Pot," 199n1
Flynn, Joyce, ethnic drama in, 118
Fouché, Rayvon, on race and technology, 163–64
*Fortress of Solitude* (Lethem), 169, 176
Frank, Leo, lynching of, 130
Frank, Waldo: Crane's letters to, 81, 100; on Edgar Allan Poe, 103
Freud, Sigmund: *Beyond the Pleasure Principle*, 102–3; "The 'Uncanny,'" 145, 147, 160

Gaines, Kevin: on class distinctions among African Americans, 140; on minstrel imagery, 159
Garrett, Leah, on railroad as Jewish form of transit, 21
Gilbert, Rufus, and the elevated train, 11
Goetz, Bernard, as representative of New York subway in 1980s, 9, 137
Golding, Samuel, translation of *Bronx Express* by, 117
graffiti, 176–78, 203n4
Great Migration: compared to earlier migrations, 21; history of, 140; Pennsylvania Station as part of, 148; reversing directions, 165; subway as vehicle of, 142
Grey, John S., advertising poetry of, 115, 125
Griffin, Farah Jasmine, on stories told from migrant's point of view, 153

Harlem, 21, 24, 156; diverse population of, 158–59; Lenox Avenue subway line and, 142–44; Pennsylvania Station as connection to, 149
Harlem Renaissance: migration narratives in, 21, 139, 164; southernness in, 154; time as subject in, 151
Harvey, Charles T., and the elevated train, 11
Harvey, David, on "time-space compression," 34
Hedley, Frank, as overseer of subway system, 48
Higham, John, on nativism, 115
hip hop, and subway as symbol of authenticity, 177–78
Hood, Clifton, *722 Miles*, 191n2
Huddle, Andrew, on African American migrants, 151
Hughes, Langston: on subway and Harlem Renaissance, 144; "Subway Rush Hour," 22; on subway as vehicle representing work, 150, 155
Hull, E. M. See *The Sheik*
Hurst, Fannie, on lack of substance in modern fiction, 55
Hurston, Zora Neale: on appeal and danger of South, 144; on class distinctions among African Americans, 141–42
Huyssen, Andreas: on modernist rejection of mass culture, 70; on nostalgia, 180

IRT. *See* Interborough Rapid Transit
immigration: in *Fortune* (magazine), 134; Johnson-Reed Act establishing quotas in, 130, 134
Ingram, John H., as Poe biographer, 103
Interborough Rapid Transit, 36; express trains, 34, 36; subway line, 3, 65, 191n2
*Interior N.Y. Subway, 14th St. to 42nd St.*, 49–50
*In the American Grain* (Williams), 100–101
intra-urban walking tour, 16–17, 30, 34. *See also* urban sketch
*The Intuitionist* (Whitehead), 15
*Invisible Man* (Ellison): and "City of Refuge," 144, 162–63; past and present in, 158–60, 162; race and gender in, 137, 155–56; the subway in, 22; underground spaces in, 28–29

Jameson, Fredric: influence of Kevin Lynch on, 39–40, 50; on postmodern literature, 188

Jewish literature, role of the railroad in, 120
Johns, Jasper, and Hart Crane, 84
Johnson, James Weldon: *Autobiography of an Ex-Colored Man*, 148; on Harlem's development, 143; on illusory freedom of migration, 139
Johnson-Reed Act, 130, 134
Johnston, John, on technology and contemporary history, 15

Kallen, Horace, on multiculturalism, 133
Kasson, John: on class distinctions in understanding technology, 55; on overhead vs. street-level point of view, 19, 45
Katz, Tamar, on postmodern community, 182
Kazin, Alfred, on graffiti as personal expression, 176; on immigrant access to city via subway, 122; on nostalgia for earlier subway, 179; on personal history felt on subway, 169, 171
Keats, John, parody of, 61
Kelling, George, and James Wilson, broken windows theory of, 166
Kennedy, Adrienne, "The Owl Answers," 116, 137
Kennedy, Randy, on impossibility of describing subway, 3
Khalip, Jacques, on elegies for Hart Crane, 106
Kilmer, Joyce, 20, 43, 54, 73, 78; "The Great Nickel Adventure," 52, 65, 67, 72; "The Subway; 96th Street to 137th Street," 65, 68–69, 106
Kirby, Lynne, on railroad in silent melodramas, 47
Kraus, Joe, on production history of *The Melting Pot*, 117
Kurlansky, Mervyn, on graffiti as protest, 177

Laidlaw, René, critique of city poetry by, 59, 68–69
Larsen, Nella: migration narratives of, 21; *Quicksand* and *Passing*, 157–58
Latour, Bruno, on obligations of critics, 9
Lee, Julia, on turn-of-the-century streetcar, 147
Lefebvre, Henri, on space as conceived, perceived, and lived, 47
*Let the Great World Spin* (McCann), 178–79
Lethem, Jonathan, 22, 165, 168, 172, 175–77, 181–82; "Speak, Hoyt-Schermerhorn," 168, 170–71, 183. See also *Fortress of Solitude*
Levine, Lawrence, on music in African American culture, 145–46
Lewis, David Levering, on southern migrants to Harlem, 143, 151
Linde, Charlotte, and William Labov, on "tour" vs. "map," 46
Locke, Alain, *The New Negro*, 149, 158, 164
locomotive. *See* railroad
Lopate, Phillip, on *The Colossus of New York*, 181
*Lowboy* (Wray), 183
Lynch, Kevin: *The Image of the City*, 39; on individual's relation to city, 50; on legibility of underground space, 44, 81–82, 98; on visual focus of cognitive mapping, 19, 40. *See also* cognitive mapping
lynching, 130, 154–55

machine aesthetics, 17
Mailer, Norman, on graffiti as protest, 176–77
*Many Are Called* (Evans), 118, 132–34
Marcosson, Isaac, on oversight of subway system, 47–49
Marsh, Reginald, *Subway Sunbeams: The Melting Pot*, 111–13, 199n1
MARTA. *See* Metropolitan Atlanta Rapid Transit Authority
Marvin, Carolyn: on body as measure of new technologies, 13; on competing technological narratives, 47; on technology connecting center with periphery, 110, 139

Marx, Leo, on literature as cultural information, 15
McCabe, Joseph, on subway as melting pot, 111
McCammack, Brian, on subway's impact on Harlem's development, 142
McCann, Colum, 22. See also *Let the Great World Spin*; *This Side of Brightness*
McCluskey, John, on dialects in "The City of Refuge," 158
McCutcheon, George Barr, on serialized fiction, 55
McKay, Claude: as modernist poet, 20, 84; "Subway Wind," 107–8
medievalism in modern culture, 57, 72–73
melodrama, 117, 131
melting pot, 118, 124, 128; subway as, 21, 109–15, 131–34, 138; vs. "salad bowl," 133
*The Melting Pot* (Zangwill), 112, 117, 127–28
metaphors: comparing southern and northern experience, 155; comparing subway to human body, 63; comparing subway ride to encounter with divine, 65; subway stories as, 189–90
Metropolitan Atlanta Rapid Transit Authority, 165
Metropolitan Transportation Authority (New York City), 36–37, 76, 166
middlebrow, publication venues, 2, 185, 187
*Midnight in Paris* (film), 179
migration: compared to circulation, 142, 150; understood as passive and active, 164
migration narratives, 139, 144, 148, 150–64, 180; the South in, 21–22, 142; southern knowledge utilized in, 152–56, 161
Mills, C. Wright, on office work, 43
minstrelsy, imagery of, 159, 180
Mitchell, Joseph, nostalgia in 169
Mitchell, Ruth Comfort, "The Subway," 18, 107
mobility: African American, 142, 163; local, 3, 73, 120–21, 164, 174, 188
mobility, urban, 168, 202n21; compared to rural, 11; sounds of, 153; tactile, 39, 86, 89, 188; women's, 199n5. *See also* automobile, the; bus, the; elevated train, the; ferry, the; stagecoach, the; streetcar, the; subway, New York City
modernism, 2, 86, 89, 191n1; commuting in, 93; defamiliarization in, 152–53, 155, 165; relation between part and whole in, 4
modernity, 6, 15, 33, 35, 38–39, 194n14; dissatisfaction with, 25, 57; graffiti and, 177; modernism and, 4, 89, 192n5; Simmel's discussion of, 54, 58, 62, 181; subway poetry and, 80; subway system as representation of, 50–51; tradition and, in African American literature, 151, 160
modernization. *See* modernity
mole, the: as urban animal, 35; mobility of, 32; subway rider as, 19, 31–35, 38–40, 171
Moore, Deborah Dash, on transportation and Jewish migration, 121
Moore, Marianne, discussed by William Carlos Williams, 90, 101–2
Morley, Christopher, "On First Looking into a Subway Excavation," 61
Morrison, Toni, on African American connection to ancestors, 152
MTA. *See* Metropolitan Transportation Authority
MTA Arts for Transit program. *See* Arts for Transit
Mumford, Lewis: on subway as underground space, 8–9, 35; on urban development in New York City, 37

9/11, 22, 165, 181, 185–87, 203n11
Naar, John, on graffiti as protest, 177
Nadell, Martha, on Poetry in Motion program, 77
National Millennium Trail, 138

nativism, 21, 111, 115, 129–31, 134
Newcomb, John Timberman, on early twentieth-century poetry, 54–55
New York City, depiction of, in middlebrow magazines, 187
*New Yorker*: essayists in, 169, 187; readers of, 187; subway rides described in, 14, 76
*New York Times:* history of, 25–27; Queens in, 138–39; subway in, 3, 19, 24, 30, 32, 60; subway riders in, 35, 38, 41, 44
New York World's Fair (1939), 134
newspapers: competing views of the subway in, 24, 26; ethnic, 111, 114, 119; subway problems described in, 9; subway tours described in, 46
nostalgia: and bohemianism, 179–80; of New Yorkers, 175; in poetry, 95; as protest, 188; for southern past, 144; for subway of 1930s–40s, 167, 169; for subway of 1970s–90s, 23
Nye, David: on competing technological narratives, 19, 56; on technological sublime, 74, 107

Oldenburg, Claes, on graffiti as personal expression, 176
omnibus. *See* bus, the
*On the Town* (musical), and New York subway, 27
O'Neill, Eugene: expressionism of, 116, formal consistency of, 118
overhead view of the city, 5, 19, 108; as impossible from subway, 48, 170; compared to street-level view, 45

Page, Max: on imagined destruction of New York City, 186; on urban development as "creative destruction," 61, 167
panoramic perception, 13, 34, 62, 64, 146
Park, Robert: on immigrant newspapers, 200n9; on neighborhood boundaries, 109
Parker, Cornelia Stratton, on working-class female commuters, 93
Patton, Margaret French: on isolation within subway crowd, 73–74; "On a Subway Train," 70–71, 197n12; as poet of public transit, 20
Peacock, Molly, "Subway Vespers," 75
Pennsylvania Station: in "City of Refuge," 153, 180; in Great Migration, 21, 148; history of, 202n9; tunnels under Hudson River to, 35, 148
personal essay, the subway in, 167
Phelps, Ruth Shepard: biography of, 196n8; "The Subway," 64–65
photography, interiority in, 133
Pike, David L., on overhead vs. street-level point of view, 45
*Plessy v. Ferguson*: as affirmation of segregated transportation, 201n3; impact of, on African American travelers, 141, 146; as symbol of social conflict, 188
Poe, Edgar Allan: "The City in the Sea," 100; death of, 103; "The Fall of the House of Usher," 99, 105; "The Man of the Crowd," 99; modernist view of, 99–105; "The Raven," 99; "To Helen," 102; in "The Tunnel," 85
poetry: and commercialism, 53–54, 60, 62, 69, 77; imagist, 59, 83, 88; interiority in, 69, 77; middlebrow, 19, 52–54, 57, 59–61, 63–66, 74–75, 78–79; modernist, 20, 59, 75, 79, 84, 86, 109; modernist, collage technique in, 80, 83, 90–91, 99, 104–6; nineteenth-century, 56–59, 67–68; religion and, 52–53, 60, 66, 75, 78. *See also* Fireside Poets; *entries for individual poets*
Poetry in Motion (public art program): attitude of, toward technology, 74; history of, 76–77
Poetry Society of America. *See* Poetry in Motion
postmodernism, 22, 167, 185; multiple perspectives in, 170, 174, 182
Pound, Ezra, "In a Station of the Metro," 83, 86–89, 197n3
Presner, Todd: on railroad's significance to European Jews, 120–22; on railway system, 47

public transportation: in Atlanta, 165; race and class in, 163–65; social conflict and, 188; as urban, 189

queer theory, readings of Hart Crane's poetry in, 92, 94, 198n12

racial uplift ideology, 141, 143, 154
racism, experienced while traveling, 141. *See also* mobility: African American; railroad, the: Jim Crow cars on
railroad, the: acclimation to, 26; in African American culture 145; American vs. British, 67; crashes on, 184; Jewish literature and, 120; Jewish mobility and, 120–21; Jim Crow cars on, 142, 145, 147; poetry of, 56, 58, 196n6; unification via, 12, 73; variety of experiences on, 7; visuality of (*see* panoramic perception)
Reed, Brian: on coherence among parts in Crane's work, 84, 86; on loss of self in machine age, 98; on subway in "The Tunnel," 82
Rice, Elmer, on first subway riders, 14. See also *The Subway*
Rocker, John, on the 7 train, 137
Rodgers, Lawrence, comparison of "The City of Refuge" and *Invisible Man*, 144
Romantics, the: image of solitary writer championed by, 70; poetic sublime of, 61, 106
Rukeyser, Muriel, "Study in a Late Subway," 75

7 train, 137–38
Sage, Russell, rejection of underground travel by, 27
Saler, Michael, on medievalism of London Underground design, 57
Sandburg, Carl, "Halsted Street Car," 68
Sandrow, Nahma, translation of *Bronx Express*, 112
Sante, Luc, on *Many Are Called*, 133
Saroyan, William. See *Subway Circus*
Saxe, John Godfrey, "Rhyme of the Rail," 67
Schivelbusch, Wolfgang: challenges to the ideas of, 64, 146; on department stores, 62; fear of train disasters discussed by, 184; *The Railway Journey* 13. *See also* panoramic perception
Schnapp, Jeffrey, on transit: individual vs. collective, 12; thrilling vs. commodified, 66
Schocket, Eric: on modernism and modernity, 4; on writing from working-class perspective, 94
Schuyler, George, "Traveling Jim Crow," 141, 146
Second Avenue subway, 22
Seiler, Cotten, on mobility: as experienced by different subjects, 115, 164; individual and collective, 42; individualist, 2; and textuality, 4
*Seinfeld*, "The Subway" episode, 137
Seltzer, Mark, on relation of body to machine, 5
Shakur, Tupac, on graffiti and subways, 177–78
*The Sheik* (Hull), 41–42
Sheller, Mimi, on physicality of automobile drivers, 4
Shikoh, Asma Ahmed, *Home* series of paintings, 172–74
Shonts, Theodore, letter to August Belmont Jr., 43
Simmel, Georg. *See* modernity, Simmel's discussion of
Simpson, Mark: on multiple forms of mobility, 3; on travel as broadening one's mind, 146
Sinclair, Bruce, on race and technology, 163
Smith, Alison, on ethnic drama, 119–20
Sollors, Werner, on assimilation, 128, 130
Sontag, Susan, on *Many Are Called*, 133
space and place, 28
*Spring and All* (Williams): "At the Ballgame," 90; "Rapid Transit," 89–90, 101–2; "Shoot It Jimmy!," 95
stagecoach, the, 10

Stephenson, John, and urban mass transit, 10–11
Stewart, Susan, on "wild style" 177
Stilgoe, John, on variety of railroad experiences, 7
Stone, Jonathan, "Song of the Subway," 57
streetcar, the, 91; advertisements in, 125; crowd, 13; horse-drawn, 10; as space of equality, 147
sublime: postmodern, 169; railroad as, 55; subway as, 19–20, 53, 55, 57, 61, 66, 73–76, 185. *See also* technological sublime
*The Subway* (Rice), 116, 186–87
subway, New York City: acclimation to, 14, 25, 79, 86; advertisements in, 4, 6, 26, 29, 76–77, 85, 197nn5–6; advertisements in, *Bronx Express*, 115–16, 124–27; collective identity formed on, 180–83; compared to other "world subways," 34; connection to southern past on, 144–145; consolidation of, 12; crime in, 7, 166; as "hole in the ground," 27, 30; as in-between space, 18, 70, 85, 94–95, 108–9, 193n27; interiority on, 124–25; in Jewish intra-urban movement, 121; as map of literary history, 20; opening of, 2; standardization of, 11–12; as symbol of continuity, 167, 170, 191n3 ; transfers between lines, 37; underground movement of, 18, 25; unification of, 36; visuality of, 13–14, 32, 38–39, 64
subway, New York City, artists of: Paul Cadmus, 137; Red Grooms, 137; Al Hansen, 172; Nina Katchadourian, 172. *See also* Marsh, Reginald; Shikoh, Asma Ahmed
subway, other cities: Boston "T," 27, 82; London Underground, 27, 57, 73, 86, 171; Paris Metro, 171
*Subway Circus* (Saroyan), 21, 116, 118, 132, 135–36, 174
subway passengers: as animals, 31, 93, 198n13; attention of, 9–10, 125; diversity of, 122, 132, 135, 182; feeling of community among, 188; isolation of, 132, 135; as part of crowd, 12, 66–74, 88–91, 112, 133; personal histories of, 168–74, 183; reading habits of, 40–42; working-class, 79, 92–95. *See also* mole, the: subway rider as
*Subway Sunbeams: The Melting Pot* (Marsh), 111–13, 199n1
subway system: connection to other systems, 19, 51, 62–66, 80, 84; unconscious mind represented by, 80, vs. subway ride, 3–6, 14, 19, 45–46, 81, 92
Susman, Warren, on "usable past," 167

3 train, 169–70
Tabbi, Joseph, on "postmodern sublime," 169
*The Taking of Pelham One Two Three* (film), 111, 183
Tallack, Douglas: on *Interior N.Y. Subway, 14th St. to 42nd St*, 49–50; on overhead vs. street-level point of view, 45
Tapper, Gordon A., on "The Tunnel," 82
Tate, Allen: elegy to Hart Crane, 106; "The Subway," 75
Taussig, Michael, on tactile perception, 86
Taylor, Frederick. *See* efficiency
Taylorism. *See* efficiency
technological sublime: in American studies, 53, 196n5; in nineteenth vs. twentieth century, 71, 106–7; in poetry, 55, 65, 73–74; in Poetry in Motion program, 76–77
technology, users of, 189
temporality: different forms of, 144, 159–60; northern vs. southern, 145, 149–52, 155, 159, 163
Thacker, Andrew: on imagist poetry, 88–89; on subway passenger's passivity, 104
Theroux, Paul: on graffiti, 176; on use of old subway line names, 181
*This Side of Brightness* (McCann), 183–84
Thompson, Emily, on sonic changes felt by migrants, 153
Thoreau, Henry David, "What's the Railroad to Me?," 58

Thurman, Wallace, and William Jourdan Rapp, on northern vs. southern oppression, 154–55
Tichi, Cecelia: on heroic engineer figure, 48; on William Carlos Williams's poetics, 89
time. *See* temporality
Times Square, 26, 33, 37, 82, 87, 189
"tour" vs. "map," 46
Toth, Jennifer, and homeless in subway, 22
traffic, as organizing urban movement, 71
*Traffic in Souls* (film), 71
train. *See* railroad, the; subway, New York City; subway, other cities
Trask, Michael: on anonymous interactions, 92; on working-class physicality, 93
travel narrative, 3, 50, 146, 192n4
Travis, Trysh, on *New Yorker* audience, 187
Trillin, Calvin, on New Yorkers' attitude toward subway, 181
Tuan, Yi-Fu, on space and place, 28

uplift ideology. *See* racial uplift ideology
uncanny, the: African American experience of, 139, 142, 162; Freudian, 145, 147, 160; Ernst Jentsch's definition of, 146–47
Underground Railroad, 21, 146, 158
underground space: in European cities vs. New York City, 29, 194n8; as place of business, 29–30; connecting subways and businesses, 33; as uncanny, 142; as underworld, 29, 171, 194n7
underworld, subway as, 8–9, 26, 28–30, 68, 192nn8–9
urban picturesque, 15–18, 34–35
urban sketch, 30–31, 168, 176, 193n25
Urry, John, on mobility: experienced by hikers, 5; imagined by readers, 16
usable past, 167

*Van Wyck Blvd; Home Series* (Shikoh) (painting), 172–74
Versluys, Kristiaan, on modernist subway poetry, 82

walking, literature of. *See* intra-urban walking tour; urban sketch
Ward, Artemas, 125. See also *Fame* (trade magazine)
Warren, Kenneth, on African American community, 143, 150
*The Warriors* (film), 137, 175–76, 179, 183
Weiskel, Thomas, on relation between self and sublime, 61, 64
Whissel, Kristin, on urban circulation, 71
White, E. B., on possible destruction of New York City, 169
Whitehead, Colson, 22, 165, 168, 172, 177, 181–82; "The Way We Live Now: 11-11-01," 185–86. See also *The Colossus of New York; The Intuitionist*
Whitman, Walt, 58, 67, 69, 99, 104, 133; "Crossing Brooklyn Ferry," 77; "To a Locomotive in Winter," 56; "A Passage to India," 56
Williams, Rosalind, on underground spaces, 28, 35
Williams, William Carlos, 20, 84, 104–5. See also *In the American Grain; Spring and All*
Wilson, Sarah: on "melting-pot modernism," 117; on metaphors for assimilation, 134
Winters, Yvor, Hart Crane letter to, 100
Woolf, Virginia, on subway passenger's sense of home, 171–72
Wray, John, *Lowboy*, 183

Yaeger, Patricia, on infrastructure, 51
Yiddish literature, capitalism in, 124

Zangwill, Israel. See *The Melting Pot*
Ziegler, Garrett, on subway passenger's relation to system, 43, 76
Zuber, Devin, on post-9/11 subway art, 185
Zukofsky, Louis, "Mantis," 75

SUNNY STALTER-PACE was born in Peoria, Illinois, and now lives in Montgomery, Alabama, with her husband, Paul, and their child, Arthur. She is an associate professor in the English department at Auburn University, where she teaches courses on American literature, drama, critical theory, and popular culture. Stalter-Pace earned a BA at Loyola University Chicago and an MA and PhD at Rutgers University. She has published articles on urban culture, technology, modernist literature, and film. Her current research projects explore the history of New York nostalgia and the international meaning of the tenement. Her proudest non-academic achievement was a three-day stint on *Jeopardy!*